THE NAKED
CONSUMER

THE NAKED
CONSUMER

How Our Private Lives Become
Public Commodities

ERIK LARSON

HENRY HOLT AND COMPANY
NEW YORK

Library of Congress Cataloging-in-Publication Data

Larson, Erik.
The naked consumer : how our private lives become public
commodities / Erik Larson.—1st ed.
p.   cm.
Includes bibliographical references and index.
1. Marketing research.   2. Consumption (Economics)   I. Title.
HF5415.2.L36   1992
658.8'34—dc20   92-14344
                                                          CIP

ISBN 0-8050-1755-0

First Edition—1992

Designed by Katy Riegel
Printed in the United States of America
Recognizing the importance of preserving
the written word, Henry Holt and Company, Inc.,
by policy, prints all of its first editions
on acid-free paper. ∞

1   3   5   7   9   10   8   6   4   2

For Chris, Kristen, and Lauren,
my sweetie pies

CONTENTS

ACKNOWLEDGMENTS

I interviewed many people for this book and owe them all my thanks, whether they want it or not. In particular: Dr. Peter "Pete" Gleason for graciously shipping me a month's worth of his junk mail; Heloise, of helpful-hints fame, who sent me a box jammed with mail forwarded by her loyal readers; Kathy Jo Brihn, for showing me around the very pretty town of Eau Claire, Wisconsin; the Poss family for demonstrating that hospitality is not dead, at least not in Wisconsin; the American Marketing Association; the Advertising Research Foundation (especially Roz, at the library); Donald Cooke; Mary Culnan; Paco Underhill; Penelope Queen; and all those friends who sent me samples of outrageous mail.

For support, concrete and psychic, I thank Gerry Marzorati, *Harper's*; Mike Curtis, *The Atlantic*; Mike Tomlinson and NOVA; and Mike Miller of *The Wall Street Journal*. Denise Shannon of Georges Borchardt, Inc. opened the door; Bill Strachan, my editor, provided a light and confident touch.

I am especially indebted to my wife, Christine Gleason: in between saving the lives of countless newborn babies she somehow found the time to read my work with her usual sharp and literate eye.

Under the spreading chestnut tree,
I sold you and you sold me—

—George Orwell, 1984.

PART ONE

OBSESSED!

THE TROJAN TEDDY

We can't tell you what they eat for dinner. But we can tell you where they live. And their phone number, who they live with, whether they have voted, and much, much more.

—Advertisement for Aristotle Industries, December 1991

Six days before my eldest daughter turned one she received the first birthday mail of her life, an eight-by-eleven envelope emblazoned with a big lavender teddy bear. Although addressed to my wife, the letter was deliberately timed to arrive for my daughter's initial birthday. It arrived, in fact, even before the birthday card sent by my daughter's godparents, who until then had been unsurpassed in their ability to mark every event in her short life with a promptly delivered card, gift, or telephone call. What interested me most, however, was that the teddy bear had been sent by a corporation. To me this letter marked a turning point in America's consumer culture, but then I take an unnatural interest in the commercial mail I receive. I like to think that I read such mail the way Umberto Eco, the Italian semiotician and novelist, reads medieval texts. I collect the best, cleverest, and most alluring pieces and study them for signs of how far America's consumer marketers have come in figuring out what makes the American consumer, that insatiable engine of America's economy and culture, run.

By the time the big teddy arrived at my house I had begun seeing signs of an intelligence guiding a lot of the junk mail crowding my box, much the way I had begun seeing the first glimmerings of real cunning in my daughter. When you notice those first hints of intelligence in your

3

children, your first instinct is to dismiss them as random events triggered by the chance entanglement of a couple of free-swinging neurons. By the time you realize that your child is indeed very smart—that the gagging cough that has brought you rushing to her crib at four A.M. every morning for the past week is a deliberate imitation of the real thing— you've already been caught in patterns of manipulation that you may need years to escape.

Someone out there was observing my little family and gauging its progress through time. But who? And how? The more I thought about it—and clearly you're not supposed to think about it, you're supposed to whip out your checkbook and start writing—the more intriguing the letter became. Somewhere a company not only had noticed the fact of my daughter's birth, but had made itself a little note to check back again in a year with a birthday letter chock full of consumer offerings, an accomplishment all the more impressive to me, who can't remember the birthdays of two children, let alone two million.

I opened the envelope. Inside I found a Sears flier containing twelve coupons for toddler-related clothing and supplies; a one-page coupon offer for Revlon baby mousse shampoo, featuring the ubiquitous Joan Lunden; and a sealed envelope that itself contained eight more special offers, including an invitation from the American Bronzing Company of Columbus, Ohio, to encase my daughter's first shoes in metal for just $7.99. I also found a pamphlet published by the Kimberly-Clark Corporation called "The Beginning Years: Your Baby at 12 months." Inside was basic advice about toddlers in ten short segments: "First Steps," "First Shoes," "Keeping Your Toddler Safe," and so forth. Most were followed by a promotional blurb extolling some virtue of a Huggies diaper related to the topic at hand. A few of these paragraphs had to cast a good distance for the Huggies connection; a section called "Teething Continues" ended with this advice: "If your baby's teething is accompanied by loose stools, the last thing you want is a leaky diaper. Huggies diapers have cuddly-soft elastic at the legs and at the waist to help stop leaking." The pamphlet included a two-dollar coupon.

Something about all these companies joining forces under cover of a lavender teddy bear to cash in on my new kid began to irk me. I didn't know it then, but consumer theorists had a name for what I felt: commoditization—the conversion of important life events into trivial commercial moments. How did my guardian corporation (I'll reveal its name later) know that my wife and I even had a child? By what mechanism did this company remind itself to send us a birthday letter full of coupons? What else did the company know?

The Trojan teddy and a few other pieces of smart mail prompted me to embark on what soon became a rather spooky journey among a little-seen but hugely influential legion of marketers obsessed with capturing, quantifying, and ultimately distilling the soul of the American consumer. With a little help from their enthusiastic allies—census bureaucrats, demographers, postal officials, ex–military surveillance experts—the marketers have built a vast intelligence network containing the names, addresses, and personal records of virtually every consumer in America, all for the lofty goal of finding more irresistible ways to sell us more soaps, laxatives, and detergents.

The intelligence this network provides is the fuel that powers such consumer colossi as Procter & Gamble, General Motors, the national broadcasters, even Hollywood. What we eat, drink, drive, and smoke is determined in large part by what the consumer intelligence community decides we might like to eat, drink, drive, and smoke. Considered from this perspective, consumer espionage may be among the most influential industries in America. The annual allocation of $10 billion in network TV advertising, for example, is determined solely and directly by the numbers Nielsen Media Research produces each night from its ratings center in Dunedin, Florida.

With the costs of introducing and selling products now so high, companies believe they cannot afford to make mistakes and that every product has to be a best-seller. They have watched the comfortable mass market of the 1950s explode into smaller micromarkets of unfathomable consumers—blacks, Asians, empty-nesters, yuppies, dinks, and so forth—who don't play by the old rules. The marketers have seen, too, how the rapid growth of cable television has eroded the power of the "Big Three" networks to reach the huge audiences they once commanded.

To make matters worse, the marketers now must wrestle with the aftereffects of their own excesses: pitch pollution—too many ads from too many places. In 1990 U.S. companies spent $238.7 billion on all forms of advertising and promotion, $23.6 billion on direct mail alone. The total is expected to rise to $331.2 billion by 1995, with roughly $10 billion of the increase due to spending on mail. Between 1965 and 1990 the number of network TV commercials shown in a year tripled to 5,400 distinct ads. The commercials, moreover, now arrive at twice the frequency allowing broadcasters to cram more ads into the same commercial time slots. In 1988, 38 percent of prime-time commercials were only fifteen seconds long, compared to 6 percent in 1984.

We not only encounter more advertising; we encounter it from more sources, some rather unorthodox. Airlines place ads on the backs of lavatory doors. Whittle Communications' Channel One broadcasts commercials directly into school classrooms. A telephone company tried inserting commercials between rings on outgoing phone calls. An Israeli company called Golden Eggs gingerly stamps advertising messages on the shells of eggs; a Chicago company puts them on hot dogs. Two dozen companies paid $30,000 each to buy space on a board game called It's Only Money. Commercials now appear on the videos we rent, spaced between the FBI warning and the movie. Buick, for example, jumped at the chance to place a leisurely commercial at the beginning of the video version of *Rain Man*, a bit redundant considering the praise co-stars Tom Cruise and Dustin Hoffman heap on the classic Buick convertible that appears throughout the film. Ads arrive unbidden on our fax machines; computerized jerks call us during dinner to pitch us home improvements and a better shot at the good life. In 1990, according to Congress, three-hundred thousand telemarketers reached out to eighteen million of us every day and touched us for $435 billion worth of goods and services, four times the total sales of 1984.

In 1991 I found myself not just the target of junk mail, but the subject. *Harper's* magazine, in its own attempt to draw attention to its mailings, put the opening paragraphs of an article of mine on the envelope of a subscription offer mailed to fifty thousand households. The article was about junk mail. "We're excited about this package," the magazine's vice-president for corporate and public affairs wrote in a letter to me presenting the mailing. "We think it will break through junk-mail clutter. . . ."

Consumers also faced a torrent of look-alike, taste-alike products. In 1990, according to an annual count kept by *Gorman's New Product News*, 12,055 new products appeared on the shelves of America's drugstores and supermarkets, 60 percent more than in 1985. That comes to thirty-three new products a day. Meanwhile, the length of time an average shopper spends in the store has shrunk, forcing new and old products to compete more fiercely for the consumer's affection.

Once stable, faithful products have begun bearing offspring with rabbity proficiency. "Take something as simple as Coca-Cola," said Mark L. Capaldini, a vice-president at Claritas Corporation, an Alexandria,

Virginia, company that pioneered the art and science of target marketing. "It's a great generic product, right? Well, in fact there are literally dozens of different combinations of packaging and even variations on the basic product. We've now got Coca-Cola and diet Coke and Caffeine-Free Coke and Caffeine-Free diet Coke. You can buy it in cans—six cans, twelve cans, or twenty-four cans. Then you can buy it in glass bottles, and the bottles come in different sizes, and then you can buy it in plastic bottles, and the plastic bottles come in different sizes. Here's an all-American product that's now available in all these different combinations, sizes, and flavors."

The combined force of all these pressures drives today's intrusive quest for the consumer. Companies dispatch their research battalions with orders to seek out any market advantage, the tiniest consumer twitch that could launch their products to stardom—even if to find it they have to hide cameras on store shelves or turn entire towns into electronically monitored consumption laboratories. The availability of new technologies, in particular huge amounts of cheap computing power, helped spur the campaign. So, too, did a fundamental science imperative, the continuing irresistible drive by marketers to transform what they do from pants-seat art to precision science and to reduce us all to "consuming units" for handy insertion into mathematical models of consumption.

The secrets prospectors are everywhere. You don't see them because so much of their probing is done from a distance through oblique means and because only a relative few of America's 250 million people are subjected to intense scrutiny at any one time (although for a while one project under way at Citicorp, the New York bank holding company, had the stated goal of creating a "census" data base that could monitor, model, and modify the consumption behavior of every upstanding American consumer).

But we continually betray secrets about ourselves, and these secrets are systematically collected by the marketers' intelligence network. Your telephone company can tell how often you travel by keeping track of how often and from what points on the globe you use your telephone calling card. (U.S. Sprint peddled such information to hotel companies and airlines.) When you register your car, you divulge an invaluable collection of socioeconomic clues, which your state motor vehicle department passes along to large data harvesters. The thirty-four states that offer this service provide the information at low cost on easy-to-use computer tapes. My motor vehicle department recently did a little marketing research of its own, mailing a survey that asked not only about the quality of department services, but about shopping at the malls in which the bureau's express offices were located. "If you did any shopping," the survey asked, "could you share with us how much money you spent?"

If you're a couple struggling with the pain and sorrow of not being able to have children, companies can know this or at least make a statistically reasonable guess. One hospital did so but made the mistake of including a *Washington Post* reporter on its mailing list. As I'll show, companies can also figure out whether or not you are gay, a nifty bit of intelligence that insurance companies find rather useful. Even the detailed answers you gave to the Census Bureau in 1990 will eventually find their way into the marketing intelligence network despite concerns within the bureau about the "less noble purposes" for which such data may be used.

Companies set clever little intelligence traps that trick us into shedding bits of information. One company adds a series of personal life-style questions to the guarantee cards that accompany TVs, stereo amplifiers, and backyard grills. The cards leave the impression that if you don't answer the questions, your warranty won't be valid. The Publishers Clearing House Sweepstakes is much more than just an offer of a chance to win a million bucks; it is also an intelligence feeler designed to help spot gullible consumers known in the trade as "opportunity seekers" and to build and update a massive data base of consumer names and addresses for its own internal use.

Some companies take the direct approach, but this can get expensive. Once, for example, my wife passed me an envelope marked discreetly with a return address on Lexington Avenue in New York. "Dear New Mother," the enclosed letter began. What really drew my attention, however, was the attached dollar bill. The envelope also contained a seventy-item consumer research questionnaire about the baby wipes we used and the television shows we watched, complete with forty little red-and-blue stickers to be stuck at various places on two inside pages. "The dollar is just a token of our appreciation—our way of saying thank you for your help," the letter said.

Competition for our secrets seems to be driving up the price we can charge. Recently a swank Boston hotel offered me five bucks to answer a survey. In 1990 American Airlines, citing plummeting cooperation rates, gave survey respondents a $25 travel certificate. The price for more specialized intelligence is even higher. During annual meetings of the American Academy of Dermatology, pharmaceutical companies pay as much as fifty dollars to any doctor willing to stop by their booths and fill out a questionnaire. A dermatologist friend told me she walked away from one such encounter with an Orrefors crystal bowl.

Newsweek took a distinctly post-Reagan approach in a brief sub-scriber survey it mailed to my wife in October 1991, when it offered to contribute an unspecified amount of money to a charity of her choosing in return for her cooperation.

Corporate surveyors buttonhole consumers throughout the country, even the world. Every three months Coca-Cola conducts a monumental global survey, interviewing at least 1,000 people from almost every country where Coke is sold. In 1989, according to the Advertising Research Foundation, marketers conducted 70,000 focus groups and did one-on-one interviews with 130,000 individual consumers.

While strolling through your favorite store you may be captured secretly on videotape. Some day soon a video crew on the payroll of a New York advertising agency may invite itself into your home to film you in the revealing act of cleaning your sink. Agents of Arbitron may try to recruit you to use a household scanner to record the price and Universal Product Code of every single product you buy. Serpentlike infrared sensors may soon begin tracking you up and down the aisles of your local supermarket—in 1991 a handful of stores already had begun testing the technology.

We are the most heavily probed, surveyed, and categorized society since the dawn of human history. The intensity of this assault has changed us, both as individuals and as a culture.

How? Why? And at what cost?

Until the 1990s marketers were able to conduct their surveillance of America without attracting too much attention. As they got bolder and junk mail got smarter, a few newspapers and magazines began chroni-cling their efforts; privacy became for the marketers an inescapable and increasingly costly issue. Lotus Development Corporation became the most celebrated victim of growing privacy angst when, in January 1991, consumer pressure caused the company to cancel its introduction of Lotus Marketplace, a compact disc containing the names, addresses, income brackets, and life-style characteristics of some 120 million households. In announcing the cancellation, Jim Manzi, the company's chief executive officer, said, "Lotus cannot afford a prolonged battle over consumer privacy," and cited the "emotional firestorm" the product had created. The cost to Lotus of overlooking privacy was a cool $8 million.

While this is not a book about privacy, before we proceed a few words about privacy may be in order.

The most influential legal argument in support of a right to privacy appeared in the *Harvard Law Review* of December 15, 1890. The writers, Samuel D. Warren and Louis D. Brandeis (later a Supreme Court justice), described it as "a general right of the individual to be left alone." Sounds simple enough, yet legal scholars still debate whether such a right really exists. Federal Judge Robert H. Bork while a nominee for the Supreme Court argued there was no such thing; soon afterward a more successful nominee, David H. Souter, gave the right, as *The New York Times* put it, his "cautious endorsement."

What is private to one individual may not be private to his neighbor; what is considered private today may not be considered private tomorrow. Today, for example, an employee of the Census Bureau can go to jail—and one employee has—for disclosing addresses or personal data collected during the decennial census, yet over the bureau's first fifty years of operation all census information was considered public property. In fact, the federal census laws of those decades required that census takers display their information, names and all, "at two of the most public places" in their territories. Federal law now considers our tax returns to be private and confidential, but from time to time Congress has enacted laws forcing the public disclosure of tax information. The Revenue Act of 1924 required the public listing of taxpayers and their incomes. Two years later Congress withdrew the requirement. In 1934, however, Congress once again allowed limited disclosure and required taxpayers to file a separate tax form, the so-called pink slip, which the public could examine at the offices of their local tax collector. These slips included name, address, total gross income, total deductions, net income, total credit against net income, and tax payable—the stuff of a marketer's dream. This obligation, however, did not go over big with the American taxpayer, and Congress hurriedly rescinded the law, just in time for the 1935 tax-filing period when the act was to have taken effect.

What constitutes an invasion of privacy? And once your privacy is invaded, how do you prove you were harmed? Can you seek damages because your neighbor happened to peek at your tax form and saw how much you made last year? Suppose one of the many families receiving lavender teddy bears had lost its child before the letter's arrival—a direct-mail nightmare that a few parents in America probably did experience with this mailing, given the gloomy fact that ten of every one thousand American babies die before their first birthdays. Could the grieving parents sue Joan Lunden, Walt Disney Company, and Kimberly-Clark for invasion of privacy? Could they make a case for financial compensation?

"Would you want to go into court with a case like that?" asked Janlori Goldman, an attorney with the American Civil Liberties Union. The difficulty in proving invasion of privacy arises from what Goldman calls "the body-in-the-street syndrome."

Goldman, director of the ACLU's Privacy and Technology Project, is a prominent member of the small but earnest cadre of lawyers, scholars, and newsletter editors who worry about our privacy even when the rest of us do not. She is a tall, direct woman with a taste for rapid-fire conversation.

"With privacy issues, victims are not obvious. Harm is not identifiable. There's no blood, there's no body, no broken bones. The harm is not tangible, you can't point to it and say 'You hurt me this way.' It's very hard to collect damages, it's very hard to make a legal case.

"It's very hard to explain to people why you just don't want to give out your Social Security number one more time; it's very hard to explain why when you get a targeted mailing you feel vulnerable; why you feel as though somebody knows something about you and you don't know why and you don't know how. You don't even know what to do about it, because you have no recourse."

She believes harm does occur, however.

"It's the kind of harm that eats away at you," she told me. "It affects the choices you make, it affects the way you live, it affects your sense of being an individual, of being autonomous, of being able to live in the world without always being watched, without always being monitored. And that is a unique American quality. We believe we can live that way. But now it's starting to sink in that we don't."

Goldman contends the monitoring systems set up by America's marketing companies already have begun to influence the ebb and flow of our daily lives. After a Washington weekly newspaper ran an article on the films Judge Bork rented from his favorite video store, Goldman got a "flood" of calls from people concerned about the sanctity of their video habits. "People are afraid to go to the video store now and rent certain movies," she said. "They don't want to rent movies that are going to identify them as certain kinds of people. They don't want other people to make decisions about them or judgments about them based on the movies they watch. It feels *so* intrusive to them, so they make market decisions that they wouldn't otherwise have made. To me, *that's* the harm."

The new marketing technologies have greatly complicated the privacy issue. Sophisticated software developed in the 1980s and the ever-more powerful computers on which it runs allow marketers to collect huge amounts of information about each of us from courts and other public repositories and to combine it all into a single data base. Companies can further "enhance" this information with details about our credit card balances, bank accounts, subscriptions, store purchases, and a host of other personal data collected discretely by companies of all kinds and then widely, avidly, and aggressively marketed to anyone willing to pay for it. The result is a wholly new kind of information, what I call "recombinant information." Is the resulting electronic file a benign composite of humdrum data or something more threatening and intrusive, a dangerous mutation?

Technology has added yet another dimension to the collection of our personal statistics. Since the mid-1980s marketers have refined techniques that now give them the ability to track millions of consumers through time. By constantly updating their data bases they can monitor shifts in our financial and personal status on a monthly basis, soon perhaps on a daily basis, and thus hit us when we are most vulnerable. They can pitch us mortgage life insurance just after we buy our homes, life insurance on the eve of childbirth.

The big marketing companies assure us they take the utmost precautions to protect our secrets. Consider, however, the findings of a study published in the *Journal of Business Ethics*, which found that today's marketing MBAs were far more likely "to engage in quasi-ethical (allowing the ends to justify the means) marketing research practices than their counterparts in the early 1980s." In particular, the study found these recent graduates to be far more willing to deceive the subjects of a marketing research poll in order to gain their cooperation. Studies done in 1981 and, appropriately, 1984 found that marketing research as a whole was rife with serious ethical abuse. "As the utilization of marketing research continues to increase," two marketing scholars wrote in 1988, "opportunities for the misuse of marketing research also increase."

If there is any doubt about the marketers' willingness to trample civil liberties, one need only read what they tell each other in their own publications and trade journals. The September 1990 issue of *Inside Strategy*, a newsletter produced by Strategy Research Corporation of Miami, printed a series of testimonials by customers who had used the company's new focus group center, where the company gathers consumers for conversations about products and other matters. It is customary during focus groups for marketers to observe consumers through one-way glass, but this center seems to have raised the practice to new heights. "State of the art!" exulted the vice-president of one client firm. "It was particularly interesting to me to be able to observe the respondents not only during the session, but before they started, in the waiting room."

Henry Johnson, while still chief executive of Spiegel Company, could barely contain his glee as he described in *Direct Marketing* magazine how computers and the new concept of psychographic marketing—an automated means of divining the attitudes of consumers—had given his company the power to see the "inner selves" of individuals.

"Through psychographics," he crowed, "we become the friend who knows them as well as—perhaps better than—they know themselves."

Such talk might have caused some marketers to worry about invading privacy. If so, they could have turned for comfort to a column by Robert J. Posch of Doubleday Book & Music Clubs, who reassuringly wrote: "There is *nothing* in the language of the Constitution that refers to any 'right of privacy' in the commercial context." (The emphasis is his.)

He went on, in fact, to chide those spineless members of his industry who cave in to criticism from privacy advocates. In particular he referred to a decision by a telephone company to drop its plan to rent lists of its customers. Posch wrote: "An industry that will voluntarily walk off its own economic plank deserves the consequences of the landing."

Some of his compatriots take a more thoughtful view. In a different issue of *Direct Marketing*, Pierre Passavant, a consultant, wrote the following: "At the risk of offending some of my colleagues in direct marketing, I must say that I have the impression that some list owners, brokers, and compilers are none too concerned with such esoteric subjects as rights to privacy and reasonable expectations of confidentiality."

He cited the case of a national medical laboratory that, for a time, rented the names of the patients whose tests it processed. "Is this the 1984 Big Brother viewing my activities via the telescreen? Or the 1984 thought police reading my mind? No, it's just my local friendly compiler.

Working with my local friendly computer service bureau. To create a
data base and interconnected data bases with information that would
make Orwell smile. . . . If suddenly our personal lives become largely
matters of public record, it will not be by government action, but due to
our uncontrolled profit motives, also known as greed. We will have only
ourselves to blame for the consequences."

My research for this book convinced me there are four universal laws
governing the flow of data collected about individuals, which I call the
"laws of data dynamics":

The First Law (also the "law of data coalescence"): Data *must* seek
and merge with complementary data.

The Second Law: Data *always* will be used for purposes other than
originally intended.

The Third Law: Data collected about individuals *will* be used to cause
harm to one or more members of the group who provided the information or about whom it was collected, be it minor (the short-term aggravation of a "junk" call during dinner) or major (the sorrow of getting a free
sample of formula just after your miscarriage).

The Fourth Law: Confidential information is confidential only until
someone decides it's not.

The impact of mass surveillance reaches far beyond concerns about
privacy. How companies use the secrets they discover causes subtle
changes in our daily culture, the world we encounter every day on our
way to work, in the grocery store, or when we watch television. Ours is a
consumer subsociety—how could so much probing *not* change our lives?

What companies learn determines how they focus their advertisements and how precisely they can isolate our deep-seated vulnerabilities.
The process takes place outside the public view. A product may suddenly
disappear from the shelves of your local Safeway; even if you noticed its
disappearance, you'd have no reason to imagine the complicated network of psychology and technology that led to it. You receive an offer for
a new credit card, but the offer tells you nothing of the sophisticated
technology that was brought to bear to pick you out of a hundred million
American consumers and to exclude your friend, who happens to live in
the wrong part of town. If you move and discover suddenly that your
junk mail has caught up with you even faster than your friends have, you

may be mildly fascinated or mildly annoyed, but you won't see any sign of the rather slavish degree to which the U.S. Postal Service has geared its technological resources to helping the likes of Lands' End and L. L. Bean keep abreast of our movements.

As consumers, we see Oz. We don't see the little man behind the curtain. We don't see how the marketers have eroded our civil rights; how by invoking the great god Efficiency they created an electronic caste system in which all of us reside and that reinforces class stereotypes and fosters a subtle new brand of discrimination based not on skin color, but on fiscal wherewithall. All this corporate probing, moreover, has produced a business culture that shies from true innovation and pays more attention to manipulating our needs, values, and shopping behavior than to giving us a better product. This dependence has grown so pervasive that it has crimped the national imagination and altered the way our product designers, directors, and politicians think.

How can you be truly creative if you're always looking over your shoulder for the approval of a panel of Baltimore housewives; if you know that any idea will be subjected to a battery of surveys, focus groups, or electronic ratings evaluations? Suppose God's product development team had first tried out His creations on a panel of average Americans— would the lobster and artichoke have made the convenience cut? Why, given all this poking and probing, are so many new products so disappointing? Ralph's Groceries, a West Coast chain, got so discouraged it considered charging "failure fees" to companies whose products took up valuable store space only to fail soon afterward. If all this snooping is so helpful, why *do* so many new products fail?

I set out to turn the tables on the consumer spies, to watch them as they went about the business of watching us. Posing as EL Enterprises, a direct-mail firm, I sent for sales material on their latest marketing lists and data bases. I subscribed to their newsletters. I invented a new mother named Angela to chart the routes by which the littlest consumers and their parents become marketing targets. I attended conferences where marketers talked among themselves of their newest and most ambitious efforts.

Some of the marketers' efforts are merely amusing, many are intriguing, a few are deeply troubling. This book aims to demonstrate how this grand and perverse obsession to understand the American consumer has shaped the world we encounter every day—to serve as a field guide to help explain why things are the way they are in the commercial landscape around us.

To build this vast intelligence network, the marketers relied on secrecy and the fact that no one was paying much attention. Above all, this book seeks to dispel the secrecy. The best elixir for that vague feeling of being watched from afar is simply to stare right back.

SEX, PRUNES, AND VIDEOTAPE

A Brief History

It may sound strange coming from a research man, but an attempt to get too many facts will often leave you without any real knowledge at all.

—Ernest Dichter, "Case Histories
in the Study of Motivation," 1951

Marketers like to get together now and then to present papers on their latest research exploits. They dress up their conferences to resemble those held by doctors, physicists, and other true scientists, but a fundamental paradox always undermines the efforts: they loathe disclosing real details of their activities for fear of tipping off the competition. At such gatherings someone inevitably quips that what the marketers could really use is a device that could be implanted secretly in consumers to provide an objective stream of information about the advertisements they see, the stores they enter, the things they buy, the displays that make their hearts pound and their brain waves spike. Anyone visiting such conferences quickly gets the impression that if such a device existed, the marketers would find a way to deploy it.

In January 1991 I attended a pair of back-to-back conferences on attitudinal and behavioral research organized by the American Marketing Association and held in the Doral Ocean Beach Resort in Miami Beach. The most striking aspect of the conferences, apart from the lovely weather and the beautiful beach, was the degree to which the marketers had built themselves a scientific lexicon just as brittle and obfuscatory as any a physicist might create. The marketers talked not about flesh-and-blood people, but about BAR scales, market penetration, cluster analysis, conjoint analysis, convergent and divergent analysis, value-structuring models, incremental sales, quality function deployment, and noninvasive respondent-driven interviews. My favorite phrase, introduced by the market research manager of General Motors' Saturn division, was "postdecision dissonance," or how a consumer feels after he has bought a lousy car. Equally striking was the adversarial nature of the jargon. Companies did not merely target us; they targeted "against" us. "Conquest rate" was the rate at which one brand was able to steal customers from another.

The marketers talk science better than they play it, however. Their jargon masks another problem that threatens to keep them from achieving their dream of becoming true scientists, while simultaneously driving their search for more and more intrusive means of spelunking our consuming souls: we consumers are quirky bastards.

As early as 1761, Samuel Johnson—Dr. Johnson—thought advertisers had learned all there was to know about peddling their wares. "The art of advertising," he wrote, "is now so near to perfection that it is not easy to propose any improvement." He was wrong, of course, and so was Claude Hopkins, an American marketer who felt moved in 1925 to proclaim: "The time has come when advertising has reached a science. It is based on fixed principles and is reasonably exact. The causes and effects . . . have been analyzed until they are understood."

Marketers had it easy in those days—consumption itself was a new phenomenon. We first became known as consumers in 1897 when Sears, Roebuck & Company identified us as such in a section of its catalog titled "Consumer's Guide." This represented an elevation from the original sixteenth-century definition in which "the consumer" was the shopper from hell, Satan himself.

Consumption as we know it today began to blossom at the turn of the century when households began the great shift from producing their own soap and sundries to buying them from rapidly growing national corporations. With markets wide open, marketing was more a matter of distribution than manipulation. The challenge was to get products out the door and into the places where people bought them. Companies nursed the naive belief that consumers were rational and would know a good thing when they saw it. To make sure they saw it, companies advertised. They pushed function, even though the claims they made tended to exceed anything any product could deliver.

As companies grew, managers began losing firsthand contact with their customers and began conducting elementary market surveillance to fill the intelligence gap. Charles Coolidge Parlin is generally credited with being America's first true market researcher; in 1910 the Curtis Publishing Company hired him to gather information that might be of use to companies who bought advertising space in Curtis magazines. His 1912 study on department stores coined the phrase "the consumer is king."

But what did the king want?

The *Chicago Tribune,* destined to be a leader in market research, conducted a house-to-house survey in 1913 to collect intelligence on the buying habits of Chicago residents. Early marketers tried other, less direct techniques as well, revealing the first glimmer of an occupational passion for indirect surveillance that would only intensify in coming years. In 1915 the Bon Ami Company invited consumers to enter a contest by sending in lists of ideas for how best to use Bon Ami cleanser. The company got twenty-five thousand lists and six thousand essays, which it then analyzed for clues as to how best to peddle the cleanser in the future. The Coca-Cola Company wrote to America's soda fountain operators offering free glasses and displays in return for the names of one hundred of their customers. Coke then mailed a letter and a coupon for a free Coke to each consumer on the lists. From 1894 to 1900 the company gave away nine million Cokes.

Sears built America's first large direct-mail data base and by 1911 was practicing an early form of today's micromarketing. The company kept address and purchase history records on every customer, which it then used as a guide in choosing which of an array of catalogs to send in the next mailing.

Marketing quickly grew more complex. As competition intensified, products in all categories began to look more and more alike. A car was a car, and every car was black. Moreover, the markets of America began to change shape and character. Soldiers returning from World War I induced demographic vertigo into previously rock-stable markets. Companies felt compelled to explore new ways of studying their markets to find new ways of getting people to buy their products. They began snooping in earnest, looking for an edge.

Albert Lasker, of the Lord & Thomas advertising agency, sent his staff door to door to figure out why sales of a new evaporated milk had suddenly plummeted. Arthur C. Nielsen, Sr., began keeping precise track of products sold by a sample of drugstores and developed the notion of market share, or the proportion of total sales of a given product category that is commanded by a single brand or company. In 1929 George Gallup, a market researcher before he became a pollster, established for Young & Rubicam what is widely considered to be the first formal marketing research department. The same year J. Walter Thompson formed a Consumer Purchase Panel designed to represent the tastes of the nation, and William J. Reilly published his *Marketing Investigations*, a field guide for conducting market research interviews.

The 1920s also saw the emergence of the kind of marketing pressures that today continue to fuel the search for new ways to understand the consumer. Companies began to worry that their markets soon would be saturated, with everyone owning everything he or she could possibly want. Automakers in particular dreaded the day when every household would own a car. Advertisers feared their messages were getting lost among the ads that so glutted the nation's magazines and newspapers. Moreover, marketers now recognized that they no longer battled only their direct competitors—they competed too against all other consumer marketers for a fixed consumer dollar.

To more effectively woo consumers, manufacturers shifted their emphasis from function to style. Suddenly consumers could buy Turkish towels in colors other than white; even toilets came in alluring new shades. Automakers began painting cars different colors; in 1927 General Motors began making annual changes in body styles, a practice that came to be known as "planned obsolescence." The stated mission of GM's research division was "the organized creation of dissatisfaction."

The men of Madison Avenue—they *were* men, with few exceptions—began experimenting with new tactics to try to raise their advertisements from the clutter. In an attempt to add a little science to their image, they called themselves "consumption engineers." George Washington Hill, America's first guerrilla adman, introduced the practice of using celebrity testimonials in advertising, persuading a host of actors, broadcasters, singers, and divas to laud the powers of Lucky Strike cigarettes to protect their voices; he also instituted attack advertising that took aim at competing products. Advertisers of the 1920s launched the first chameleon ads designed to mimic surrounding editorial layout designs and type styles.

Some advertisers went right for the adrenal gland, launching brazen "scare" campaigns intended to frighten consumers into buying their products. In 1928 Scott Paper Company warned of the dangers that might befall the hapless consumer who chose another company's toilet paper. "A single contact with inferior toilet tissue may start the way for serious infection—and a long and painful illness." Listerine, which earlier invented the socially undesirable affliction "halitosis," warned now that more than embarrassment might befall those who did not gargle. In one ad, titled "Her Last Party," the company told the wrenching story of a woman who caught a chill on her way home from a party and failed to take a prophylactic slug of Listerine.

She died.

The 1920s saw the start of another lasting trend: disdain for the consumer. The consumer was still king, but now the king was considered none too bright. Advertisers reminded each other repeatedly that the consumer had the mind of a child and placed the child's age somewhere between nine and sixteen. This national dimness justified deception. "To tell the truth might make no appeal," warned John Benson, president of the American Association of Advertising Agencies, in 1927. "It may be necessary to fool people for their own good. Doctors and even preachers know that and practice it. Average intelligence is surprisingly low."

As marketers sought to stir dissatisfaction and promote demand for products, critics condemned the new consumption ethic as wasteful and morally damaging. The marketers countered with an argument they would dust off again in the 1990s as a response to rising privacy concerns: they were merely exercising their constitutional right to "freedom of speech."

Radio too emerged in the 1920s and provided the first demonstration of how fiscal and competitive pressures can drive marketers to new levels of intrusion.

The marketers of the late 1920s stood in awe of radio's ability to penetrate to the heart of the household. They warned each other against sullying the new medium with anything as crass and crude as advertising. In 1925 *Printer's Ink*, a prominent advertising magazine, cautioned that radio advertising would cause only "ill will" and added: "The family circle is not a public place, and advertising has no business intruding there unless it is invited." It was okay, however, for advertisers to *sponsor* radio shows—that is, to drop a company name now and then at the edges of the programs the advertisers funded.

The marketers' reluctance was short-lived. Radio was simply too tempting a medium for lifting one's messages from the clutter. The marketing imagination went to work looking for ways to maintain the appearance of discretion while stepping up the promotional heat. Soon, for example, sponsors began inserting their names directly into programs, having characters use and discuss the products. In the pursuit of more and more visibility, some sponsors worked the names of their companies into the stage names of the musical groups that performed on their shows. Thus early radio listeners were treated to performances by the Ipana Troubadors, the A&P Gypsies and two Palmolive soloists given the stage names Paul Oliver and Olive Palmer.

By the late 1920s economic conditions had become more precarious, and a downturn in 1927 reignited worries about overproduction and advertising saturation. Radio became a gleaming beacon. In 1928 the American Tobacco Company, makers of Lucky Strike cigarettes, halted most of their print advertising to test the power of radio and watched sales rise 47 percent in two months. Lord & Thomas, the ad agency handling the Lucky Strike account, proclaimed the value of using radio "frankly and fiercely."

The mass market was born. Cities were still sharply stratified by class and ethnic origin, and different regions of the country still had different tastes, but radio—and, beginning in 1941, television—ignored the differences and for the first time allowed marketers to reach virtually everyone in America with the same message. By the 1930s marketers turned their attention to trying to understand the behavior of this mass market by adopting the new techniques of scientific polling, a tool tailor-made for gauging the mass appetite.

Marketers did not yet fully appreciate just how peculiar consumers really were. Prunes were still only prunes; Marlboro was still a bright red ivory-tipped cigarette meant only for women.

The really sexy phase of marketing—the era that would change forever the way products were sold in America—was about to begin.

To the uninformed the prune is a dried and wrinkled food having all the charm of castor oil. To Ernest Dichter, founder of the motivation research movement of the 1950s, the prune was rather more complex. It was a "scapegoat food" shunned because of all the dark psychological freight people subconsciously piled on its back.

And no wonder, Dichter found, after conducting two hundred in-depth psychoanalytic interviews: the prune was a "witch."

"It is interesting to observe," Dichter wrote, "that the witch invariably is visualized as a wrinkled, ugly, sterile old spinster whose witchcraft has to make up, as it were, for her lack of 'normal,' human, giving qualities. The witch, too, is an undesirable freak, whose services we could seek clandestinely in the dark of night. The implication in regard to the prune is obvious."

The prune was also a "Puritan" perceived as "meager, rough, and joyless," utterly alien to our steamy sexual selves. "The adult eater has retained the deep sensuous desire for sucking, for squeezing a thick, luscious, meaty food and making it yield its rich and satisfying content. . . . Prunes, when they are raw, certainly do not gratify the desire for lusciousness."

Dichter suggested a solution: Picture the prune in the company of a "wholesome, fresh-looking girl."

Vance Packard, in his 1957 best-seller *The Hidden Persuaders*, attributed the shift toward motivational research to three factors: the fear that most people already had everything they needed; the increasing similarities among products; and the recognition that consumers were not rational beings. This irrational streak among consumers had confounded marketers who relied on the research techniques of the prior decade with their emphasis on surveys and straightforward interviews. The trouble with the previous "nose-counting" approach, Packard wrote, "was that what people might tell interviewers had only a remote bearing on how the people would actually behave in a buying situation when confronted with a three-legged stove or almost anything else."

Science, in this case psychology, provided the marketers with new tools—Rorschach tests, word association, psychoanalytic interview techniques—to turn this irrational streak to an advantage and to skirt the grave danger of a populace suffering from too much satisfaction. Motivation research, MR for short, captured the imagination of marketers. By 1957 eighty research companies claimed to specialize in motivation research, among them Dichter's Institute for Research in Mass Motivations. Dichter, in his book *The Strategy of Desire*, claimed that by 1959 his company had conducted over 1,200 studies on "the phenomenology, the psychology" of cars, soap, toothpaste, toys, dictating machines, surgical supplies, baseball gloves, weed killers, cigarettes, pencils, TVs, hats, bras, girdles, shoes, doilies, even coffins. Among coffin shoppers, Dichter found, the greatest concern was that the lid close firmly.

The motivation researchers saw deep meaning everywhere. Gum chewers were "frustrated breast-feeders." Smoking was a "safety valve for autoerotic impulses." People liked soup because it took them back to the warmth of babyhood, perhaps even earlier: "Its deepest roots may lie in prenatal sensations of being surrounded by the amniotic fluid in our mother's womb."

Cars, of course, were not merely vehicles that got you from place to place. "A motor car," Dichter said, "is one of the most perfect psychological devices for sublimating our subconscious wish to kill or be killed."

Dichter realized that even look-alike products could be made to seem different and compelling by endowing them with distinct personalities that might shed a positive glow on their buyers. Inanimate objects, he wrote, "possess a definite psychic content, a 'soul' which plays a dynamic emotional role in the daily lives of individuals." Product images could be engineered to induce the "tension differential" that arises when people strive for social or career advancement beyond their immediate reach. He urged marketers to use the powers of motivational research "to make people constructively discontented by chasing them out of the false paradise of knowledgeless animal happiness into the real paradise of the life of change and progress."

One celebrated success of motivational research was the sexual transformation of Marlboro cigarettes. In the mid-1950s, when men began turning to filter-tip cigarettes, Philip Morris decided the women-only market for its Marlboro filters was too limiting. Louis Cheskin, another noted motivation researcher, redesigned the Marlboro box in macho red and white. Leo Burnett, the famous Chicago ad man, designed an advertising campaign that featured rugged, tattooed hombres of all kinds—deep-sea fishermen, sailors, mechanics, not just cowboys—doing manly things in Marlboro country. The cowboy later became the main Marlboro man and drove the brand to success as the best-selling cigarette around the world.

The great power of motivational research, however, was that it offered a seemingly scientific way to make sense of the irrational behavior of consumers. Managers could now point to hard evidence set down in reports written by Ph.D.'s and rely on these instead of their own judgment. In a 1960 *Harvard Business Review* critique of motivation research, Theodore Levitt, the reknowned marketing scholar, worried that too much attention to such research had induced "a paralysis of the imagination" among managers. "Management has let itself be seduced largely because it does not consider what happens a seduction," he wrote. "Rather, it considers the whole affair highly scientific. And this has been a particularly congenial submission because management has always sought formulas and prescriptions for easier decision making. But calling this science is like confusing a spade with a steam shovel."

The 1960s brought a new shift in consumer espionage, this time toward the application of exotic technologies in hopes of capturing objective, quantifiable information about consumer behavior. Can it be mere happenstance that during the decade spy shows were the favorite TV genre, with "I Spy," "The Man from U.N.C.L.E.," and "Secret Agent"? Like Dichter, this group of researchers sought a means of getting past what consumers said they did to what they really did, but they approached the problem from the outside rather than the inside.

Marketers hooked consumers to lie detectors to see what effect different commercials had on galvanic skin response. They experimented with "pupilmetrics," a technique of measuring the opening and closing of the human pupil, billed as a scientific means of gauging how much attention consumers really paid to advertising. Marketers filmed shoppers from hidden cameras as they examined packages in store aisles; they installed movie cameras on TV sets to see how people really watched television.

Soon the marketers took their hunt for the consuming soul directly to the brain itself. In the early 1970s they began pasting electrodes to the scalps of consumers to study how the electrical patterns of their brains varied in response to advertisements and other commercial stimuli. As neuroscientists refined the techniques of electroencephalography (EEG), the marketers began applying those techniques to more complex studies of consumers' brains, hunting now for changes across varieties of wave frequencies—alpha, beta, delta, and so forth—and between the right and left hemispheres of the brain. As EEG techniques grew more sensitive, however, the patterns they captured grew more confusing. The 1980s saw a resurgence in EEG studies by neuromarketers; by 1990 most had concluded that EEGs eventually would prove useful in testing consumer reactions, but not for a very long while.

Meanwhile the same old fears that had dogged marketers since the 1920s were kindled again. Again manufacturers grew concerned that too many products hawked through too many ads were spreading the consumer dollar far too thin. Now, however, there was something new to worry about: the mass market had begun to decay. By the late 1980s marketing pundits were writing its obituary—a bit prematurely, perhaps, given that most national brands continue to be marketed to the masses using traditional techniques, but nonetheless capturing the evolving pressures in the marketplace. "It is my belief that the 'mass market' is dead," wrote Philip Kotler, a Northwestern University marketing professor. America, he argued, had entered the "era of mass customization" in which "computer technologies and automation capabilities within factories now allow us to bring out affordable, individualized versions of products—every consumer's dream."

To fulfill this dream, however, would require a degree of market intelligence gathering never before achieved. Marketers would have to shift from targeting the masses to targeting masses of individuals; from mass marketing to mass surveillance. Boston Consulting Group coined a phrase to describe the new thrust: "marketing to a segment of one."

For help in locating and identifying so many individuals, the marketers again turned to science, this time adopting the targeting technology born of the mother of all intelligence agencies: the U.S. Bureau of the Census.

GROUND ZERO

3

THE CEMENT ELEPHANT

*With the census you and I tell our government about our-
selves. This is then used by businesses to locate customers.
There is something amiss when I tell the government that I
work and have young children, and then I'm subjected to an
advertising campaign by Pampers.*

—Andrew Hacker, professor of political science,
Queens College, City University of New York

At a cocktail party, names are just a formality. The question that really
starts the social chemistry brewing follows next: Where do you live? It is
the linchpin of a far more complex underlying search for information. In
that one question we ask: Who are you? How do you behave? Are you
someone I could love or easily hate? We ask about place in order to get an
immediate, advance sense of newcomers and their motives; our habit of
asking is probably the vestige of some early-warning system built into
prehistoric man and reinforced over time by the terrible things massed
groups of strangers have done to each other throughout history.

In large cities like New York and San Francisco, neighborhoods array
themselves along a life-style continuum containing both glaring con-
trasts and subtle shadings. In San Francisco to say you live in the Castro
district instantly conveys the impression that you are gay; to say you live
in the Marina, that you are straight, young, probably single. Once you
have lived in San Francisco for a while, however, you discover more
subtle gradients: you find that every neighborhood—Forest Hills, St.
Francis Wood, the Outer Richmond, Telegraph Hill—applies its own

29

stamp to the way you view its residents. During my most recent stay in San Francisco I lived at a corner formed by the edges of three distinct city neighborhoods: Diamond Heights, Glen Park, and Noe Valley. I lived in Noe (pronounced No-ee), and I knew *exactly* what that meant: I was a young family man with a taste for cappuccino and funk. A little funk, mind you; the only all-black outfit I owned was the tuxedo I wore when I got married. The other two neighborhoods evoked markedly different life-styles. To break up my workday occasionally I took a walk up to Diamond Heights—straight up, as a matter of fact—via Harry Street, a long wooden stairway running up a cliff forested with cypress and eucalyptus. The climb ended in a 1960s Brigadoon, a suburban realm of detached homes, garages, even concrete pavement. On occasion I skipped Harry Street and instead walked onward into Glen Park, a solidly middle-class neighborhood of Victorian cottages. Family, but without the funk. In San Francisco, Miami, New York, Baltimore, anywhere, your geophysical location betrays something about you, providing a vivid index of your tastes, dreams, and, of course, personal finances.

There is no richer collection of information describing the places we live than the vast stockpiles collected every ten years by the U.S. Bureau of the Census. After every census we read about change and controversy. Our newspapers chronicle the shifting demographics of the nation, running front-page stories as each new installment of data is published. What we seldom read, however, is the degree to which the Census Bureau became the fundamental tool, and a most willing ally, in the marketers' quest for America's consuming soul. It developed the technologies that now support the corporate intelligence network arrayed to capture our slightest consumptive whims. In fact, the bureau and its vast stockpiles of information spawned the data collection industry; its generous policies on data distribution made a lot of money for a few very nimble companies. One deal—"the sweetheart deal of the century," as a participant called it—sharply increased the precision with which marketers can now target consumers. We subsidized this advance three different ways: first, with our taxes; second, with our information; third, with the money we paid for the products being marketed.

The marketers' use of census data has brought direct, pervasive, and persistent change to the cultural landscape; census data is the foundation of every major marketing campaign in America. It determines the contents of your mailbox, the location of the nearest McDonald's, even whether your local radio station is staffed by flesh-and-blood people or is one of a new breed of robotic outposts whose sole mission is to sell advertising time.

Marketing companies are now so good at what they do that the bureau plans to study them to determine what data collection techniques, if any, the bureau might be able to adopt for the year 2000 census. At the same time, the bureau finds itself in the ironic position of having to protect its confidential information against the threat that one of these data-rich marketing companies may one day apply its technical might—its ability to merge and match large amounts of diverse data—to the task of uncovering the identities of individual census respondents.

Such steadfast defense of our secrets against even this remote threat would be reassuring, if not for the fact the bureau has sidestepped a more immediate and pervasive challenge unique to this information age. New strains of information—recombinant data—created when companies blend census data with records from their own consumer files challenge the bureau's narrow notion of confidentiality. David Burnham, author of *The Rise of the Computer State,* testified on the subject before a joint congressional committee considering the 1990 census. "The Census Bureau has little control over how the marketing companies enhance the census data," he told the committee. "But the merger of general census data with specific information developed by private companies and state licensing agencies may result in serious invasions of personal privacy. . . ."

How did our demographic secrets make their way into the consumer data bases of America? How are they used? How have they changed America?

The story of how the Census Bureau came to play such a key role in the pursuit of the American consumer is best told in the converging histories of two demographic institutions: the bureau itself and a man named Jonathan Robbin, a statistical lothario whose passionate quest for the mathematical underpinnings of human behavior made him a wealthy man.

"I cannot resist what I do," Robbin told me in one of several conversations at his home in the Mohican Hills of Bethesda, Maryland, just west of Washington, D.C. "It's like being married to a beautiful woman where every night you discover something new about how lovely she is."

■ ■ ■

Sex is a primal drive, but so too is man's urge to count himself and his peers. The earliest written records of census taking date to ancient Egypt, although it seems likely that even prehistoric man took a rudimentary count of sorts, giving his hunting companions a quick and probably worried glance to see if together they really did have the manpower to bag that mastodon they had just cornered.

Throughout history man's more formal counts have been bracketed by controversy—charges of overcounts and undercounts, warnings that a census would betray a country's weaknesses or bring heavenly retribution. Heaven became a factor in 1017 B.C. when God ordered King David not to count the people of Israel. David disobeyed and launched what is easily the most controversial census in the history of man. He counted 1,570,000 men, a total that quickly became one of the earliest examples of an overcount when God, angered by David's defiance, unleashed a pestilence on the men and killed 70,000 of them. Word spread that Satan himself had caused David's abysmal behavior. The event had a lasting effect on the census activities of governments for the next twenty-eight hundred years, the power of the taboo undoubtedly reinforced throughout the Dark Ages as governments repeatedly counted their populations to see who had survived the latest plague. In 1753 a critic of a proposed English census worried that the count could bring "public misfortune or epidemical distemper." Even to the maverick population of America the threat of punishment from God was no small thing. The Founding Fathers worried that the biblical taboo might diminish response rates. They overcame their doubts and wrote into the U.S. Constitution a requirement that the government count its population once every decade, beginning in 1790. James Madison lobbied to make the census a detailed probe of society but was overruled, probably a good thing given the logistical nightmare of just finding early Americans—such no doubt charming respondents as Boston Frog, Booze Still, Trulove Sparks, Wanton Bump, Hannah Cheese, Madsavage, Tripe, Fish, Hash, Murder, Tombs, and Demon—in the hollows and forests of early America.

Over the next fifty years the census became a far more intrusive and controversial vehicle, its original purpose gradually broadened to take account of other pressing needs, such as determining whether the country had enough manpower to defend itself against foreign enemies. By

1840 census takers were asking how many Americans could read, what jobs they did, who was deaf, dumb, blind, insane, and "idiotic." The 1860 census asked citizens to divulge the value of their personal estates.

Census officials began treating the collected information as confidential, although no law required them to do so. The custom didn't keep the Union Army from turning census data into a weapon, however— thereby providing one of the earliest proofs of the second and third laws of data dynamics: that information produced for one purpose *will* be used for other purposes and eventually *will* cause harm to those who supplied the information.

In 1864 Union General William Tecumseh Sherman concocted an audacious plan—a full-force march from Atlanta to the sea, which Civil War historian Bruce Catton called "the strangest, most fateful campaign of the entire war." Sherman set out not to engage another army, but to destroy the Confederate economy and to convey the message that the United States, in Sherman's words, "has the right, and also the physical power, to penetrate to every part of the national domain, and that we will do it . . . that we will remove and destroy every obstacle—if need be, take every life, every acre of land, every particle of property, everything that to us seems proper." With the help of the census office—it was not yet called a bureau—he made a pretty fair try at fulfilling that promise.

He planned a fast, lean march. Doing so meant he would not be able to maintain conventional lines of supply; in those days before helicopter gunships and Harrier jets, an army was only as good as its ability to protect the roads, rivers, and railroads down which it had already traveled. Sherman would have to live off the countryside to a degree no Union or Confederate army had done before.

From the start of the war, Census Superintendent Joseph C. G. Kennedy had been earnestly providing the war effort with maps and census information on southern population and industry but had sparked only limited interest. Sherman, however, saw in Kennedy's annotated maps the key to his campaign.

In practical effect Kennedy had provided Sherman with a kind of Mobil guide for the plunder of the Confederate countryside, using data produced in more settled times by the very people Sherman encountered along his route. He gave his troops explicit orders to forage, a practice that until then was technically against the law. The army's mission included destroying mills, cotton supplies, railroads, anything of economic or military value. An Illinois sergeant wrote that his colleagues seemed "to take savage delight in destroying everything that could by any possibility be made use of by their enemies."

After the campaign, Sherman dropped Kennedy a thank-you note: "The closing scene of our recent war demonstrated the value of these statistical tables and facts, for there is a reasonable probability that, without them, I would not have undertaken what was done and what seemed a puzzle to the wisest and most experienced soldiers of the world."

The Civil War slowed the rate at which America's population grew, but from 1870 to 1890 America made up for lost time, boosting the population by 25 percent or more per decade. As the population grew, so too did the government's curiosity and its difficulties in managing the crush of incoming information. In 1870 census takers asked 156 questions on 5 different census forms; by 1880 they got downright snoopy, poking around for answers to 13,010 questions on 215 forms. Most of these questions had nothing to do with the general population and were directed instead to surveys of industry; nonetheless, the bureau wound up trying to process a couple of billion shards of information, all to be recorded, tabulated, and organized by hand. The 1880 census, in fact, brought the system to its knees. Some planned volumes of census information simply never were published.

What the bureau needed was a room full of mainframe computers. What it got was a young Columbia University engineering graduate named Herman Hollerith, whom one historian has dubbed "the forgotten giant of data processing."

Hollerith joined the 1880 census effort as a "special agent" assigned to collect information about the use of steam and water power in heavy industry. Statistics were just then becoming a sophisticated science, and the census office drew the top talent of the nation, young bucks and war heroes, a reflection perhaps of the degree to which we Americans always have been obsessed with who we are and how we live.

Statistics were both job and pleasant diversion for Hollerith. Strictly "as an amusement" he helped tabulate vital statistics for Colonel John Shaw Billings, a famous Civil War surgeon who by then ran the census office's vital-statistics division. Hollerith also dated the colonel's daughter, a fact that might cause hard-core skeptics to wonder if there might have been another motive lurking behind Hollerith's statistical passions.

Miss Billings invited Hollerith to her family's home for dinner one Sunday, a meal not often discussed in historic circles but one that ought to rank among the great serendipitous events of all time. The evening must have been scintillating, because before long the colonel and young Herman were talking about statistics.

At one point Colonel Billings actually did tell Hollerith, "There ought to be a machine"—something to help speed the brain-deadening task of hand-tabulating millions upon millions of census forms.

Billings suggested that punch cards might form the basis of such a machine. The idea had been put to use in commercial weaving to guide the new Jacquard looms, and railroad conductors clipped a punch "photograph" of each passenger, nipping boxes that indicated color of hair, color of eyes, even the size of a passenger's nose, a vital statistic by anyone's definition.

Hollerith did not get the girl, but he did get down to work, and by 1887 he had patented the main elements of his "census machine," including a keyboard card puncher and an electromechanical tabulator that registered data by thrusting metal pins through the holes in punch cards until the pins touched electrical contacts at the other side. Hollerith had sired what would later become that brilliant, if vexsome, invention, the computer punch card.

The census office adopted Hollerith's machine for use in tabulating the results of the 1890 census. It is hard to appreciate now, given the rapid advance of technology, but Hollerith's machine quickly became the technological marvel of the day and the foundation of America's data-processing industry. In 1911 he merged his Tabulating Machine Company with three others to form a wholly new company, a hardy little enterprise that a decade or so later would change its name to IBM.

America's fledgling consumer products companies began using census data as a marketing tool around the turn of this century. In 1905, in *Modern Advertising*, Ernest Elmo Calkins and Ralph Holden described how companies had begun the innovative practice of working population statistics into their marketing plans. Their book further documents the earliest roots of marketing's drive to become a rigorous science. "The present-day tendency on the part of experienced advertisers is to get at the facts—to reduce the art of advertising to a science—to develop what may be called the mathematics of advertising."

The bureau published its data grouped by large chunks of geography. To help direct the taking of the census, however, it broke the country into far smaller divisions, such as census tracts, which include an average of four thousand people, and census blocks, the smallest divisions, which include about eighty-five people in cities, thirty in rural areas. Until 1960 census takers interviewed every single American in person. By dividing the nation into such small hunks, administrators could keep better track of which households had been surveyed, which had been missed. By 1910 Herman Hollerith's technology made it practical for the Census Bureau to begin tabulating its data by such small units: eight cities requested special counts broken down by census tract. In 1940 the bureau tabulated (but did not publish) housing information at the block level for 191 cities.

By breaking its data into small units, the bureau immediately gave companies a more focused look at what kinds of people lived within their markets. The bureau had designed its tracts and blocks to take account of natural geographic features such as rivers, creeks, and forests, barriers that tended to define the boundaries of neighborhoods and thus to enclose more or less homogeneous populations. Over time, and especially through the efforts of Jonathan Robbin, each census block would become a clear window into the mind of the consumer.

By 1940 the bureau faced a tsunami of information. Hollerith's machine and his punch cards had kept the bureau ahead of the wave, but as the population grew and census tabulations became more complex, even this technology had reached its limits. World War II and another chance encounter between a man and a woman soon brought the solution.

During the war, the army hired two University of Pennsylvania engineers, John Mauchly and J. Presper Eckert, to build a computing machine capable of handling the intricate mathematics of ballistics. Their effort eventually yielded a monster of metal, wire, and eighteen thousand vacuum tubes called ENIAC, or the Electronic Numerical Integrator and Calculator, generally considered the first electronic digital computer. In 1944, while the project was still locked in secrecy, Mauchly happened to meet a female army ordnance official who was married to a census statistician. She introduced Mauchly to her husband, who in turn introduced him to Morris Hansen, one of the bureau's brightest statistical stars and a pioneer in the art of using a random sample of population to make projections about the whole population. (Today even our daily newspapers conduct polls based on sampling theory, but in the 1940s this was novel stuff, the statistical equivalent of a Madonna video.) Hansen was quick to recognize how much time and labor such a sophisticated machine could save.

In 1946, largely through his lobbying, the Commerce Department and the National Bureau of Standards commissioned Mauchly and Eckert to design a new computer just to handle census statistics.

In 1951 the Census Bureau took delivery of the first of Mauchly and Eckert's creations, the Universal Automatic Computer (UNIVAC), the world's first commercial digital computer. It was a thing of statistical, though not physical, beauty. Punch cards still supplied the raw data, but these cards were now fed into a device that transferred the information onto a magnetic tape, which then streamed into the gigantic computer. UNIVAC arrived too late to help much in processing data from the 1950 census; by 1960, however, UNIVAC computers were doing virtually all the bureau's calculations. Even so, the bureau still failed to recognize how truly novel and powerful this new technology was; it put UNIVAC to work doing the same tasks, only faster. What the agency failed to see was that UNIVAC, its magnetic tapes in particular, offered an opportunity to build brand-new combinations of statistics—customized census reports—cheaply and without sapping the bureau's limited energy and budget.

Changes outside the bureau would soon bring the agency to appreciate UNIVAC's hidden powers. The new computer technology had begun to draw the attention of corporations and social researchers. Computers became more powerful, more compact, more affordable, and a lot easier to use. At the same time, companies were becoming far more aggressive about the collection of market intelligence. Competition for markets had increased; consumers had a vast array of products to choose from, many having similar functions and attributes. Companies found they had to spend more heavily to win the consumer's attention; they had to figure out where the consumers were, how they thought, why they chose one product over another. In 1932 only 29 companies had formal market research departments; by 1969 the number had risen to 1,235.

Meanwhile something very strange had happened to Jonathan Robbin, then a literature major at Harvard. He had fallen in love with computers: crude things; multicolored ganglions of wire and hot band steel; lovely things; precise; as elegant in concept as the sonnets of William Shakespeare. Robbin became one of the earliest computer jocks, a whiz kid long before Steve Jobs and Steve Wozniak lodged the species in the American psyche. Soon he would revolutionize marketing and become "the king of zip codes," and the landscape of our consumer culture would be changed forever.

■ ■ ■

Three folding tables surround Jonathan Robbin. One contains a forest of
manila folders, one serves as his desk, another supports the collection of
softly purring, creamy gray boxes that constitute his computer. If packed
together in one container, Robbin's system would take up as much space
as a living room TV, yet he estimates it has at least one thousand times
the power of an early UNIVAC, which would have filled his basement
office and most of the house above.

If physical appearance governed choice of occupation, Robbin
would be the manager of a Cambridge, Massachusetts, toy store for very,
very smart children. He is a midsize man who dresses in Brooks Brothers
casual: khaki pants, blue oxford shirts, loafers, and fine-rimmed tor-
toiseshell glasses. On a first encounter you might be tempted to call him
jolly, but this would miss the mark. Rather, he seems powered by an
overheated reactor in danger of spreading statistical shrapnel, such
oblique demographic correlations as the fact that people who listen to
religious radio do not eat salted nuts.

In conversation he takes it for granted that you, his listener, also have
read a thousand books on fractal geometry, multivariate statistical analysis, and mathematical taxonomy; that you too are on intimate terms
with the classification of Bahamanian sediments and the effects of
rotatory inertia on rocket hulls. Robbin speaks in sudden, complex
plumes, rushing the explanations of his statistical inventions as if they
were the most obvious innovations on earth, ideas anyone with even half
a brain, an *eighth* of a brain, could appreciate.

He is quick to vow that he has no interest in probing the personal
lives of individuals. "I don't give a *shit* about that," he says, giving way to
his habit of now and then inserting microbursts of profanity into conversation, as jarring in this esoteric landscape as a land mine exploding in
Harvard Yard. "All I care about is predicting outcomes, predicting
marginal propensity to buy. The higher my multiple-r, the higher my
huddle and T square, that's where I get my kicks. I get my jollies from
being more accurate. My business is engineering systems that help
people make money. That's all I do."

A fundamental notion has colored Robbin's for-profit career: Given
the right variables, scientists ought to be able to predict the behavior of
communities of people. "I've often thought there may be some way to
describe the aggregation of human beings much as you would the

physical process of aggregation of particles, to come up with something like a 'gluon,' the unit of attraction whereby people meld together." The motherload of predictive human variables, Robbin knew, was stockpiled in Suitland, Maryland, at the headquarters of the U.S. Bureau of the Census.

Robbin gained an intimate appreciation of census data in the 1960s, when, as founder and president of General Analytics Corporation, he became a subcontractor for the Office of Economic Opportunity and thus helped wage the war on poverty. No one will ever accuse Robbin of thinking small. In his role as poverty warrior he devised a program that took 1960 census data and merged it with information collected from some twenty-nine other agencies to produce a narrative portrait of socioeconomic conditions in all 3,134 U.S. counties. In published form the volume ran a modest 187,000 pages.

Robbin also produced a riot predictor, his "Index of Susceptibility to Civil Disorder." He ran a computer analysis of social conditions existing in all the cities that experienced race riots in 1968, then isolated a set of variables that seemed to him most responsible for causing the riots. These, he argued, could be used to predict where the next riots would occur.

The statistical shtick that gained him most notoriety was large-scale multivariate statistical analysis—simply put, the science of making sense of large masses of information. He refined the techniques as a graduate student at Columbia and New York universities. In particular he tinkered with the art of cluster analysis, which he would later harness to build Claritas Corp., his most successful company. Cluster analysis breaks masses of seemingly homogeneous data into small, manageable groups of information that capture the features common to the components of each group but also highlight the differences among each group. Its power, and the feature that so enthralled Robbin from his first encounters, was its capacity to produce surprise by exposing phenomena no one could have expected. Where standard scientific method requires a scientist to guess in advance what he is going to discover, cluster analysis harnesses serendipity.

One of Robbin's first uses of the technique involved an analysis of a large number of very similar artifacts at the Metropolitan Museum of Art in New York. The museum suspected some were clever forgeries, and through cluster analysis Robbin was able to distill the features that bona fide artifacts had in common and thus weed out the counterfeits.

Marketers discovered Robbin's skills. Throughout the 1960s he conducted studies for IBM, Pepsi, Lever Brothers, Ford, Merck, Warner-Lambert, and several major advertising firms. The Southern California Gas Company hired him to figure out where it should install gas pipelines to take advantage of the region's rapid growth. Robbin analyzed customer files to determine what characteristics identified the company's best, highest-volume residential customers, then figured out which census tracts held the highest concentrations of such customers. Next, taking into account geographic barriers such as freeways, mountains, and canyons, Robbin projected the directions in which each community would be likely to expand.

"My fun in this life is epistemology, dancing around on the horizon of knowledge," Robbin told me. "I'm fascinated with the things that draw people together into communities. Utopia is not such an unthinkable concept. It's absolutely possible, and achievable by the rational use of human knowledge for altruistic ends. Part of that rational use is the kind of thing I've been working on and developing all my life. It's a sad commentary that it really has to be dedicated to the problem of selling things in order to make a living."

Sad commentary or not, somewhere along the way Robbin discovered he liked making money.

A stranger passing the tawdry miracle mile that fronts Census Bureau headquarters in Suitland could easily confuse the compound, with its high fence and orange-vested armed guards, for a federal prison. Until the late 1960s the look of the place mirrored the Census Bureau's attitude toward the outside world. No formal mechanism existed for helping researchers make the best use of the data the bureau took so much time and effort to collect; users for the most part had to take the data as it was published by the bureau. Everything else was excess demographic baggage. Jonathan Robbin nicknamed the bureau of this era "the cement elephant."

But the bureau would soon change its attitude and in the process kick off a marketing revolution.

In the sixties, computer technology advanced quickly; by 1963 domestic sales of computers passed the billion-dollar mark. IBM introduced its classic System 360 series of computers; National Cash Register built a computer just for small businesses; the first minicomputers appeared, most notably Digital Equipment Corporation's PDP-1, promising low-cost, high-speed performance in a compact machine that would not require its own office. Now able to manipulate large masses of data more readily than ever before, companies began demanding special combinations of census data tailored to their specific needs.

A few entrepreneurial census officials pushed to make the bureau more responsive. In 1967 the bureau established the Data Access and Use Laboratory specifically to explore ways of making census products easier for outsiders to use. The bureau began selling, for $70 a reel, the actual magnetic tapes from which it produced its own routine publications. In 1967 the bureau organized its New Haven Census Use Study, whose mission included the development of software that would allow computers to draw digital maps and to scour a data base to find a match for a given address, technologies fundamental to marketing as performed today.

The process of digitizing maps—converting them to a numerical description a computer could manage—proved to be complex, like trying to convert an intricate jigsaw puzzle into a collection of numbered intersections and doing it so precisely that a computer could then make an exact copy of the puzzle. The resulting software was dubbed the DIME file, for "dual independent map encoding," a tool that for the first time allowed users to produce powerful visual representations of census data quickly and cheaply, and without having to hire vast armies of draftsmen.

Donald Cooke, who guided this portion of the use study, discovered just how powerful, and how sensitive, such maps could be. In the course of the study, medical researchers from Yale–New Haven Hospital got wind of the bureau's new mapping capabilities and stopped by with files of computer tapes packed with sensitive personal medical records. They asked Cooke to make maps showing the incidence of certain diseases and conditions by the address of each patient; they insisted the records be stored in the project's data vault when not in use.

"I'm a little uncomfortable about saying exactly what kind of health phenomena we were mapping because the maps never saw the light of day," Cooke told me. "They were done strictly for doctors; they were done off confidential health data. What you have to do, you have to figure out what would make Don Cooke uncomfortable talking about these things twenty-five years later. Like what if we had individual incidence of syphilis, or something like that, and the Census Bureau was mapping it. That's the kind of thing an epidemiologist would love to see, but that clearly would be a terrible infringement on the rights of the individuals and the kind of thing the Census Bureau would like to distance itself from."

He did describe one map, an address-by-address plot of birth weights. "You could see that the low birth weights corresponded spatially very strongly with the ghetto areas," Cooke said. "You could graphically see these socioeconomic health phenomena just jumping right out of the maps. It was very powerful stuff."

Address matching, another of the project's goals, at first seemed an elementary challenge, and in a perfect world, Cooke told me, the process would indeed be simple. "But the world isn't perfect. People will write 275 Main, and you have to know whether that's Main Avenue or Main Street. Maybe it's really Maine, as in the state, but they write it Main. Or they've taken John F. Kennedy Boulevard and made it JFK Boulevard or Kennedy Boulevard. In concept, address matching is trivial; in practice it's fiendishly complex."

Just how fiendish became apparent when Cooke left the Census Bureau and with two partners founded Urban Data Processing of Cambridge, Massachusetts. Its first customer was *Reader's Digest*, which hired Urban Data to build an address-matching program to cover some of the more complex addresses of its millions of subscribers. "We had this very narrow view of the world that you get when you grow up in New England. We thought New England was representative of addresses. We had heard about how in New York the numbered streets went up to 250 or so. And that was fine. But we had no idea that in Utah the numbered streets went up past 5000. We had *no* idea about Queens [in New York]. A typical avenue address in Queens might be 119-59 37th Avenue. What that means is you're on 37th Avenue and you're in house number 59, in the block between 119th and 120th streets. And of course we had never come across the addresses you get in the Southwest or in Los Angeles. Avenida de los Robles! *Reader's Digest* had them all."

The cement elephant was coming alive, but a geographic barrier still kept most companies from taking full advantage of the power of census data.

Jonathan Robbin recognized that a fundamental chasm existed between the way companies saw the world and the way the Census Bureau saw it. The companies functioned in a geography defined by the post office—streets, addresses, and, beginning in 1963, zip codes. The Census Bureau's geography, its blocks and tracts, couldn't have been more different.

The two geographies clashed at the level of their fundamental building blocks. Each census block is essentially a rectangle with four faces. Each face consists of addresses from only *one* side of a street. The basic component of the postal system, however, is the carrier route. And carrier routes, as every suburban resident knows, include *both* sides of the street. Moreover, the physical boundaries of zip zones and census territories simply don't coincide. No software existed to apportion census data among the nation's 38,000 zip codes, though the Census Bureau made the first attempt to produce such a geography-bridging tool in 1972 when it released a special tabulation of its 1970 census data known as "the Fifth Count," a file that clustered a portion of the data by zip. The Fifth Count, however, was deeply flawed.

By now Robbin had founded Claritas, Latin for "clarity." He set to work on the mind-numbing task of correcting the Fifth Count and of extending the file to include every zip in the country. True to form, Robbin did not stop at anything as trivial as a mere collection of census data broken down by zip codes. He included a then little known cache of IRS information on income already tabulated by zip. The result was a three-thousand-page set of volumes called *REZIDE, the National Zip Code Encyclopedia*. One prominent feature was Robbin's "zip quality rating," which ranked every zip by a score that took into account household income, education, home value, and occupation. An early *REZIDE* volume describes this ZQ rating as "a highly sensitive tool for the instant recognition of lower-, middle-, and upper-class areas."

Time Inc. put Claritas on the map. Claritas used its statistical know-how to demonstrate conclusively that *Time* magazine reached the country's most affluent consumers. *Time* had been saying this all along, but now the magazine could prove it with concrete numbers. Claritas found, for example, that almost 90 percent of *Time*'s New Jersey readers fell into the top 40 percent of households as ranked by zip quality. This finding allowed *Time* to focus its subscription drives on zip codes of comparable quality throughout the country. Soon *Time* would rely on Claritas data to create a special edition, dubbed *Time Z*, targeted just at the richest neighborhoods.

"We made a lot of money for them," Robbin told me.

In turn *Time* made a lot of money for Claritas. At one point Claritas raked in a million dollars a year from *Time* alone, Robbin said, but Time Inc.'s patronage had an additional value: what was good for *Time* proved rapidly to be good enough for many other companies.

Robbin still was not satisfied, however; zip codes were too broad and imprecise. He began looking for a way to use census data to describe specific neighborhoods.

Meanwhile the Census Bureau had begun to look and behave suspiciously like a business. Perhaps too much so.

Throughout the 1970s and 1980s our tax dollars directly subsidized a revolution in marketing that let the marketers find us, target us, and persuade us far more efficiently than ever before.

One need look only at the backgrounds of the men, and the sole woman, appointed to run the bureau over the past two decades to get a sense of why and how this trend arose. In 1969 President Richard Nixon named the first hard-core marketer to the post, George Hay Brown, director of marketing at Ford Motor Company since 1960. Vincent Barabba, chief executive of a political polling firm, followed and ran the bureau from 1973 to 1977, installing formal procedures to promote use of census data. He was succeeded by Manuel Plotkin, previously chief economist and market research manager for Sears, Roebuck & Co. Barabba returned in 1979, then left in 1981 to become director of marketing at General Motors Corporation. In 1984 Ronald Reagan appointed a past president of the American Marketing Association, John G. Keane, to run the bureau, and George Bush appointed Barbara Everitt Bryant, previously senior vice-president of Market Opinion Research in Detroit.

In the years following the 1980 census, the bureau and private industry worked out some nifty deals, lawful arrangements that nonetheless raise fundamental questions about who owns America's data and how the information should be made available.

The classic example took place in 1981, when a group of ten companies, following Jonathan Robbin's earlier lead, joined forces to ask the Census Bureau to do a special tabulation of 1980 data broken down by zip code. Requests for special counts had by then become common, but the consortium's deal was unusual. It gave a select group of companies exclusive control over a body of public information in heavy demand—control that brought them windfall profits and a major competitive advantage, and gave taxpayers a lot more junk mail.

The bureau had planned to produce a zip-coded file in 1980, a much improved version of the basic Fifth Count file it produced after the 1970 census, but a major cut in the bureau's budget forced it to scrap the plan. The bureau told the consortium it could produce the new file for $250,000, a price designed to recoup only the cost of actually apportioning the 1980 data among the 38,000 zip codes and of producing the necessary computer tapes. The price would not recover a dime of the $1 billion the bureau spent to conduct the census itself.

The bureau also agreed to withhold the resulting zip file from general public use for eighteen months. The consortium, meanwhile, granted each of its members a license to use the zip file to provide zip-coding services to other marketing companies interested in adding census data to their own consumer data bases. "We made a fortune on that, as you can imagine," said Edward Spar, president of Market Statistics Inc., New York, a member of the consortium. "Each of us paid $25,000 for it, and I can tell you right now I made a hell of a lot more than $25,000 on that file."

Even the members of the consortium were surprised that the bureau kept the file from the public. "Everybody knew that was going to be the sweetheart deal of the century," Spar said. "We didn't try to talk the bureau into not producing the file for everybody. We were dumbfounded when they didn't."

A murkier instance of private control of public data arose when the Census Bureau wound up having to buy from a private company the right to use geographic software the bureau had been about to produce on its own.

Well before the 1980 census was taken, the bureau announced plans to produce a computer file containing the digitized boundaries of all the country's census tracts, then had to postpone its development. Donald Cooke, who by now had left Urban Data and founded Geographic Data Technology, knew the tract boundary file would be a hit with marketers. It would allow companies to make those fancy marketing maps that have now become so commonplace: those mosaics of bright colors showing the buying patterns and affluence levels of the country as broken down by census tract. Cooke saw a chance to "scoop" the bureau, as he puts it, and in the process make a profit.

He recruited a group of other marketing and mapping companies to chip in $10,000 each to help him cover the costs of developing the software. His company would own the final product, but each member of the consortium would be licensed to use it. Ten of Cooke's employees completed the digitizing process in five months at a total cost of roughly $120,000.

The product was so successful, the Census Bureau never did produce its own version. In fact, the bureau quietly asked Cooke if it, too, might buy a license for $10,000. Cooke agreed. The licensing agreement allowed the bureau to use the software only for its internal needs and barred it from distributing the file to anyone else. The only way other companies and social science researchers could use the software was to buy access to it from members of Cooke's consortium.

Maneuvers like this prompted Andrew Hacker, a professor of political science, to observe: "Our own computer revolution may be bringing us full circle. Just as once only the wealthy could afford manuscripts, now electronic information is being supplied to elite buyers on a first-use basis. . . . That this is happening with census data, itself a product of citizen cooperation, is both sad and unsettling."

One gray winter afternoon I found myself sitting in a cool, glass-enclosed room at the Alexandria, Virginia, headquarters of Jonathan Robbin's company, Claritas, waiting for my life—or at least a mathematically optimized hyperspatial impression of it—to appear on a computer screen. The location was perfect for a target-marketing company, I decided. The adjacent building, now a warren of artists' studios, was once a torpedo factory that tested its wares by launching them across the Potomac.

Beside me sat Doug Anderson, a young Claritas vice-president, who had typed the zip code of my first Baltimore neighborhood, "Original Northwood," into the machine. I also had entrusted him with two other chunks of my life—my zip when I lived on Nob Hill in San Francisco and the zip of my childhood, the somewhat less exotic streets of Freeport, Long Island, a suburb of New York probably best known as the last exit before Jones Beach.

Anderson tapped a couple of keys. "The moment of truth," he said.

A chill wind blew through the room. Whatever appeared next on the screen would be the fruit of Jonathan Robbin's efforts to to find a way by which marketers could get an instant picture of every neighborhood in the country without ever stepping away from their computers.

In building his clusters, Robbin had taken a thousand census variables and applied the principles of cluster analysis to distill the variables into a manageable collection of categories that captured the essence of neighborhoods. After trying a dozen different approaches, Robbin settled on a set of forty different clusters, neighborhood types that seemed to possess a great deal of power for predicting the consumer behavior of their inhabitants. He called this new targeting system "geodemographics."

The idea got off to a slow start. The theory and mathematics were arcane, the statistics unorthodox, the uses difficult to comprehend. "When you talked about target marketing by neighborhood life-styles," one Claritas executive recalled, "people just scratched their heads."

The biggest breakthrough, at least in terms of Claritas's own well-being, had little to do with statistics. In 1978 a new Claritas executive, Robin Page, hit on a way to make the system easier to grasp. He devised an evocative name and concise capsule description for each cluster, names now well known within the marketing community, such as Blue Blood Estates (the richest cluster), Public Assistance (the poorest), Pools & Patios, Shotguns & Pickups, Tobacco Roads, and Bohemian Mix. These names also captured the imagination of the lay press. A *New Yorker* writer interviewed Robbin for the magazine's "Talk of the Town" section; *The Wall Street Journal* profiled Claritas in a page-one feature. The Pools & Patios cluster even trickled into the script for the movie *Power,* which starred Richard Gere. Claritas named the system PRIZM, for Potential Rating Index for Zip Markets.

Robbin's geodemographics at last took off. By November 1981 Claritas had one hundred customers, including ABC-TV, American Express, Publishers Clearing House, Coca-Cola, Colgate-Palmolive, the Massachusetts State Lottery Commission, R. J. Reynolds Tobacco, even the U.S. Army.

Robbin calls it a "prosthetic" device for the mind, a means, simply, of extending perception. A direct-mail company seeking to find fresh targets for its products could divide a list of its customers into PRIZM clusters, see which clusters represented the best customers, and then target those clusters throughout the country. "The whole idea is that you can now assign every neighborhood in the United States to one of these forty types," Robbin said. The Blue Bloods of California will behave much like the Blue Bloods of New Jersey; the Pools & Patios set in Massachusetts will swoon for the same stuff the patio crowd goes for in Louisiana.

The PRIZM system is now firmly embedded in the marketing landscape. The massive intelligence systems built by Nielsen, Arbitron, and other big-data companies allow customers to do PRIZM analyses. The army used PRIZM to help it locate its recruiting centers in the most receptive areas. The new Saturn division of General Motors used PRIZM as a small part of its vast market research campaign to figure out what kind of car to build and how to sell it. But perhaps no corporation relies on the system more directly, and with more direct impact on the daily lives of millions of consumers, than Satellite Music Network, a Dallas-based subsidiary of ABC/Capital Cities.

The company began broadcasting music by satellite in 1981 and now transmits ten different show "formats"—hard-rock, contemporary hits, and so forth—each with listeners who fit a distinct demographic profile. Stations pay a monthly fee and in return receive twenty-four-hour-a-day broadcasts. Freed of the messy business of actually having to hire disc jockeys and program their own shows, these stations operate on a shoestring. Satellite Music targets dead and dying stations as likely customers.

The company uses PRIZM first to figure out just who listens to which format. Listeners throughout the country betray their particular tastes when they call in requests for songs to the 800 numbers designated for each format. The operators who take these requests ask each caller for his zip code. Satellite Music then checks to see which PRIZM clusters dominate those zips. Patterns emerge that show the musical formats each cluster prefers. Thus when a new radio station signs on, Satellite Music can analyze the zip codes in the station's broadcast territory to see which clusters predominate and which formats those clusters like best. It knows, for example, that people in the Gray Power cluster tend to like "Stardust," known in radio jargon as an MOR, or middle-of-the-road, format. If the zip codes of a new affiliate show a predominance of Gray Power clusters, Satellite Music can then suggest the station choose the "Stardust" format.

The network transmits national advertising directly to listeners through the local stations, but automatically fills a portion of the advertising time with prerecorded local advertising sold by each station's own salesmen. The local ads are stored on automatic tape machines activated by a signal from Dallas. Satellite Music's national DJ's even do voice promos for the local stations, and these too are broadcast on electronic cue. Listeners hear a seamless broadcast that, for all they know, originates in the station's hometown.

One ailing client was WMMW, a floundering AM station in Meriden, Connecticut. The station chose "Stardust" and quickly became a ratings success, albeit at the expense of a few jobs. Where once the station needed fifteen full-time employees and ten part-timers, suddenly it only needed five full-timers and two part-timers. The station's operating cost fell to $6,000 a month; previously its payroll alone was $15,000 a month.

What secrets would Robbin's clusters reveal about me? What demographic skeletons would PRIZM unearth?

"All right," said Doug Anderson at Claritas headquarters. A list of clusters had appeared on the screen. "You've got a big mix of people here," Anderson said.

The cluster most heavily represented in the zip for my Baltimore neighborhood was Downtown Dixie-Style, downscale souls ranked fifth from last in terms of affluence. About 15 percent occupied cluster 32, Public Assistance, the bottom rung. (For various reasons the numbers assigned to each cluster do not correspond to their affluence rank.)

All in all, my zip showed elements of thirteen different clusters. We needed to get closer to my neighborhood, to a smaller portion of my zip. Anderson typed in the number of my census "block group," a unit of census geography built of census blocks.

In census-speak I lived in state 24, county 510, census tract 902, block group 4. In PRIZM that made me a member of cluster 27, Levittown, U.S.A.

Levittown.

I confess, I was just a tad disappointed. I had seen my neighborhood in different terms, an enclave of sixty-year-old houses under a forest of still-surviving elms and occupied by an eclectic crowd that included an oceanographer, a homicide detective, an assistant attorney general, even a violinist from the Baltimore Symphony Orchestra.

Levittown connoted something else: boxy homes on a broad, treeless plain.

Things appeared on the screen I'd never known about myself:

I was an ice hockey fan. I bought a lottery ticket one or more times each week. I went bowling more than twenty-five times last year. I belonged to a union, installed my own faucets, most often frequented pancake houses and doughnut shops. I was not at all likely to chew tobacco or buy comedy tapes and records.

Anderson next began typing in the block groups of my past. How far I'd fallen! In San Francisco I belonged to cluster 37, Bohemian Mix, six notches higher on the affluence scale than Levittown.

I traveled by railroad and bought disco tapes. I drank malt liquor and imported brandy. I visited Europe and went to four or more movies in ninety days. I drank Pepsi Light. I did not own a chain saw, drive a pickup, or panel my own walls.

Finally we ventured into the deep past. State 36, county 59, census tract 4143.02, block group 5. Freeport, Long Island.

Cluster 27. Again.

Levittown redux.

"You've really gone full circle," Robbin told me later. "From a family back to a family. I mean, that's what I would suppose. Are you married with children?"

"Yes."

"That's it. You want your kids to live in a house. Do you live in a house?"

"Yes."

"But when you were in Bohemian Mix you probably lived in an apartment, right?"

"Yes."

"I mean, look—is that easy to say or is it not? I went through the same damn thing. I hated suburbia. I was brought up in a suburban area of New Jersey, a nice manicured little town called Summit. . . . I *hated* it. I think I was assigned to read *Madame Bovary* about twenty times in my career. I couldn't even find that book in a bookstore in Summit, New Jersey. Now of course it's different. It's upscale. Back then everybody was a troglodyte. And it was *dull.* It's odd that I now live in something very similar. I live in *Bethesda.* I've come full circle back to suburbia. I've never been able to escape it."

Robbin's clusters struck me as being a convenient way of stereotyping consumers from afar, but when I suggested this during one of our conversations at his home, he bristled.

"As a matter of fact," he snapped, "I take exactly the opposite point of view—that there's no such thing as an average person. You have to take a multivariate point of view to be able to describe neighborhoods. Look, I'll give you an example. Cluster 37 is Bohemian Mix. It's a bimodal distribution, U-shaped: it has a lot of poor people and a lot of rich people; it has starving jazz musicians living in the basement and rich psychiatrists on the top floor, but there's nobody in the middle. You can't average the two together and say 'Oh, this place has an average person making $25,000!' "

Even Robbin, however, occasionally slips into talk that seems to belie this multivariate stance. During a visit to Phoenix, he took a side trip to Sun City, one of the country's largest enclaves of the Gray Power set.

"I was amazed, amazed," he said. "I loved it. It was fascinating. It was like being driven through a necropolis. Nobody was moving, nobody was on the street. Nobody was walking, not even with a dog. I only saw one soul out of a thousand households that I passed, and it was this one guy sitting on his front lawn sort of watching the sprinkler go around and around. Maybe he was trying to see if the grass was growing? We went into a shopping mall to make a phone call, and sure enough here were all these spry oldsters pushing carts around and gumming at each other— all these women in their lime green pants and harlequin glasses. Just as I *expected* they would look."

I asked Robbin if ever he had walked into a neighborhood only to discover his clusters were off the mark.

"Never," he said without hesitation. "It's a testament to the accuracy of the census data. They really gathered the facts."

The Census Bureau created the modern marketing machine, but it did so without breaking its strict code of confidentiality. It never releases the names or addresses of people who answer census questionnaires, and it masks information considered so distinctive as to be likely to give away a respondent's identity. The increasing sophistication of corporate marketers, however, has forced the bureau to confront a new specter of the information age—the danger, albeit clearly remote, that somehow the new marketing intelligence technologies will be used to extract individual identities from the masses of summarized data the bureau publishes.

The bureau began protecting against the accidental disclosure of information with the 1940 census, when it "suppressed" some summary data that was distinctive enough to have given away the identity of the citizens it described. This could happen, for example, in a thinly occupied chunk of census geography where just reporting the age of a very old resident might betray his identity. The risk of accidental disclosure became most acute in 1960 when the bureau for the first time released a file now called the Public Use Microdata Sample, or PUMS, containing the actual responses of a random sample of citizens to the long form census questionnaires, with all names and addresses deleted.

The fear is that some data-rich company could compare the personal records stored in its files against the details disclosed in the microdata tapes and match enough of them to identify the people who answered the questionnaires. Gerald Gates, the bureau official in charge of keeping an eye on the growing technical powers of marketers, believes the risk of such a match occurring is extremely low. On the other hand, he said, the marketers' growing prowess and increasingly rich files have put the bureau on its guard. "The more files there are out there," Gates told me, "the harder it gets to release data."

To cover itself, for the 1990 census the bureau applied a technique known as data switching, where especially distinctive records are simply swapped with statistically comparable records from another geographic region. For its microdata files the bureau discloses only the geographic locations of each respondent by census geographies containing one hundred thousand or more people, thus sharply reducing the chances that some demographic hacker could find a match. The bureau applies a series of other masking techniques as well.

In so valiantly defending our individual identities, however, the bureau overlooks a far more immediate problem: the threat the marketers pose to the privacy of *groups* of people.

One computer file of 1990 census data breaks down the data to the level of individual blocks for the entire country. This was the first time the bureau had done so on such a comprehensive scale, and although marketers cannot match this data to names in their files, they *can* use it to flesh out such files. The resulting body of recombinant data can present a vivid portrait of individuals living in a given block regardless of whether or not the bureau disclosed their names.

During World War II, America saw firsthand how group data can harm people. The bureau doesn't reveal much about the episode—it is conspicuously absent from a time line published in the bureau's newsletter to commemorate the one hundredth anniversary of the census—yet it continues to stain the bureau's collective memory.

On December 7, 1941, Japan invaded Pearl Harbor. War hysteria quickly spread through the far West, complete with rumors of Japanese submarines passing under the Golden Gate Bridge. By February the Western Defense Command began planning the "evacuation" of all Japanese-Americans from the western half of California, Washington, and Oregon and from most of Arizona.

Under the Second War Powers Act of 1942, the bureau could have turned over the specific names and addresses of Japanese residents. The bureau refused. In a 1980 book on the Census Bureau, author Dan Halacy described this refusal as "the most heartwarming example" of the bureau's commitment to protecting individual identities.

The bureau's subsequent behavior, however, was rather less than exemplary.

On February 25, 1942, the Western War Command requested assistance from a variety of civilian agencies, including the Census Bureau, to help bolster the West Coast's defenses against a possible attack. The bureau wasted no time. Immediately it dispatched Calvert L. Dedrick, chief of the division of statistical research, to San Francisco. Dedrick did not supply addresses but provided the next best thing—a compromise that preserved the bureau's reputation for protecting the confidentiality of individuals and yet would soon cause heartbreak and despair for 110,000 American citizens whom even J. Edgar Hoover did not consider particularly threatening.

One official of the time, former U.S. Supreme Court Justice Tom C. Clark, was interviewed in 1975 by the Berkeley Regional Oral History Office about his role as civilian coordinator to the Western Defense Command. He recalled how census data was put to effective use:

"The Census Bureau moved out its raw files. As you know, they take the census every ten years, and it just happened that it had been taken in 1940, the year before. So, they had excellent data to work with because it was almost current. They would lay out on tables various city blocks where the Japanese lived, and they would tell me how many were living in each block. . . . The army would designate certain city blocks where the Japanese lived. A processing station, as it was called, would then be opened up in the designated area. . . . On the day the army selected for removal, these people would report to the processing station with their clothing, personal effects, and so forth, and the army would move them by buses or by train to the camp where they were to stay for the duration."

By August 7, 1942, 110,000 Japanese-Americans had been shipped to Army Assembly Centers or to War Relocation Authority centers, such as the large internment camp at Manzanar in California's Owens Valley.

In testimony before a joint congressional committee considering the 1990 census, author David Burnham testified that the Census Bureau's participation illustrated how "in some circumstances aggregate information about a given race or ethnic group can be almost as dangerous as data concerning the name and address of specific individuals."

The merger of summary census data with privately held individual records raises a confidentiality issue that simply did not exist until the last decade or so. Canadian census officials found themselves grappling with the problem in 1990 when one of Canada's official data distributors—companies deputized to package and distribute data from Statistics Canada, Canada's census office—asked permission to merge a data base of individual names with a file of census data and to sell them together as a distinct product. The question shook the agency and forced it to consider the new realities of data-base marketing. The agency refused the request and promptly began considering a formal addendum to its licensing contracts forbidding any such blending of data. There was something unseemly about the government's deputies producing such products, an official of Statistics Canada told me. At the same time she acknowledged that the agency would be powerless to stop other companies, those beyond the ring of quasi-official distributors, from doing so.

Officials of the U.S. Census Bureau tend to shrug off the problem. The bureau's duty, they argue, is to produce and disseminate data, not to police its use. I asked Marie G. Argana, assistant chief of the bureau's User Services Division, whether the bureau had ever considered trying to regulate its customers. "If we do that, who decides what's good use and what isn't?" she answered. "Do we set ourselves up as censors of data use? That's real heavy stuff."

In 1985, however, Lawrence Cox, then a senior Census Bureau statistician, raised the issue in a bureau paper. Even summary data, he wrote, "can be used in ways that affect the well-being of an entire group or class of people as opposed to a single individual. One example is the use of summary data to target the delivery of 'junk' mail to certain zip codes. In such cases it may appear that a breach of confidentiality has occurred. . . ."

A few pages later he made specific reference to Claritas Corp. "Another indirect threat to privacy is presented by those who combine census data with data from other sources to form detailed demographic and economic profiles of a small geographic area. One such mixer of census data with other data is the well-publicized 'geodemographic' data base. . . . Whether such a political or marketing device as geo-demographics is an invasion of privacy or not, the Census Bureau faces the problem that its data, normally used as an instrument of good, could be used for less noble purposes."

Talk like this causes Robbin's temper to flare. "It's a conflict," he said, his speech accelerating. "People have an interest in their privacy, they have an interest in being consumers. Now, what are they going to trade off?"

He slapped one hand against the other, the report like that from a small pistol.

"Everybody has these conflicts of interest that they can't reconcile. They want one thing, they want another thing, and one cancels out the other. One person doesn't want to see a billboard along a road because it desecrates the scenery. On the other hand, there's this guy coming down the road who wants to know if there's a place to stay in the next fucking town."

Clusters raise an even less tangible issue. Our laws seek to eliminate discrimination by age, race, sex, and creed. Yet in any of the hundreds of data bases that have incorporated the PRIZM system or competing cluster systems, masses of consumers are grouped by their level of socioeconomic achievement. Have we replaced brute discrimination with a far more subtle variety?

All of us have been classified and installed in a digital caste system through which we systematically are included in or excluded from the daily flow of consumer culture. In contrast, before this age of market fragmentation and segmentation, the growth of the mass consumer market had an egalitarian effect. "Everybody could join the 'class' of consumers in the marketplace," wrote Susan Strasser in *Satisfaction*

Guaranteed: The Making of the American Mass Market. Today's rush toward market segmentation, she argues, "codifies increasing class distinctions."

Who cares? What's the harm?

"Our big concern," said Janlori Goldman, the ACLU attorney, "is that the market is going to make certain decisions about people without ever meeting them, without ever talking to them, without ever really knowing who they are. The biggest danger in that kind of a situation is that those decisions will be discriminatory, that they will be based upon their race, their sexual preference, their religion, or their gender. A bank in Boston refused to provide mortgages to people who had a certain zip code. Just like that! If you lived there, you didn't get a mortgage. Well, who do you think lived in that zip code? Low-income blacks."

David Miller, a Claritas senior vice-president, told me clustering techniques pose a danger only when misused. "By nature segmentation is discrimination. I'm discriminating against people I don't think are willing to buy my product. I don't think anybody's going to complain all that much if Citibank chooses to promote jumbo CDs to wealthy neighborhoods as opposed to poor neighborhoods. That's pretty innocuous. It's a whole different story, however, if somebody decides he's going to promote a *necessary* service only to one group and deny the opportunity to a second group. That's the redlining question."

Most companies, he argued, have a powerful motive to steer away from such exclusionary strategies. "Virtually everyone out there is trying to get everyone *into* their sales," he said. "Every single person we've dealt with has a legitimate question—how do I reduce my costs, make more money, become more profitable, and increase my market share? For good or bad, that's the wave of the future for the United States."

Throughout the 1980s census data was the raw material the marketers used to predict the behavior of consumers. In coming years, however, census data will become less and less important. The biggest data-marketing companies have now refined their abilities to track our behaviors, needs, and dreams to the point they may no longer need census data.

"In the 1990s, the census data is almost irrelevant," said Peter Francese, an early data-marketing pioneer and now publisher of *American Demographics* magazine. "The consumer data bases have gone so far beyond census data that census data is, believe me, incidental music. That's not to say it's not important, because you can't take any surveys without benchmarking them against the census. But it used to be the whole enchilada. I liken it to a car: census data used to be the whole car; it's now just a component of the engine."

Ed Spar, the president of Market Statistics, agrees. "The way things are going," he told me, "the private sector won't even want the census. They'll have their own census. The big players, the Equifaxes, have zillions of names. They can count the hair on a man's ass."

4

NAKED CAME
THE CONSUMER

*The process we're witnessing now is in fact the capitalist
society trying to squeeze out of each person, like blood from a
stone, whatever commercial value that person may possess.*

—Marc Rotenberg, Computer Professionals
for Social Responsibility, December 1991

If a stranger asked me how much I paid for my house, I doubt I'd tell
him. Likewise I don't routinely discuss the credit limit on my Visa card
or the balance in my checking account. But these financial artifacts and
hundreds of other bits of personal information have become routine
commodities in the data bazaar, blithely collected and traded by marketers for the supposed good of the American consumer. The biggest data
collectors run digital trap lines from coast to coast and know more about
us, in some respects, than our friends and lovers do—they can know, for
example, what brand of condoms you charged at your local Rite-Aid or
that you picked up a pregnancy test today. They can know too about your
secret life, the flowers you buy that your wife never sees, your practice of
staying in gay guest houses whenever you go away on business. These
companies grow more and more knowledgeable with each passing day,
and they are not shy about their growing powers. In 1991 during a
marketers' convention in New York I picked up a flier that described a
new, all-inclusive consumer intelligence service offered by the Elrick &
Lavidge unit of Equifax, the credit-reporting company. They called the
system "OmniVision" and boasted: "We think we know more about your
own neighborhood than you do, and we'd like to prove it!"

Dozens of companies now specialize in collecting and merging the shards of personal information we consumers leave behind. We see the fruits of their efforts each day, however fleetingly, when we sort through the stacks of junk mail that collect in our boxes each morning. In 1990 the mailers unleashed 63.7 billion pieces of mail on the mailboxes of America, one billion more letters than in 1989. Together it weighed 7.6 billion pounds, roughly fifty-seven times the weight of the *Queen Elizabeth II*. Most of it, I am convinced, came to my house.

I have developed a pretty good eye for separating junk mail from the real thing, and most of what I get goes into the trash unopened. I cull my mail using an informal statistical process that tells me that any letter that arrives with a couple of "YES!" and "NO!" stickers on the envelope is probably not going to be a letter from an old and dear friend. I am careful always to save the catalogs for my wife, who has been known to bring L. L. Bean, J. Crew, Lillian Vernon, and Hanna Andersson to bed with her at night, sometimes all at once. She is also a deep believer in the long shot; any letter with Ed McMahon's face on it is priority mail. She is a doctor, and people with causes to advance and gadgets to sell adore doctors.

Together we make one hot couple, at least from a marketers' perspective. Our names have been rented, matched, merged, purged, deduped, stockpiled, downloaded, parsed, and sorted; we have been scavenged by data pickers who sifted through our driving records and auto registrations, our deed and our mortgage, in search of clues to our needs and dreams, such revelatory data as the make and year of our cars and the equity we hold in our house. The scavengers pass along this information to central computers, which in turn merge it with other streams of individual data—the magazines we subscribe to, the organizations we support, the places we travel, the kids we raise—and then spit it all out to virtually anyone willing to pay for it.

Lists are the raw materials. There are "compiled" lists built of records bought wholesale from state governments or amassed piece by piece. There are "response" lists created whenever people subscribe to magazines, order products through the mail, or enter a contest. Advertisers can rent lists that tell what car you bought, whether you like dried fruit and nuts, whether you are Catholic, Jewish, black, pregnant, or gay.

Until the 1980s there was only so much a mailer could do with such lists. By the middle of the decade, however, computers and advanced software had become cheap enough and powerful enough to allow the

data collectors to manipulate lists containing tens of millions of names
and to match them and merge them with whatever other lists they could
get their hands on, thereby turning the spare skeleton of a single list into
a robust file of consumer portraits.

Suppose your name appears on one hundred lists (a conservative
estimate, by the way). If combined, the data on those lists would take on
a descriptive and predictive power far beyond the mere sum of the
individual list fragments. Such "superlists," as they have been called, are
like strands of genetic code that determine how we consume, where we
shop, what we eat, whom we are likely to vote for in the next election.
The number of people now stockpiled in corporate computers is staggering. TRW, another big credit-reporting company, keeps monthly tabs on
165 million consumers, or roughly 90 percent of all consumers over the
age of eighteen. Donnelly Marketing Information Services tracks 125
million people and enriches its data base by mailing surveys to 30
million households at a time, ten times a year. Wiland Services of
Boulder, Colorado, built a system called ULTRAbase that stores "1,000
demographic, geographic, and behavioral data elements" on more than
215 million individuals.

On whose lists, I wondered, did I reside? How did I end up there?
How much did the market researchers know about me and my family?

I set off to find out. I packed a powerful question: Where did you get
my name?

I began the search for my direct-mail self on the top floor of the Clarence
Mitchell, Jr., Courthouse in Baltimore. Here in a mundane room of
ocher walls and brown tile my life as a commodity began. Microfilm
files 1611-278 and 1611-281 stored such details as what I paid for my
house, the amount I borrowed to buy it, and how much I was able to
scrape together for the down payment. Our real estate transactions are in
the public domain, and should be; as it is, developers and ordinary
homeowners do some pretty sneaky things to have their way with the land
of America, and it is nice to know there are public places where we or our
attorneys can go to review their deals. The information, however, doesn't
simply stay in the courthouse serenely shrouded in dust. It migrates; it
coalesces. It becomes an integral part of wholly new strains of recombinant information never envisioned by those who drafted our real estate
disclosure laws.

One day data prospectors from Rufus S. Lusk & Son Inc. stumbled on my land records and snatched them up.

Lusk, headquartered in Silver Spring, Maryland, collects real estate data primarily in Maryland, Virginia, and Washington, D.C., scavenging exact home equity and tax information, indexing it, cross-referencing it, then selling it to realtors, landscapers, interior decorators, the FBI, the IRS, even *The Washington Post*—to anyone, in short, with an acute interest in the comings and goings of people.

Rufus S. Lusk III, grandson of the company's founder and its current chief executive, is an unabashedly enthusiastic trader of other people's information. He is a former minister of the United Church of Christ and looks it, with a pleasant open face and a tendency to talk just a bit too loud as if every room had a hundred pews and he had to reach the wounded soul in the very last one.

The FBI uses Lusk's data to keep track of suspicious resident aliens. The IRS uses it to help validate the tax returns of well-heeled taxpayers. *The Washington Post* routinely scans Lusk's records of expensive housing transactions to monitor the arrivals and departures of VIPs. But when Lusk gave *Washingtonian* magazine the vital statistics of a Georgetown home purchased by Ben Bradlee, then managing editor of *The Washington Post*, Bradlee phoned Lusk and angrily lectured him about privacy.

Lusk was unmoved. "Freedom of information and embarrassment go hand in hand," he likes to say.

In my search for my marketing self I stopped by Lusk's Timonium, Maryland, office and met Carol Stewart, vice-president in charge of the office. I asked to see my records. She agreed and assured me, "It's all public information."

To test her conviction, I asked to see the real estate records of Kurt L. Schmoke, Baltimore's mayor. No doubt I'd have needed hours of prodding to get the mayor's address from his press office, let alone the amount of his mortgage. An employee loaded the appropriate microfiche card into a reader. (Lusk also maintains on-line searching systems.) Suddenly there it all was, right there on the screen: 3320 Sequoia Avenue, zip 21215. Owner-occupied. Single-family dwelling. Acquired November 1983 for $125,000, with a $112,500 mortgage from Yorkridge-Calvert Savings & Loan. He paid $3,553.36 in annual state and local property taxes.

My heart leapt.

I asked now to see my own records, and these too appeared. Of far more interest to me, however, were the adjacent entries, the homes of my neighbors. Yes, this was all public information—but why did I feel I was being let in on a secret?

Ah, Richard and Carol, Fred and Betsy, Nancy, Margaret! I knew more about you, your buying power, your budget constraints, than you ever suspected.

Seeing my name and the names of my neighbors all toiling in their own small way to help Lusk make a profit gave me an odd feeling. My affairs were being monitored, yet until my visit to Lusk I had known nothing about it.

Who else was watching?

That afternoon I called the Maryland Motor Vehicle Administration to see what they might have on me. I was steered to Ed Seidel, a public information officer who was happy to be of help and who confessed that he himself was fed up with the amount of information he was being asked to cough up these days. He told me the state kept two "headers" on me and on every other Maryland driver: one contained my registration and title information, the other my license and driving record. Both are available to anyone who wants to see them, both are collected routinely in national sweeps by private companies like data giant R. L. Polk.

Seidel asked for the "Soundex" number from my driver's license. As I read each digit, I heard him call it out to someone else sitting near him in his office. A printer whined at me through the earpiece of my phone.

This made me a little nervous, although I'm not sure why. "I hope there's nothing embarrassing there," I said.

"Embarrassing!" Seidel said. He chuckled. "You don't know embarrassing. Sometimes the list is as tall as my boss."

What could one glean from my driving record? My address, of course. And the vital statistics of me and my car: I was at the time thirty-six years old, stood six one, and weighed 185 pounds. I drove a 1984—that year!—Honda Civic Sedan, plate number WGN103. My car weighed less than 3,700 pounds.

All this, except maybe the weight of my car, can be useful to marketers.

The age of my car clearly indicated I was a likely target for a new one. My age, in the parenting range, probably meant I wouldn't be getting any mail about those hot little Mazda Miatas—more likely a Dodge Caravan or Jeep Cherokee. A long list of violations on my record might have caused my insurance company to boost my rates or cancel my policy outright; such revelations, however, might also have caused high-risk insurers and accident attorneys to consider me a hot prospect.

"It also includes an indication if anything's been flagged," Seidel said. "Which yours is."

He paused for effect. "You've got a little parking ticket for 12/15/88, city of Baltimore."

"I paid that," I said.

With a kind of weary delight he asked, "Are you sure?"

Every organization seems to have a list. Whenever you subscribe, give, or buy, your name is put on the lists of those you've subscribed to, given to, bought from. Chemlawn rents its list; so does the Minnesota State Lottery. Sunoco rents the names of its credit card holders. No one is spared, not even subscribers to *The New Yorker.* The magazine began marketing its readers for the first time in 1988. Catalog companies, magazines, and other upright concerns could rent the list, upon approval, for $90 a thousand names, although the magazine expressly barred its use for such crass endeavors as sweepstakes, real estate offers, politics, and fund-raising. Also in 1988, U.S. Sprint began trading the names of its more than six million customers. Anyone who rented this list could select customers who were female, who made international calls, or who traveled a lot. The company tracked customers' travels by their use of Sprint's "Fon Card," a telephone credit card designed to be used on the road. A Sprint executive told me the company began offering the list in order to trade it for lists owned by other companies.

Even kids are a commodity. *Sesame Street* magazine rents its subscriber list; so do *Snoopy* magazine and *Mickey Mouse.* Hasbro Toys peddled the 454,427 names of individuals who sent in proof of purchase labels to get a rebate on My Little Pony games, Jem Doll cassettes, and GI Joe figurines. There is also a list of the forty thousand children who bought Grow A Frog, a mail-order frog-breeding kit that includes a tadpole.

Some lists can betray private details about our health and, perhaps most valuable to marketers, the degree to which we worry about our health. Dependable Lists Inc. of Bellwood, Illinois, rents a list called "Back Pain Sufferers," containing the names of five million Americans with back trouble. Phillips Publishing Inc., Potomac, Maryland, rented a list of people who subscribed to *Cardiac Alert* magazine. RMI Direct Marketing of Hawthorne, New York, marketed a list of over two million Americans who had simply *inquired* about getting a hearing aid.

In April 1991 I received an announcement for a new list called "Health Ailments" intended only for the eyes of direct-mailers. The flier was sent to a really shady corporate entity called EL Enterprises—me— by LBMI Direct Marketing Services Inc., a New Rochelle, New York, concern that manages hard-core commercial lists. The "Health Ailments" list offered the names of up to 984,000 Americans a year who, by answering direct-response surveys, had disclosed some form of chronic condition, including rheumatism, arthritis, and high blood pressure. The cost was $65 per thousand names; for $10 extra you got the 82,000 fresh names generated by the list each month. Such monthly lists are known in the business as "hotlines"; list managers charge more for these on the theory that consumers now and then slip into acquisitive moods, and when they do it is best to strike fast.

My favorite health list was managed by George-Mann Associates of Hightstown, New Jersey. The company marketed the names of the 22,000 members of an outfit called the Bureau of Protective Analysis. These people paid an annual fee and in return got quarterly urinalysis reports so they could keep tabs on what the bureau calls "the eighteen potential trouble spots."

I called George-Mann Associates because I could not help but wonder about the logistics of all this. Did the people on this list pack up their urine every three months and ship it off through the post office? What *were* the eighteen potential trouble spots?

"I don't have too much information," said Monica Fine, one of George-Mann's list managers. "When they join they get a newsletter, they get these reports, and they are people who are conscious about their health."

"These reports are done by the bureau?"

"By the bureau. Right. Part of the fee."

I persisted. "How can I reach the bureau?"

"We don't give out that kind of information."

"Well, can you tell me where it's located?"

"No," she said. "We're not really allowed to. We protect the anonymity of our list owners."

The names of the bureau's 20,000 urologically preoccupied Americans, however, were available for $60 per thousand.

■ ■ ■

Lists are a marvelous vehicle for helping companies locate and target America's suckers—although marketers are careful never to use so crude a term in public. They call these consumers "opportunity seekers."

My wife qualifies as an opportunity seeker, if only because of her passion for entering contests where the odds of winning equal the odds that Carl Sagan will be struck dead by a meteor while peering through a telescope.

As a result she gets an unusual mix of mail. One day she may get an update on communicable diseases from the Centers for Disease Control in Atlanta, the next she hears from the likes of Professional Systems Corporate Headquarters, North Hollywood, California.

Professional Systems sent her a piece of junk mail that looked like a serious official communication from a bank—one of those computer-generated envelopes that you have to pull apart. The front was distorted by black hash marks as if to mask an enclosed check or automatic teller identification number. Inside was a "Final Notice" intended "to advise you of goods being held in your name."

My wife hadn't ordered anything, yet Professional Systems was holding a camera for her. From the description included in the notice, it had to be a pretty sophisticated little number, too—a "Meikai 35-mm camera, including 50-mm optical lens, lens cap, tripod mount, film counter, hot shoe synchronized for electronic flash, in black moisture-resistant carrying case with strap."

All she had to do was pay $12.95 to get it.

Cheap cameras, cheap jewelry, and fake diamonds fall into a category known in the junk-mail trade as "consumer technology." Opportunity seekers betray their gullibility when they order such devices through the mail or those 900-prefix telephone numbers that flash repeatedly across our TV screens late at night in the commercial breaks of rerun movies. For a glimpse of how the mailers view this class of consumer, consider LBMI's announcement for a list of names generated by an entity that called itself Consumers Technology:

"Would your client be interested in consumers that spend between $4.99 and $19.99 for Tiffany Heart Gold Chains, 35-mm Cameras and Water Filter Systems? . . .

"These opportunistic buyers are a slice of middle America. They love to read gossip stories about Roseanne Barr and Rob Lowe in publications such as the *Star* and the *National Enquirer.* However, they always make time for the money-saving 'opportunities' in the back of each issue. . . ."

People in financial trouble or with unrealistic dreams of financial success are also considered hot direct-mail prospects. LBMI sent me word of lists chock full of such hard-luck souls, including its "National Credit Hunters" roster of 1.6 million people who had applied for Visa or MasterCard credit cards but had been turned down. Interested parties could rent the names of 400,000 such disappointed people every two weeks for $70 per thousand.

"National Credit Hunters is a brand NEW file of bargain-hungry and opportunistic people!" the company announced.

Within two weeks of being turned down, the notice continued, "these credit-hungry men and women are available for rental."

Advertisers prey on credit hunger. Poverty and hard times make for good hunting. LBMI announced that another list, the "Cash Galore" list, generated "150,000 names every week from a postcard offer that targets the lowest end of the socioeconomic spectrum. Each consumer makes a phone call to a '900' telephone number at a cost of $13.95 to find out how 'they too can get credit.' Then they make a second call for $29.95 to apply for The Cash Galore credit card."

What I find most interesting about such announcements is the degree of disdain that percolates from the text. LBMI tried to interest me in a list of 210,000 people who ordered *The Wealth Guide*, a guide full of tips for winning and claiming prizes.

"Respondents sent in $8.95 to fulfill the chance of a lifetime. They receive step-by-step instructions on their way to fame and fortune.

"Each and every mailer with a highly promotional offer should test *The Wealth Guide*. The typical *Wealth Guide* buyer truly represents middle America," which to LBMI meant that each had a household income of $20,000, and "is blue collar, ethnic, and believes without a doubt they'll tap into newfound wealth."

Fraud investigators have a nickname for lists of gullible consumers: they call them "goose" lists. Recently my wife received a letter that clearly demonstrates how direct-mailers perceive the people included on such lists.

It was a chain letter, with a twist. As is customary in chain letters, the writer urged her to send a dollar to each of five people named at the end of the letter and then to remove the top name and add her own at the bottom. Next, however, the writer told her to make two hundred copies of the letter and to "obtain a list of 200 or more names of OPPOR-TUNITY SEEKERS from a mailing list company." The list would arrive printed on mailing labels, which my wife was to stick to each envelope. "Within 60 days," the letter continued, "you will receive your $50,000 in cash, guaranteed!"

The direct-marketers tread on more sensitive ground when they begin compiling and peddling lists of marital status, sexual appetite, and religious affiliation.

One recent list, for example, held the names of 296,402 unattached people who had responded to offers aimed at singles. A list called "Private Lives" opened a window on the suddenly not-so-private lives of some 44,000 subscribers to an adult newsletter. Lists of gays are especially sensitive.

Sean Strub, a gay direct-mailer, is the country's foremost compiler of the names of homosexual men and women. He founded Strub/Dawson Inc., a direct-mail fund-raising company in Westchester, New York, and Strub Media Group Inc., New York City; Strub Media built the gay list used by both companies. Every three months Strub Media mails two packets, the "Community Cardpack" and "Sapphile," to 90,000 gay men and 30,000 lesbians, respectively. Each contains dozens of three-by-five cards bearing ads for gay bookstores, magazines, and organizations; AIDs-related charity events; and such gay entertainments as all-female cruises and videos of nude men wrestling and boxing.

New York provides the most gays for Strub's list, 37,117; North Dakota the fewest, just 24. Strub acquired his names from gay guest houses, bookstores, and magazines and through shared-name arrangements with other direct-mailers and organizations that target gays. (In a shared-name deal, Strub finances another mailer's campaign and in return gets the names of people who respond.) Strub also harvests names from neighborhoods known to be gay, a tricky tactic given that gay neighborhoods typically include some decidedly nonhomosexual vestiges of families who lived there long before the gays arrived. In the Chelsea neighborhood of Manhattan, Strub said, gay and Hispanic families may share the same block; in San Francisco's Castro district gay couples and old-time Italian families struggle up the same hills. To help tell who is who, Strub passes his list against large commercial data bases to see if any of the people on the list have kids. If so, he bumps them from the file, considering presence of children to be a pretty good indicator of heterosexuality. He also conducts address-matching searches to identify same-sex couples sharing a single address.

Gay men, it turns out, are a lot easier to find than gay women, Strub said. The psychic barrier between straight and gay men is far less permeable than that between straight women and lesbians. Straight men tend to avoid gay functions and organizations, while straight women participate in both straight and gay events. Straight women, moreover, often choose to live with female roommates, thus defeating Strub's address-matching tactic.

Most direct-mail companies keep a list of customers who have died in order to avoid sending junk mail to grieving relatives. Strub's "don't mail" list now contains some 70,000 names and has become a de facto indicator of the lethal advance of AIDS. About 7,000 of these names, however, belong to people who have written back angry letters—Strub calls them "homophobic"—demanding to be taken off his list.

Strub considers himself a careful steward of the list. He told me he will not provide names for sexually explicit advertising or to political causes that make him uncomfortable. He is solicitous too of gay sensibilities. In one Community Cardpack he included a lengthy apology for allowing Burroughs-Wellcome, the pharmaceutial company that makes AZT, to insert in an earlier mailing an ad that encouraged gays to be tested for the presence of HIV antibodies in their blood. "Burroughs-Wellcome has a right to advertise," Strub wrote, "but I wish we had provided space to [express] an additional viewpoint. . . .

"Personally, I think it is a good idea for people at risk to know their HIV status and T-cell count. However, Burroughs-Wellcome's $25 million ad campaign's purpose is really designed to get people to start taking AZT.

"The result will be thousands of people starting AZT without knowing its extraordinary toxicity, the serious concerns about AZT's efficacy, or anything about alternatives available."

Direct-mailers target religion and race by renting lists from churches and from religious and ethnic associations, or by analyzing surnames for clues to their ethnic and religious heritage. They can select 900,000 Catholic surnames from Spiegel's vast mailing lists. A California list-management company marketed a list called "Christian Zealots" consisting of half a million former donors to ten evangelical ministries.

One company, AB Data Ltd., of Milwaukee, Wisconsin, specializes in collecting the names of Jews. Its *National Jewish Household* directory contains about 1.3 million households. Two or three times a year AB Data runs the names of virtually every consumer in America through a search program that analyzes geography, census data, and surnames and picks out the names and addresses of people most likely to be Jewish. The selection process is not as obvious as conventional wisdom might indicate. "A lot of people think the names Schwartz and Klein are Jewish names," said Avram Lyon, an AB vice-president. "In fact, Schwartz is only 47 percent Jewish. These were names that were taken from census work in the Middle Ages. People would come into villages and towns and divide the population between *schwartz* and *weiss*—black hair and white hair; and *klein* and *gross*—short and tall. That's how these names evolved."

A single letter can mean the difference between AB. Data counting you as a Jew or a non-Jew. AB expects 18 percent of people named Aaron to be Jewish, but 100 percent of those named Aaroni. Eighty-six percent of America's Cohens should be Jewish, 43 percent of the Cohans. Statistically speaking, former president Ronald Reagan had a 1 percent chance of being Jewish; if he had dropped the last "a" and substituted an "e" to form Reagen, he'd have increased his chances to 8 percent.

Many Jews adopted the names of cities as their last names. Nine percent of people named Paris are Jewish, by AB's calculations, compared with 25 percent of those named London. A name like Recanti would seem at first glance to identify an Italian and thus, perhaps, a Catholic. By AB's reckoning, however, virtually all Recantis are Jews, Recanti being a classic Sephardic name.

Why are American Jews so attractive to marketers?

"They're well-to-do and highly assimilated," Lyon told me. "They have a lot of disposable cash in the sense that their income is higher than the norm. There is a social tradition within Judaism toward charity. They tend to read more than the general public. There's only one group that has succeeded more than the Jews in terms of their economic and social assimilation into American society, and that's the Japanese."

I asked Lyon if he had ever received requests from fundamentalist types hell-bent on a little direct-mail evangelism.

"Have there been inquiries?" he repeated carefully. "The answer is 'yes.' "

AB, however, declined to cooperate.

The list game can be a treacherous one, for there is little honor, apparently, among direct-mailers. Most list owners insist on knowing what direct-mailers want their lists for and on seeing copies of the offer to be mailed. To insure that list renters use names only as often as agreed, list managers routinely seed them with false names—the names, for example, of pets and people long dead whose addresses, however, are actually addresses of living employees. If these employees receive more than one letter addressed to a particular defunct consumer, they sound the alarm. List owners even copyright their lists, thereby winning the right to sue anyone who might try to make unauthorized use of the names—even though we consumers never gave them direct permission to use our names in the first place.

Typically, direct-mailers are reluctant to say just how they acquired our names. Soon after my first daughter was born, I received a letter from Globe Life & Accident Insurance Company, in Oklahoma City, offering me the opportunity to buy life insurance for my daughter. The letter called this insurance "the most valuable gift [parents] could give their children—the 'gift of a lifetime.' " Never mind that child life insurance is intended for one thing—to cover funeral expenses and otherwise soften the blow should the child die. Globe Life is no slouch as a correspondent; it mails consumers over fifty million letters a year.

I phoned Globe Life and asked first to speak to the man whose signature appeared in the closing: Mark S. McAndrew, executive vice-president. Admittedly this was a rather naive thing to do. I never talked to McAndrew; he or someone in his employ shunted me to another male executive, who then passed me to Globe's manager of lists, Cynthia Cooke, a Globe employee for eighteen years, whose voice evoked cigarettes and tumbleweed.

I asked her how she got my name and, for that matter, how she knew I was a father.

"I can't give that to you," she said.

I was ready with an argument of awesome, primitive power. "Why not?" I asked. "It's my name."

She laughed. "We have agreements with other people that we won't disclose that. And even if we didn't, we look upon that as proprietary information. We paid for the use of it, and—it's hard to be delicate about this—it's our business."

She exhaled into the phone.

I was able to piece together a couple of other trails, however. I learned that Amnesty International had rented me from *The Atlantic*—on the belief, I suppose, that *Atlantic* readers care enough about human rights to contribute. The Quality Paperback Book Club, in search of quality readers, also got my name from *The Atlantic*. In return, *The Atlantic* probably got one of two things: rental income or the right to borrow chunks of the house lists maintained by Amnesty and QPBS. The book club, of which my wife is a quality member, rented her to *Mother Jones* and to *Lear's* magazine, bringing the trail full circle, from magazine to book back to magazine. *Lear's* sent my wife a subscription pitch after first running her name through one of the giant national data bases of consumers' ages. *Lear's* learned that she was thirty-five years old or older—a *Lear's* kind of woman—and fired off a letter. (A list exists, too, that allows you to select women by weight. Sexist, you say? Then how about this—there's another list that targets short men.)

A flesh-and-blood customer apparently referred us to Hanna Andersson, a Portland, Oregon, supplier of high-ticket kids' clothes, and Hanna graciously passed us on to Lillian Vernon, whose catalog offers everything from nightgowns to cabinet knobs. The Baby Store gave our names to the Grolier's Beginning Readers' Program and to the Right Start catalog, a kind of Sharper Image for babies. The Right Start beat our baby home, arriving one month before the little consumer was born.

That my wife is a voracious consumer must now be obvious to most marketers in America; less well known, however, is her distaste for politics. Little did she know she would wind up in the thick of it just by ordering, by mail, a package of frozen beef from Omaha Steaks.

Omaha Steaks rented her to the GOP Victory Fund of the National Republican Congressional Committee and, on a separate occasion, to the National Security Political Action Committee. Each committee tapped the list on its own, without first trading notes.

Is there some affinity, then, between Republicans and red meat? I decided to call the woman who had signed her name to one of the letters, Elizabeth Fediay, chairman of the National Security PAC.

"I think that's an absurd statement," she snapped. "At some point

someone probably assessed that this list has been successful with political fund-raising and political activism."

I find the meat theory far more compelling.

Marketers are not always so oblique in their pursuit. Often they simply
ask us for our most intimate secrets. In return for a handful of coupons or
a shot at winning a contest, we tell them everything they want to know.

Direct-mailers and their allies often mail out surveys to millions
upon millions of consumers at a time, trolling for new names to add to
their data bases and for additional information about those who already
reside there.

One company, National Demographics & Lifestyles, managed to
persuade many manufacturers to attach a brief consumer survey to the
warranty materials they packed with their products, such things as
radios, TV's, and other so-called consumer durables, and in the process
built itself a data base containing the hobbies and passions of twenty
million Americans.

Recently I found a life-style survey that included a list of fifty hobbies and interests packed in the box of my new charcoal grill. I was to
check off the things that I liked to do on a regular basis. Among the
choices: bicycling frequently, hunting/shooting, grandchildren, Bible/
devotional reading, entering sweepstakes, and casino gambling.

The idea of attaching the survey to warranty cards was an artful
tactic. Consumers worry that if they fail to fill out the questionnaire,
they will lose the warranty protection.

More intrusive probes arrive squeezed into those packets of coupons
we all see so often in our mailboxes. These packets are known in the
industry as co-op mailings because ads from many different companies
share the same envelope. Typical of these are Donnelly Marketing's
"Carol Wright" mailings and Larry Tucker Inc.'s "Jane Tucker" series.
GRI Corporation of Chicago came up with a kind of direct-mail club,
called the Shoppers' Association for Value and Economy, or SAVE.
You'll find an offer to join tucked into most of the co-op mailings that
arrive at your home. According to the terms of one recent SAVE mailing, if you fill out the survey and send in a buck, you will get a fifty-piece
earring collection right off the bat—and probably several hundred billion pieces of junk mail in the future.

In these surveys any detail, no matter how personal, is fair game.

Select & Save Inc. of Hicksville, New York, recently sent me a co-op mailing bulging with coupons and offers for an eclectic selection of items, everything from Disney books to burial insurance. Included was a survey that asked seventy-eight sets of questions. "FINAL NOTICE," the survey warned. "YOUR FREE SAMPLES & COUPONS WILL STOP . . . unless you complete this survey."

Here is a sampler of questions they wanted me to answer:

- Has anyone in your household ever used estrogen therapy (Premarin)?

- How often is mouthwash used in your home?
  (more than once a day, once a day, 1–2 times a week, 3–5 times a week, less than once a month, 1–2 times a month?)

- Does anyone in your household use any of the following tampons? (Kotex, o.b., Playtex, Tampax Petal Soft [plastic], Tampax Original [cardboard], other?)

- Which tampon absorbency?
  (regular, super, superplus?)

- Which type of tampon?
  (non-deodorant, deodorant?)

- Does anyone in your household suffer from

    Alzheimer's Disease,
    Angina,
    Bladder Control/Incontinence,
    Bleeding Gums/Gingivitis,
    Blindness/Visual Impairment,
    Bronchitis,
    Diabetes,
    Emphysema,
    Epilepsy,
    Frequent Headaches,
    Gastritis,
    Hearing Difficulty,
    Migraines,
    Osteoporosis,
    Physical Handicap.

I was to check the ones suffered by me, by my spouse, and by "other." This health sequence, by the way, was but one of the seventy-eight questions.

A few dozen questions later the survey came back to matters of health, this time asking me to reveal who in my household suffered from

Allergies/Hay Fever,
Arthritis/Rheumatism,
Asthma,
Heart Disease,
High Blood Pressure,
High Cholesterol,
Sinusitis,
Thinning Hair/Balding,
Ulcer.

The surveys may ask what pregnancy test you bought, what denture cream you use; they demand the names and ages of your children and the smoking habits of every smoker in your household.

The surveyors are deeply concerned, apparently, about the state of the American bowel. The Select & Save survey asked, "In the past six months, which bulk fibers or laxatives have been used in your home?" (It listed ten choices.) Donnelly's "Carol Wright" survey asked point-blank, "How many times, if any, did you medicate for diarrhea in the past year?" A recent SAVE survey probably deserves the award for cutting to the core of consumer need: "What is the likelihood that you would use a premoistened towelette in addition to, or as a replacement for, bathroom tissue for personal cleansing and refreshing?"

In my search for self I stumbled on an alarming tendency of personal data to migrate and coalesce. Data companies seem driven by an imperative akin to the forces that drove America to expand to the Pacific. Across the land, data bases now swell like thunderclouds.

The Dutch publishing giant, Verenigde Nederlandse Uitgevers-bedrijven, known more commonly and conveniently as VNU, is becoming a global information superpower. Its U.S.-based Consumer Marketing Information Group owns Claritas and a host of other consumer data companies. Dun & Bradstreet Corporation, in 1984—*that* year!—acquired the A. C. Nielsen Company, the world's largest market research concern. Nielsen produces national and local TV ratings and owns Donnelly Marketing Information Services and its data base of 85 million households. Nielsen Marketing, a Nielsen division that produced $940 million in revenue in 1990, has recruited 15,000 households to scan their groceries whenever they shop so that a computer can report the findings back to headquarters; the company plans to increase this panel to 40,000 households.

The nation's big credit-reporting bureaus have merged and altered their missions to produce what may be the two most powerful data-base marketing companies in the country, if not the world.

In 1985—they had the good sense not to pick 1984—Equifax and TRW quietly shrugged off their traditional roles as mere reporters of fiscal virtue and set up formal marketing divisions. Both aggressively acquired data and data companies, thereby enriching their already robust files. They brought a powerful new tool to marketing—the ability to track monthly changes in virtually every consumer's fiscal behavior. But in transforming themselves from simple reporters to avid marketers, they shattered the fragile compact between themselves and consumers that once had governed their operations.

In 1991 Equifax, acknowledging that such secondary use of credit information was not quite fair, abandoned its $12 million business of selling lists derived from its credit data base, but it continued to provide banks and retailers with lists of consumers for use in making prescreened offers of credit. TRW saw no reason to leave either business, despite a suit brought against it by the attorneys general of nineteen states that challenged its information-handling practices, among them its use of credit data to build direct-marketing lists. A settlement reached late in 1991 discharged the suit but allowed TRW to stay in the list business.

I acquired my credit report from TRW for $5. I'd always imagined my report to be a kind of Deathstar in high elliptical orbit, periodically casting its shadow over my life. In fact it was an innocuous printout of credit lines, credit limits, and account balances, with columns of coded information indicating whether or not I paid my bills on time. The report did, however, give me a sense of the sweep of my life—there was my Wanamaker's Department Store account from my two-year stay in Philadelphia; my account at Emporium Capwell in what Jonathan Robbin would call my "Bohemian Mix" days; and my account at Granat Brothers' San Francisco branch, the jewelry store where I paced the soft carpets for hours agonizing over the right diamond for my wife's engagement ring.

Innocuous enough, but misleadingly so. It's *how* the credit bureaus began to use this information that gave it life—and gives one pause.

TRW won't provide a marketer with copies of any actual credit reports. This would be too brazen a violation of existing fair credit laws. Instead TRW compiles a list of consumer names that reflect the credit data. L. L. Bean, for example, could request a list of all consumers who possess a bankcard with $5,000 or more of available credit. (TRW does not allow a search by specific brand of card; neither did Equifax.) TRW would then search its files and pull a few million names. The company, however, would not return that list directly to Bean, but rather to a third-party printer, ostensibly to protect the privacy of consumers who fit the search criteria (but also a dandy way of keeping unscrupulous clients from running off with the names and using them again).

TRW also uses its credit files to build statistical models of consumers. Say L. L. Bean wants to know if people who do not respond to its catalogs share some common trait. Bean gives TRW a list of its "nonresponders." TRW finds those lackluster consumers in its files, pulls up all the credit, demographic, and auto registration information it can on each one, and then tries to find the common thread that makes these people so recalcitrant. In effect, TRW builds a model of the typical nonresponder. The company then produces a new and expanded list of potential Bean customers from which everyone matching the nonresponder model has been eliminated.

TRW does not have to scavenge for its credit data. The information arrives in a monthly monsoon from creditors who by agreement report to the company every thirty days. This in turn allows TRW to detect immediately when a consumer gets more credit, assumes a new mortgage, or experiences some other change in status—change being the stuff of marketers' dreams.

Change rejuvenates consumers. We gambol about like colts in the dew of a new dawn—ideally in front of a new house that needs a couple of new down comforters from The Company Store, an armoire from Conran's, a set of kitchen chairs from Williams-Sonoma.

Word that some lucky soul just got a new credit card can set the direct-mail world aflame. A newsletter sent to me by Listworld, a broker of credit-related lists in Huntsville, Alabama, put it this way: "The holder of a new credit card is a perfect target for just about everything."

My friends at LBMI Direct sent me an announcement about their list of 10 million "new credit card issues," with a monthly hotline of 950,000 names. "Generally, American consumers 'welcome' the arrival of their newly issued bank credit cards by indulging in a spending spree. A direct marketer's DELIGHT!"

The trouble is, when Equifax and TRW entered the marketing business in 1985 they changed the rules of the credit game and without telling anyone or asking anyone's permission. In the old days they were simply passive receivers and reporters of information about the creditworthiness of consumers. When my bank searched deep into my financial past, I resented the intrusion but considered it the bank's right—after all, I was asking for a loan of $100,000. I was thankful the credit bureaus were there to speed the process. My wife and I tolerated being digitally poked and prodded and evaluated because we stood to gain something valuable in return: a loan and, through this loan, a house.

Without any agreement from me, however, TRW and Equifax began actively peddling my credit history—not to provide me with credit, but so that someone else could try to *sell* me something. TRW, for example, turned my wife and me over to CPC Associates, a list company in Bala Cynwyd, Pennsylvania, which in turn rented us to American Mailing Co-Op in Minnesota, which decided we were a "special" family and offered us a peek at "Wilderness Resort," fifty-four miles outside Washington, D.C.

TRW even tries to *predict* how long we consumers are likely to stay financially viable. It provides marketers and financial institutions with lists that forecast whether we will go bankrupt within the next twelve months.

In its marketing past Equifax provided a similar service, its Delinquency Alert System, and claimed to have identified "30 key indicators associated with a high risk of bankruptcy and delinquency." Using these indicators, Equifax assigned each of us a numerical index—our propensity to go belly up. "In developing our model," an as yet unrepentant Equifax had crowed, "we benefited from 100,000 actual files on persons who had gone bankrupt."

It is probably no accident that the cover of one Equifax list brochure featured a fierce bolt of lightning striking from a deep purple sky.

But, really, what's to worry? Who could possibly get upset about a new catalog turning up in the mailbox? If you don't like it, the companies advise, just throw the thing away. What's the harm? You might even find something you'd like to buy, or subscribe to, or support.

We are supposed to like this individualized attention. As Joe Dawson, executive vice-president of Equifax Marketing Services, told me back in the days when Equifax was still peddling what it called its "Power Lists": "Consumers are shouting they want to be identified as individuals. They want their specific wants, needs, preferences to be satisfied."

A nice thought; what happens in practice is a bit more controversial.

5

MOTHERS AND OTHER TARGETS

The switch to target marketing has brought an unforeseen consequence: everyone is after the same targets, so these lucky people are subjected to a barrage of advertising out of all proportion to their importance in the total market for most products.

—Leo Bogart, sociologist and marketer,
Journal of Advertising Research, 1986

As any new mother knows, breast-feeding is no picnic. Amid the usual postpartum hormonal storms, mother has to cope with a vast array of unexpected assaults to her resolve. The milk does not come right away; nipples get sore; baby shrinks. For weeks mom is haunted by the fear her baby isn't getting enough to eat.

Suddenly, magically, coupons or free samples of Gerber and Carnation infant formula appear in her mailbox. Brilliant, the marketers say: this is exactly the kind of precision marketing that is going to help American companies survive the fragmentation of the mass market. "Insidious," the pediatricians say (the American Academy of Pediatrics chose the word): these companies are exploiting an obviously vulnerable population.

Welcome to the brave new world of "synchographics," a marketing technique now coming into vogue that allows companies to pitch us products timed to such personal milestones as puberty, marriage, and the acquisition of a new home. Companies can now track us from the dawn of our days to the last good night. One week after my second daughter was born I stepped out my front door and found a sample package of Luvs disposable diapers, made by Procter & Gamble, fluttering on my stoop. The package bore no mailing address and no postage and had arrived well before the regular mail delivery—which meant that someone other than the mailman had dropped it off. Shortly after my first daughter turned three, she received a catalog called Pleasant Company addressed specifically to her and featuring lots of charming and very expensive dolls, official notification, apparently, that she could now become a bona fide consumer. My father-in-law gets a lot of mail asking him to voice his support for Medicare and Social Security.

I already have my first funeral offer.

"Come up to the sky," the brochure offered rather menacingly. I was thirty-six and living in San Francisco when Skylawn Memorial Park of Burlingame, California, sent me the offer, not the likeliest age to die, but just the right time, apparently, to begin paying "as little as $19 a month" to save my place under the grass or, if I preferred, in the aboveground mausoleum. I quickly checked the "More Information" box for Skylawn's "Economical Double-Depth Program," but I never heard back.

At times the marketers are capable of pinpoint accuracy. On the very day a friend of mine turned forty he got an offer for the newsletter *Sex Over Forty*. This was forbidding mail indeed. "As a man," the letter read, "you may be slower to have an erection. As a woman, you may be slower to lubricate. The character of your orgasms may change. And so may the tempo of your lovemaking. The frequency of your desire may alter. And there are likely to be other changes as well."

Synchographics lets marketers in a sense read our minds by letting them track the events most likely to consume our thoughts. It lets them drop seductive little handkerchiefs in our life paths. But synchographics also raises troubling questions that old-fashioned mass-marketers never had to worry about: When is timing too good? When does a company cross the line from timely delivery to crass exploitation? And who is responsible when such targeting leads to a broken heart?

The Gerber and Carnation campaigns are prime examples of the kind of synchographic targeting we are going to see more of in coming years.

These companies even know when you're pregnant.

. . .

Among pediatricians, breast milk has attained near sacred status. It costs nothing, the supply is virtually endless, and it has magical effects on baby's immune system and psyche, properties synthetic formula cannot hope to match. The World Health Organization (WHO), in its 1981 formula-marketing code, acknowledged this superiority and urged companies never to promote formula directly to the general public. The United States did not sign the code, but the American Academy of Pediatrics endorsed it. So too did Ross Laboratories, Mead Johnson Nutritionals, and Wyeth-Ayerst Laboratories, who shared monopoly control over the U.S. market for routine formula until the entry of Gerber and Carnation. The Big Three promoted their flagship brands, Similac, Enfamil, and SMA, only through doctors, hospitals, and medical journals—the "ethical" way, according to the American Academy of Pediatrics. Sales of formula through grocery stores alone totaled $1.6 billion in 1990, up 22 percent from 1989.

Carnation, a subsidiary of Nestlé S.A., historically the evil genius of formula marketing, began advertising its new Good Start formula directly to consumers in January 1991. Gerber began its campaign in September 1989 when it introduced its Gerber Baby Formula. (Gerber did not actually make the formula; it was produced, in a failed attempt at an end run around the WHO guidelines, by none other than Mead Johnson.)

Carnation and Gerber both take great pains in their advertising to emphasize that indeed breast-feeding is best and that any decision to switch to formula should be made on the advice of doctors. Both, however, send mothers coupons or actual samples in mailings timed to arrive as early, according to the AAP, as three weeks after birth. The academy feared the timing would accelerate the already declining incidence of breast-feeding among American mothers. "If you're going to send it to a mother two months down the road, that's one thing," said James E. Strain, executive director of the academy. "She's probably well established on breast-feeding, she knows what she's doing. But three weeks is a very critical time. That's when most mothers are apt to give up on breast-feeding, and I think the formula companies recognize that."

One Gerber spokesman confirmed that Gerber's samples would begin arriving as early as three weeks after birth; another quoted a Gerber policy directive that said six to eight weeks, the point, he said, by which mothers already have made their decisions about whether to continue breast-feeding.

Gerber and Carnation argue they must reach parents as early as possible if they are to have any chance at all of breaking down the powerful brand loyalties mothers develop in the hospital. One study, conducted at the University of California at Los Angeles Medical Center, found that mothers almost always wind up using the same brand of formula they encountered at the hospital and most often use the same preparation—ready-to-feed—which happens to be the most expensive. The Big Three formula makers know a good tactic when they see it: they supply their formula to hospital nurseries free of charge. They also see to it that nurses provide every mom with a free "discharge pack" containing a quart can of the pricey ready-to-feed version, a smaller four-ounce jar of the same, and such other goodies as a toy, a pacifier, or maybe a baby bottle and nipple.

Carnation and Gerber charge that such practices are a lot more insidious than their direct-mail campaigns. A discharge pack, a Carnation marketing official complained, "gets there first, earliest, and with the implied hospital endorsement. And it's there from day one." Steve Poole, a Gerber spokesman, said his company at least lets mothers get out of the hospital. "We have given them a chance to get home," he said. "We've given them a chance to begin breast-feeding, to make up their minds, unlike when formulas are distributed in the hospital or even used in the nursery." (In fact, as I'll show, Gerber manages to slip its coupons to women even before they give birth.)

Central to the matter of timing, yet surprisingly absent from the AAP debate, was the question of how Carnation and Gerber, and a host of other target marketers, acquire the names of so many pregnant women and new mothers in the first place.

Often mothers simply *tell* companies the news, but they do so indirectly and probably without being aware they are doing it. There is no more elaborate consumer intelligence system than that set up to capture the gravid status of women.

The first and most obvious way that women let companies know they are pregnant is when they subscribe to baby and parenting magazines or buy clothing at maternity shops. It is remarkably easy for companies to find out who's got the names of new and pending mothers. I went to my local library and took a look at the mailer's bible, the *Direct Mail List*

Rates and Data directory, a volume the size of a big-city telephone book describing thousands of lists, their owners and managers, and the prices they charge. I looked up "Babies."

Here's a partial list of the name merchants listed: *American Baby* magazine, the Baby's Gallerie, *Baby Talk* magazine, Doubleday List Marketing, TRW, Graco Children's Products, Heart Thoughts Inc., Lifestyle Change Inc., Metromail, *Mothering* magazine, Motherwear, Natural Baby Company, One Step Ahead, Page Boy Maternity, *Pampers Baby Care* magazine, Perfectly Safe catalog, Right Start catalog, and R. Duck Company (owners of the "Rubber Duckies New Mothers Mail Order Buyers" list).

One reckless afternoon I decided to transform myself into the slightly nervous husband of a woman named Angela, a lovely young thing about to have a baby. Of course, being first-timers, we needed information to reduce our terror. I called *American Baby* magazine to order a subscription in my new wife's name.

The subscription operator was cordial and accommodating. Right off the bat she told me the magazine happened to be offering a six-month free subscription to any woman expecting a child.

"Sounds good," I said.

She got down to business. "First baby?"

"Yes," I said over a tremor of excitement.

"Due date?"

"May 15, 1991." Two months away.

The *American Baby* list machine quickly went to work.

On May 28, barely two weeks after the due date, Angela got a letter from a company calling itself the Federal Record Service Corporation in Washington, D.C. The letter looked official to Angela and just a tad scary. Like me, she usually throws out most of her junk mail unopened, but this she kept. Inside was a letter with bold black print that read **BIRTH RECORDS DIVISION.**

Then, just below, again in bold black:

IMPORTANT NOTICE:

New Federal Legislation requires that all dependents reaching one year of age by the end of the tax year must be listed by Social Security Number on your income tax return.

In the next textual breath it warned:

> Your newborn child may not have been registered with the
> Social Security Administration.

The letter offered to do the work of getting Angela's baby a Social
Security card and number for $15—a task mothers can readily accom-
plish in the hospital free of charge.

Three days later Angela's first issue of *American Baby* arrived. It was
packed with advertisements and welcome advice and came with a per-
sonalized suggestion that Angela now begin a real, *paid* subscription to
the magazine. "WELCOME TO AMERICAN BABY, ANGELA LAR-
SON," the offer said. "FIRST TIME MOTHERS LIKE YOU HAVE
SPECIAL NEEDS FOR INFORMATION ON BABY (AND NEW
MOTHERS) CARE—AND WE WANT TO BE WITH YOU EVERY
STEP OF THE WAY TO HELP YOU AND THE NEWEST MEM-
BER OF YOUR FAMILY!"

Soon afterward Angela got a special edition of *American Baby* called
First-Time Parents, including articles aimed at helping mom and dad get
through the first three months and at helping Hasbro Inc. sell a lot of
toys. The magazine had only eleven advertisements; all, including three
full-pagers, featured toys made by Hasbro's subsidiary, Playskool Inc.

Two weeks later Angela received her own copy of the Right Start, an
upscale catalog of children's toys, clothing, and equipment. "WOW!"
cried a computer-generated note on the back cover. "A new addition to
the LARSON family. BALTIMORE will never be the same!! And neither will your lives."

The mail kept coming. In the thirty-three weeks between mid-May
1991, when the first letter arrived, until the middle of January 1992,
when I stopped counting, Angela received forty-seven letters, catalogs,
and phone calls, including five co-op mailings—the cluster bombs of
advertising—whose contents increased the total of distinct offers to 151.
That works out to 4.6 offers per week. Among the most prolific mailers
was Grolier Direct Marketing of Danbury, Connecticut, which made
nine attempts to interest Angela in its Walt Disney and Dr. Seuss
children's book clubs. By December the company clearly had grown
frustrated with Angela's refusal to order. On Thursday, December 19,
Grolier telephoned to pitch the Dr. Seuss program; two days later the
company called again to offer the Disney program, then threw up its

hands altogether and dispatched a copy of Dr. Seuss's *The Foot Book* free of charge. It arrived exactly one week after the last call.

I of course took the calls. I asked the first caller how she got Angela's name. "It's just here in the computer," the woman answered. I was struck by how chummy some of Angela's callers were. Just having a first name, it seemed, empowered them to behave like old friends. "Hi," a perky female voice greeted me at about ten A.M. one Tuesday morning. "Is Angela there?"

"Speaking," I answered, then quickly corrected myself. "I mean, I'm her husband."

She didn't want to talk to me, however. "Just tell her its Allison from *American Baby*," she sang, and the line went dead.

Some of the mail seemed precisely tuned to human frailty and the terrors that beset mothers soon after childbirth. In July, when Angela's baby was roughly two and a half months old, she received the "Bundle of Joy" co-op mailing containing twenty-five offers. Among them:

- An offer to try a "miracle" skin cream called XM 1200 made by an unidentified company with a return post office box in Berea, Ohio. "Your mate will marvel at your touch," the ad cooed. It promised explicitly that the cream would "bring back the radiant smooth body skin of your youth."
- A pitch from the National Institute of Weight Control in Cleveland, Ohio, to try their diet pill, called the Primary Tablet, which caused rapid weight loss by triggering the "Fat-Evaporation Effect."
- A warning from Water-Tech Industries' Child Care Products Division that unfiltered water could be the undoing of Angela's baby, because lead and toxic contamination had become a chronic problem nationwide. "Research indicates that nearly all young children are threatened and as many as 1 in 5 are seriously affected." Among the apparently widespread problems caused by this contamination were "inability to learn, stomach pains, hearing loss, skin rashes, and more." The solution, of course, was the Water-Tech "Baby's H_2O" water filter, for $29.95.

The Bundle of Joy mailing also included a somewhat macabre offer from American Baby Products of Lincoln, Nebraska, for "Copy-Tot," which lets parents make casts not merely of their babies' first shoes, but of their hands and feet, and to impart to these mementos a fake bronze look. The results in the brochure looked downright strange, with tiny bronze fists and feet emerging from desks and tabletops, some skewered with pens to show how they can be converted to desk sets. The cost was $14.95, which included a "Total Happiness Guarantee."

By August the mail took a distinct turn toward the morbid. United of Omaha, an affiliate of Mutual of Omaha, invited Angela to insure her baby's life. "It's real life insurance," the letter reassured her. "It's not accidental death insurance. The $6,000 is paid regardless of whether life is lost because of an accident or an illness."

This *was* a relief. Angela read on. "Before your child is 25, *you* are protected from spending many thousands of dollars of your own money for funeral and cemetery costs." The company made it clear that the policy would pay nothing if Angela's baby committed suicide within two years of the opening date. An accompanying pamphlet, however, put one of Angela's other concerns to rest. Yes, the pamphlet said, death on the playground is covered. "Guaranteed!"

Two weeks after this the SIDS (sudden infant death syndrome) Alliance of Columbia, Maryland, dropped Angela a no-nonsense request for bucks that sent her rushing to her baby's crib to listen for breathing. "Before today is over," the Alliance wrote, "20 apparently healthy babies will die peacefully in their sleep."

Three weeks later another co-op mailing arrived, this one "Jane Tucker's Supermarket of Savings," with twenty-six offers including a one-sheet flier designed to look exactly like a cover of *Newsweek* but called "Newsbrief" instead. "WHAT HAPPENS IF YOU DIE. . ." the fake cover roared, "AND LEAVE NO WILL?" (Once again the ellipses, a favorite tool of direct-mailers everywhere, was provided by the advertiser.) Angela could solve the problem by paying $6.95 for a make-your-own-will kit from an outfit called the State Will Company.

That very same day Angela received . . . a Trojan teddy!

This too had come from *American Baby* magazine, the source of the birthday greeting I described in the first chapter. But this teddy had arrived eight months too soon.

Had something gone wrong? The time had come to pay a visit to *American Baby.*

At *American Baby,* based in New York and published by the Cahners Publishing Company, timing indeed is everything. The magazine won't settle for just ordinary mothers. "It's very easy to find postnatal names," said Patricia Calderon, marketing director of American Baby Group. "We don't need them. We need to get them when they're still pregnant."

She casts her net wide, collecting names from 23,000 sources including subscription cards displayed in 10,000 doctor's offices and from sign-up sheets passed around at childbirth classes, all asking the due date of the expected baby and whether it's the first, and all offering the magazine's standard six-month free subscription. *American Baby* then markets lists of its names through its own rental division and sells them outright to Metromail Corporation of Lombard, Illinois, one of the largest collectors of consumer data. Metromail, in turn, rents the list to whomever it wishes.

American Baby uses three million of the names to mail Trojan teddies—more formally, the "Especially for Mothers" co-op mailing—to new mothers. Calderon explained the mystery of why Angela's teddy arrived early: in 1989 *American Baby* scrapped the one-year greeting to concentrate instead on mothers of four-month-olds, considered prime targets because when babies reach that age their mothers begin shifting them to solid foods. The four-month stage, moreover, fell smartly within the primary window of opportunity for tapping the "birth market."

"When you find out you're pregnant," Calderon began, launching into her marketer's view of maternal development, "you're going to be very concerned with yourself. You're going to be feeling morning sickness. You're going to be uncomfortable. That baby isn't real yet. You're sick. You don't feel good.

"By the second trimester, the baby starts to become a little more real. . . . The excitement is building, but you're still not in a serious acquisition headset.

"Third trimester, you're down to the wire. That baby's coming. *You go on a buying spree!* . . .

"Once the baby arrives, of course, you start massive acquisitions of everything."

At about the six-month point, however, the spree begins to subside. All the big stuff's been bought. You're down to routine maintenance: diapers, food, baby wipes.

"So an advertiser wants to be there from the sixth month of pregnancy to the sixth month postnatal," Calderon said. "He wants to *barrage* that woman with impressions."

The magazine itself is a targeting marvel. Thanks to the technology of selective binding, which allows a bindery to create different issues of the same magazine without interrupting production, American Baby has printed up to two hundred different editions in a single month, each with different advertising content and having one of two editorial thrusts: articles geared to pregnant women or to new mothers, with a core set of articles shared by both. The subscriptions shift from a prenatal focus to postnatal in the month the baby is due. Roughly 514,000 pregnant women and 636,000 new mothers receive their respective issues each month.

The magazine could target readers even more precisely than it does, Calderon told me. "We have the capability of running 'Your Three-Month-Old Baby' articles in here, so that when your baby is three months old your issue will have an article just for her that is not in the issue of a neighbor with a six-month-old."

Advertisers, however, had not yet been willing to foot the higher costs of such precision.

I ordered Angela's subscription rather late by American Baby standards, so her first copy was the June issue, which arrived June 1. The magazine sent Angela all six issues but seemed reluctant to let her go. The sixth issue—November 1991—warned, "THIS IS YOUR LAST ISSUE, ANGELA LARSON. NOW IS NOT THE TIME FOR FIRST-TIME MOTHERS LIKE YOURSELF TO BE WITHOUT THE EXPERT ADVICE AND HELP OF AMERICAN BABY MAGAZINE."

The same warning came with the next issue.

With the eighth free issue, however, the magazine gave up even the warning. When I last checked, we'd received two more issues, the last being the May 1992 edition.

American Baby offers advertisers other opportunities to fine-tune their targeting beyond mere timing. It sends them a list of upcoming articles to allow them to choose where they want their advertisements to appear. "They'll want to be adjacent certain kinds of editorial," Calderon told me. "For instance, if you're a formula maker, you may want to be opposite a breast-feeding article. Or near it."

Placement gets dicey, however. Like warring siblings, advertisers prefer to keep their distance from competitors—to be precise, six pages of distance. "In a one-hundred-page magazine where it's all baby advertising," Calderon said, smiling weakly, "that can be very difficult to accommodate."

■ ■ ■

Hospitals play a key role in the migration of information about pregnancy and birth. They don't, as a rule, disclose the names of patients registered with their labor and delivery suites, but they might as well do so for all the obliging, indirect assistance they provide to the data scavengers.

The process begins when the hospital's own Lamaze or birth-education instructor passes out free coupons, samples, and information to impending parents. It is here, for example, that mothers typically encounter those sign-up sheets from *American Baby*. Here, too, they are likely to come across subscription lures cast by *Growing Child*, a newsletter whose issues are timed to arrive at different stages of a child's development. Interested parents-to-be fill in their names and the expected delivery dates of their babies, which information eventually makes its way into the "Growing Child Prenatals Database of First-Time Mothers-to-Be," managed by 21st Century Marketing, Farmingdale, New York. A data card supplied to interested direct-mail companies lists prices and other particulars. "DON'T MISS OUT ON THESE HIGHLY RECEPTIVE FIRST-TIME MOTHERS," the card exhorts. "YOUR OFFER CAN BE IN THEIR MAILBOX WITHIN THE FIRST MONTH OF THEIR NEW BABY'S ARRIVAL. . . ."

Such first-timers have an especially warm place in the hearts of formula makers. As one formula manager confided in a burst of marketing exuberance: "If she's a first-time mom, she's scared to death. She thinks this stuff is medicine. She's really scared. If the doctor told her to start doing back flips, she'd do back flips." He complained, however, that collecting first-timers remains a difficult task. "I can't get that right now. I can't separate first-time moms from second-time moms."

The intelligence network again comes to life when mom delivers her baby. Most hospitals offer a baby-photo service operated right in their nurseries by an outside contractor. At most hospitals that service will be First Foto, a division of Hasco International Inc. of St. Charles, Missouri. Any mother who orders a First Foto package winds up in Hasco's new-mother data base, which Hasco then markets to other companies.

Occasionally mothers make their way into prenatal and postnatal data bases even though their babies have already died, a gloomy but statistically plausible situation. (About ten of every thousand children born each year don't survive past their first birthdays, according to the

National Center for Health Statistics.) Allen Bacher, Hasco's senior vice-president, acknowledged that now and then the company does get a report of what he termed a "postnatal occurrence"—meaning a baby's death. The company finds out about it when the grieving parents are deluged with offers for baby-related goods or services.

"Of course they'll contact us," Bacher said, "and we'll treat them with a very high degree of sensitivity and make sure they get no more referrals in the future. We have that capability."

First Foto gives new mothers a chance to choose not to be included in its data base—a tiny chance. In print exactly the size of the E *Pluribus Unum* on a nickel, First Foto states: "If you would prefer not to receive additional information on baby-related items, check here."

I asked Bacher if he really thought this "negative option" line was sufficient, especially given the turmoil and scrambled emotions associated with birth.

"We think it's enough," he said.

Hospitals help the data scavengers again when they bid new mothers good-bye and hand each a postpartum "gift pack," a sealed plastic grab bag stuffed with coupons, offers, and free samples. (Unlike "discharge packs," these contain no samples of formula.) My real wife, the doctor, spirited two such gift packs from her hospital nursery, one produced by Bounty Gift Pax Inc. of Trenton, New Jersey, the other by First Moments of Greenvale, New York. *American Baby* produces a third called the "American Baby Basket for New Mothers." The makers of all three packs claim they each reach anywhere from 3.5 million to 3.9 million of the 4 million new mothers who give birth each year.

In addition to the usual fare—the offers of bronze baby shoes, free film, kids books, and Gerber life insurance for babies—I found lots of little reply cards clearly designed to get mothers to disclose their pregnancies and births. In Bounty's bag, Ortho Pharmaceutical Corporation offered new mothers a free sample of "Conceptrol," a contraceptive gel it calls "the ideal choice for new mothers." The reply card asked for the mother's name, address, and the age of her youngest child or the due date of her expected baby.

At my request—this time I posed as myself, a curious citizen—First Moments sent me a copy of the marketing materials it uses to recruit advertisers for its gift bags. I discovered how heavily First Moments plays up its close relationship to its host hospitals, a relationship that seems to have escaped the angry gaze of the American Academy of Pediatrics.

"Delivered at hospital bedside by a nurse . . ." proclaims the cover of this brochure in bold black letters. Inside there is a photograph of a nurse presenting a First Moments bag to a brand-new family. The adjacent blurb exults: "It's the perfect climate to build lasting brand loyalties!"

Gerber turned up in the First Moments bag with a flier offering coupons for Gerber Baby Formula worth up to $14. As "a special added bonus" mother could write for three more $1 coupons—all she had to do was fill out a brief market survey asking her name, address, age group, and whether her new baby was her first child. If not the first, the flier asked, please check the ages of your other kids. Also tell us your baby's name and birthday and tell us whether or not you currently are feeding your child formula.

Then came the clincher: Gerber asked mom to rat on her friends. Responding mothers were invited to turn over the names of as many as three other pregnant women. Give their names, addresses, and due dates, and they too would get coupons!

Gerber and Carnation get most of their names, however, from the grand master of synchographic targeting, Metromail Corporation. "It's the only game in town," a Carnation manager said. "They're the ones who are most successful in compiling names. They don't have a competitor."

Metromail keeps a lush data base called the National Consumer Database, which draws information from 3,500 different sources to track the affairs of 85 million American households, just shy of the number the Census Bureau tries to contact for each decennial census. The data base can hold up to twenty-five pieces of information about every individual named within, including presence of credit cards, mail-order responsiveness, and political orientation. The company gets its credit information through data swaps with at least one of the major credit-reporting companies, according to George Bardenheier, vice-president of sales. He wouldn't identify which company, however.

Babies, impending or born, wind up in Metromail's Young Family Index. Each year this list produces the names and addresses of 900,000 pregnant women and 3.6 million brand-new mothers. In 1990 mailers could rent the prenatals for $75 a thousand, the new moms for $55.

Metromail builds its prenatal list from names supplied by various sources, including *American Baby* and maternity-wear retailers who ask women to list their due dates. The company "ages" these records for later inclusion in its files of completed births, which are compiled using an elaborate and exhaustive intelligence-collection process.

Several hundred Metromail employees, all working from their homes near Metromail's St. Louis data center, receive copies of every newspaper published in America, some two thousand dailies and weeklies. They quickly turn to the birth-announcement pages, where they find the name and sex of each baby born and the name and address of the parents. Using special typewriters that allow them to type each name into a cartridge that can later be loaded directly into a computer, these workers record some seventy thousand births each week.

Next the workers drop off their cartridges at Metromail's St. Louis data center. Metromail then double-checks the addresses against postal records to make sure zip codes are correct and that a given street is really a street and not a road, court, drive, circle, or avenue. Metromail also adds income information derived from Census Bureau tapes. The income data, far from exact, is the average household income reported by residents within a census block group, a unit of census geography consisting of some 340 households. Metromail also blends in names and addresses supplied by those local governments that consider birth records to be public, and by maternity shops and other far-flung sources.

All this information would be virtually useless if not for the advent of sophisticated "merge-purge" software that allows companies to match names and addresses, purge duplicate records, and merge additional names and data. In the process of compiling its data base, for example, Metromail tallies about 6 million births, or 2 million more than the 4 million that actually took place. Through the merge-purge process it winnows the duplicates and refines the list to 3.6 million births.

Metromail continues to follow these babies as they grow into children and young adults, taking special note of such consumer milestones as when they turn sixteen and when they become eligible to drive. (Time to offer car insurance!) The company's High School Student Index stores the names of some 5.2 million students and replenishes the list from over 350 different sources. Metromail also tries to figure out if the teens in its data base are likely to go on to college. Guidance counselors around the country help out by sending Metromail lists of the names of college-bound students. Where such information isn't available, the company takes a statistical stab at guessing a kid's propensity to consume four years of college by reviewing the education and income levels of his parents and his neighborhood.

Just as teens graduate from high school and head for college, so too do they graduate from the High School Student Index to Metromail's College Student Index, fed by data from 850 sources, including college directories. This list contains the names of more than 60 percent of America's full-time college students. It offers the school addresses of 4.9 million and the home addresses of 3.7 million. Interested mailers can even ask Metromail to select names by the amount of tuition each kid pays.

A student's digital right of passage comes when he at last wins an entry in his local telephone book under his own name. At this point Metromail confers upon him the information age equivalent of manhood: his very own, distinct file in Metromail's adult data base.

Metromail continues to keep in chronological step through its National Family Index, a list of 20 million households with kids.

By following consumers through time, Bardenheier said, Metromail allows companies to practice "life-event marketing." Birth, he believes, is the most powerful life event in terms of prompting consumers to consume. New parents buy life insurance, expand their homes, take out lines of credit to cover all the baby things parents have to buy: cribs, strollers, life insurance, and crashproof Volvo sedans.

"When you have your first child, all of a sudden you're thinking about things you never thought of before," Bardenheier said. "There's a major need for planning. You've got this little nine-pound baby looking at you, and you've got to take care of it."

For life-event marketing to succeed, companies must keep continuous track of their targets, even through the many moves we Americans tend to make in our lifetimes. In 1989 18 percent of us moved, according to the Census Bureau; from 1960 to 1989 nearly all of us—91 percent—did.

The marketers have become very good at keeping up with us, as witnessed by the fact that our junk mail is now likely to find us even before our personal friends do. Shortly after my latest move, from San Francisco to Baltimore, I gathered my mail and was astonished to see Ed McMahon's face grinning from the pile. He was pitching yet another sweepstakes for American Family Publishers, and he already had my new address. Suddenly it occurred to me that somewhere along the way the list of life's inevitabilities had increased to three: death, taxes, and Ed.

But how did he get my new address? He wasn't on my list of people to notify. There was no yellow forwarding label stuck to the envelope: my current address and my name appeared through one of the *four* plastic windows. How did he find me?

The fact is—and it is a little-known fact outside the marketing industry—companies could not practice life-event marketing without the willing and able cooperation of the U.S. Postal Service. When people move they typically fill out a change of address card and file it with their local post offices. The old and new addresses wind up in one central postal data base, called the National Change of Address (NCOA) Masterfile. The postal service licenses a group of private-sector companies to use this file to provide address correction services to the direct-mail industry. The agency made the file available in order to help reduce the amount of undeliverable mail. The licensed companies scan the mailing lists of their clients, look for matches, and insert the new addresses. As of January 1991 there were nineteen licensees, including Donnelly Marketing, Equifax, TRW Inc., Metromail, R. L. Polk & Co., and Wiland Services.

The file gets a workout. In 1990 the nineteen companies used it to process some twenty-five billion addresses.

Each NCOA licensee pays only $80,000 the first year for rights to market address correction services using the data base and $48,000 each year thereafter. Yet each company turns the data base into a profit-making operation, part of the array of services it offers its direct-mail clients. These clients, in turn, use the service to boost the marketability of their own data bases and to create new ways of targeting those of us who paid for the stamps that made the whole arrangement possible in the first place.

One such list, created by running an existing list through the NCOA file, is called "Park Avenue Direct Change of Address" and is marketed by LBMI Direct Marketing Services.

The basic "Park Avenue Direct" list consists of the names of opportunity seekers who respond to such promotions as the "Park Avenue" designer watch offer, whereby savvy consumers can pick up a designer watch for three dollars.

"The Park Avenue Direct Change of Address file brings direct-marketers a one-two punch that's tough to beat," LBMI wrote on its rate sheet for the file. "The highly successful Park Avenue Direct data base is passed against an NCOA file every thirty days. This results in a 35,000 monthly hotline of super responsive and promotionally oriented men and women who have just MOVED. New movers are always in a BUYING MOOD."

The cost to rent these opportunistic monthly movers was $65 per thousand names, or six and a half cents per name. The most the postal service could have received in revenue in 1991 from NCOA license fees was $1.5 million—or roughly six one-thousandths of a penny for each of the twenty-five billion addresses actually processed through the NCOA system.

In 1991 the postal service began putting the finishing touches on a new file that promises to make the junk-mailer's job even easier. For the first time, the postal service began compiling a central, master list of every address in the country. (Previously only carriers and local post offices knew the exact addresses of routes in their jurisdictions.) The postal service began developing the new address bank, tentatively called the National Address Directory, to speed the process of sorting and thus of delivering mail. As of 1991 each mail carrier still spent half his day manually sorting mail to conform to the exact path he walked. The directory will allow the post office to assign a specific bar code to each address and thus to sort the mail by optical scanning machines. The file won't contain names, just addresses.

The postal service expects to license this file, too, just as it did the NCOA file. Once in place, the new directory will allow a direct-mailer to deliver his entire mailing list to a directory licensee, who in turn will correct and update the *entire* list—not merely the addresses of the new movers, as in the plain vanilla NCOA system. Each licensee would do all this, of course, for a fee.

The biggest data companies don't rely just on the postal service for address changes. Metromail, for example, tracks movers by purchasing address changes from magazine publishers, mail-order houses, and other direct-marketing sources whom the movers may have notified. TRW Inc., the giant credit-reporting company, offers a new mover file based on address changes reported by credit customers.

Equifax, before it abandoned direct marketing in 1991, claimed it could know even when we consumers were *considering* a move. There was nothing supernatural about the process, Equifax's Joe Dawson told me. "If you were contemplating moving, you would go out and start looking for financing," he said. "Someone would make an inquiry about you for financing, or a level of financing, that was abnormal to whatever your regular pattern might be."

The direct-mail companies are fond of saying that junk mail is simply misdirected mail and that we should be happy about their newfound targeting finesse because it means we will get less junk mail and more offers for the things we really want.

I am not convinced. Rather, targeting seems to bring an awful lot of repetitive offers from companies all pursuing the same prime targets. To test this notion, I asked my father-in-law to save one month's worth of his junk mail and send it to me. He sent me all thirty pounds. As I sliced open the box I realized how truly rare the opportunity was—as rare, I decided, as seeing a baby pigeon. How often do we get to see, touch, *riffle*, another guy's junk mail?

For analytic purposes I pretended that a surprise volcano had buried the city of Rochester and its surrounding suburbs, including Brighton, where my father-in-law lives, and that a future archaeologist had stumbled on this box. In considerable awe, the archaeologist mulled over the first question to leap into his mind: What mental disorder had caused this poor soul to begin saving his own junk mail?

Putting that aside, my archaeologist would quickly appreciate the significance of his find, especially if he knew about synchographic targeting. The box would open a window on the life of this man; forever after he would be known as "Brighton Man." I know him as Pete.

The mail arrived in January 1991; Brighton Man had received at least two hundred pieces in a single month.

What secrets did the mail betray?

Brighton Man was a doctor. To be more specific, he was a radiologist. He got a lot of medical mail with brightly colored pictures of the inner geography of people. He'd been precisely targeted all right. *Thirty* pieces of mail were brochures for medical conferences and seminars in such sober, scientific environs as Palm Springs, Maui, Interlaken, Laguna Niguel, Aspen, and Disney World.

Brighton Man was upscale. He received a general travel brochure from Cunard offering cruises on the *Queen Elizabeth II.* Investment advisers wanted his business. A land company tried to interest him in a hunk of "waterfront" property in the Ozarks.

Brighton Man was a conservative. In that single month he received fourteen requests for contributions to such lofty causes as making English the national language, sending Bibles to Russia, and blocking Washington, D.C., from becoming a state in order to keep the "radicals" Jesse Jackson and Marion Barry out of Congress. The Republicans sent him a plastic ID card and asked for money. The conservative *National Review* wanted him to subscribe. The National Committee to Preserve Social Security & Medicare sent him the largest piece of junk mail, a real forest eater with an envelope measuring 16½ inches by 17 inches; the envelope and contents together totaled 10.6 square feet of paper. The committee wanted his money and his psychic support for its campaign to preserve Social Security and Medicare benefits.

Here is what my archaeologist concluded: If that volcano hadn't buried Brighton Man, his targeted mail soon would have.

6

WHOSE NAME IS THIS ANYWAY?

Thank you for your note requesting that we delete your name from our mailing list. We regret that this request cannot be accommodated, as we rent all of our mailing lists and therefore exercise no control over their content. . . . I would be more helpful, but my hands are tied.

—Stuart Cohen, president,
Baywood Publishing Company
Letter, July 1991

Lately companies have begun invoking the Constitution in defending their rights to probe our private lives. They talk now of the right of corporate free speech. "You can't have a free-market economy, truly free, without the free flow of ideas and information," argues Peter Francese, the data-marketing pioneer who founded *American Demographics* magazine. "You can say we ought to reign in corporate free speech, but the problem with doing that is, where do you stop? You stop, I believe, at the point where somebody—*anybody*—says, 'Hey, I want that information. I, me, the individual, want to make the choice whether to throw a letter into the wastepaper basket or to read it and buy whatever it offers. I don't want you, the government, making that choice for me. Otherwise I'm not free.' "

The data keepers, moreover, say we have nothing to fear, that they are scrupulous about protecting our records. They would rather shoot their mothers than betray us to unworthy causes. They insist, further, that they have no use for dossiers on individuals and use the detail available only to help target broad markets and to know the "hot buttons" that make those markets respond. "It's too much trouble for me to look up your record, and even if I wanted to, I'm not sure that I could do anything with it," said David Miller, a senior vice-president of Claritas Corp., the Alexandria, Virginia, target-marketing company. "What am I going to do? Laugh? I don't get any great thrills out of that. All I'm trying to do is build a decent model that helps other people target their advertising."

But personal data has a way of being used for purposes that no one ever intended—my Second Law of Data Dynamics. Two classic proofs of this law took place in 1984, of all years. The mere fact the parties involved didn't appreciate the significance of the year should itself give us pause.

In 1984 Farrell's Ice Cream, a chain of ice-cream shops, ran a special promotion whereby customers could get free ice cream on their birthdays. All they had to do was sign up, by providing their names, addresses, and, of course, their birth dates. Farrell's amassed a large list of such names and began peddling the list through brokers.

One customer was the U.S. Selective Service. In August 1984 the agency rented the list, in particular the names and addresses of all males soon to turn eighteen. It then sent them all reminders to register.

Also in 1984, the Internal Revenue Service concocted an experiment to find out whether commercial mailing lists could be used to track down people who failed to file their taxes. The IRS planned to test this idea in the four IRS districts that cover Brooklyn, Queens, and Long Island, New York; Indiana; Wisconsin; and Nevada.

The IRS approached Donnelly Marketing and two other data giants, but they refused, arguing such use would invade people's privacy. The IRS, however, eventually found one loyal American list broker, Dunhill of Washington, willing to supply the needed names. Dunhill provided the addresses, incomes, ages, and dwelling types (single or multifamily) of two million people.

A question comes to mind, possibly an irresponsible one: Just how much can we trust an industry that, to ensure the honesty of its members, seeds its lists with the names of pets and long-dead men? If there is nothing to worry about, if all this digital poking and prodding is a corporate right, how come it feels so wrong?

The data keepers do not like to talk to writers and reporters these days, because they know the wretches in short order will be peppering them with questions about privacy. "When you're in a direct-marketing company and you hear there's a reporter on the line, there's not a big incentive to call him back," said Metromail's George Bardenheier, vice-president of sales. "We're gun-shy because people really have maligned the industry."

I contend, however, that the data industry itself is largely responsible for the growth of suspicion about its motives and practices. It collects its information in oblique ways, snatching it from our credit files, banks, and hospitals, harvesting it from surveys that don't explain how the information will be used. If all this is so good for us, why don't TRW, Metromail, and the other data keepers come forward and drop us all a note explaining the true extent to which they use our names?

Something like this, perhaps, in bold black letters:

WE AND A COUPLE OF HUNDRED OTHER COMPANIES ARE GOING TO APPROPRIATE YOUR NAME, MATCH IT, STORE IT, RENT IT, SWAP IT; WE'LL EVALUATE YOUR GEODEMOGRAPHIC PROFILE, DETERMINE YOUR ETHNIC HERITAGE, CALCULATE YOUR PROPENSITY TO CONSUME. WE'LL TRACK YOU THE REST OF YOUR CONSUMING LIFE, PITCH YOU BABY TOYS WHEN YOU'RE PREGNANT, CONDOS WHEN YOU'RE FIFTY. IN RETURN FOR THE USE OF YOUR NAME, WE WON'T PAY YOU A PENNY. SIGN HERE.

Somewhere along the way, the data keepers made the arbitrary decision that everyone is automatically *on* their lists unless they ask to be taken off. This was a deft bit of work redistribution. Instead of companies having to work at persuading us to hop into their data banks, we consumers have to work at keeping ourselves out of them. We have to write to the Direct Marketing Association to ask to have our names taken off mailing lists; we have to petition our credit bureaus for a look at our own credit files (and must pay for the privilege—although in 1991 TRW broke ranks and announced it would provide credit reports at no charge). In order to compel companies like Lotus Development not to distribute our secrets on handy little compact discs, we have to band together in on-line guerrilla groups, like the Computer Professionals for Social Responsibility, and write thousands of electronic-mail protest letters.

There is an easy way for America's data establishment to shake itself free once and for all of pesky journalists and to reassure consumers.

Invert the underlying premise—assume we're all *off* the lists unless we request specifically to be put on. Then woo us. These are, after all, our names.

Equifax took a step in this direction when it launched Buyer's Market, a program that invites people to fill out a "Consumer Preference Checklist" setting out the kinds of mail they would or would not like to receive. The program survived Equifax's decision to leave the credit-derived list business and became a hallmark of the new consumer-friendly Equifax. By 1992 Buyer's Market had one million members and had begun selling lists based on explicit consumer preferences. Never one to miss a trick, Equifax began charging consumers a fee of $10 to $15 to join the program. As of January 1992 the company still did not know if Buyer's Market would prove a success; clients were busy testing the lists to see if consumers really were interested in getting their mail. "We always wondered, do people really do what they say they're going to do?" said John A. Baker, Equifax's senior vice-president, in a telephone interview. "If they do, this will be a hot product."

This too may be irresponsible, but I propose that the marketers go a bit further and pay us for the privilege of using our names. If the mailers and data keepers are so intent on building a national consumer intelligence network, let them in their next mass mailings send us all a licensing agreement wherein they agree to pay us a set royalty for each and every use of our names and a rental fee for the privilege of having us in their data bases in the first place.

Each of us would become a little private industry—not just micro-markets, but microcorporations. We could have logos on our doorbells. We could even hire agents to represent our names and make sure they appeared only on the finest lists.

Best of all, those checks peeking from the plastic windows of our junk mail would at last be real.

Fortunately the direct-mailers are not nearly as omniscient as their brochures might indicate. Even though I am married and have two kids, I still get direct-mail offers from a dating service. I also get junk mail intended for a man named Nels Larson. Somewhere along the way the intelligence network decided that Nels and I lived at the same address; even the postal NCOA service merged our direct-mail fates. Nels's mail has followed me coast to coast, twice.

The data keepers also continue to be stymied by women like my wife who choose to keep their own names. Often we get two copies of offers, one addressed to her, one to me. Occasionally we even get mail for a phantom occupant of our house who uses Larson as a first name and my wife's maiden name as a surname.

The consumer intelligence community is getting smarter, however. Pinched by market pressures, enthralled by the newest mass intelligence technologies, companies are rushing to install far more sophisticated and immediate surveillance systems. What they would like most is a way of observing our consuming behaviors day by day—or, better yet, moment by moment.

The A. C. Nielsen Co., for example, wants to install TV meters that "see." Our groceries already have become stool pigeons; our supermarkets, as a result, have been changed radically, however invisible the changes may be to the naked consumer. Someday soon even our wristwatches may be pressed into service as monitors of our consuming affairs.

PART THREE

THE WIRING
OF AMERICA

7

SEEING IS BELIEVING

We don't read week by week which cars sound best, which barber is shaving more faces, but we do read what show is attracting more viewers. Television is berserk with that, the crawling around like crazed insects scrambling to climb this tree to be number one. In such a system there is no room for innovation or creativity.

—Norman Lear, producer, 1983

A great mystery has gnawed at the hearts of advertisers ever since the Bulova Watch Company aired the first TV ad on July 1, 1941: Just how many people really do stick around for the commercials? Advertisers have always had to come at the question from an oblique angle, measuring the audiences for programs surrounding their commercials, but not the commercials themselves. The A. C. Nielsen Co. brought technology to the business of estimating audience size in 1942 with the first mechanical meter, the "Audimeter," which used a stylus to scratch out a record of where a radio dial was tuned. The system was crude by today's standards but faster than the competition's surveys and quickly gave Nielsen monopoly control over the business of national ratings. Most viewers know Nielsen only as the maker of the bullets that killed such shows as "Star Trek" and "Twin Peaks," but to think of its ratings exclusively in terms of their show-stopping power is to underestimate the depth of Nielsen's influence over the culture, content, and business of television and, therefore, over the evolution of our consumer culture itself. Nielsen *is* television. Imagine a company like IBM ceding to an outside party decisive control over whether it has a profit or loss in a given quarter, and you'll get a glimpse of Nielsen's peculiar hold over broadcasting.

Nielsen kept competitors at bay through the timely, deft use of technology, but each fundamental advance caused far-reaching change throughout the landscape of television. Its engineers have always pursued TV's golden fleece, the elusive "passive" audience meter, a device capable of recognizing each TV viewer and recording even his briefest exit. Audience engineers have dreamed of such a device ever since that epiphanic instant in 1952 when a Toledo, Ohio, water commissioner realized that a sudden citywide drop in pressure coincided exactly with the commercial break in "I Love Lucy" and joked that someone should invent a "flushometer." The men from Nielsen tried weight-sensing scales and electric eyes and sophisticated weapons technology of the kind we saw put to work so vividly during the Gulf War. Still, some insurmountable obstacle always seemed to get in the way—big dogs, for example, the bane of any audience engineer.

Throughout the 1980s Nielsen could afford to pursue this quest at a leisurely pace. Late in the decade, however, Nielsen's three largest customers, ABC, CBS, and NBC, began charging publicly that Nielsen's existing "people meter" technology was unreliable, perhaps obsolete; in 1989 they conducted a monumental investigation and discovered that their $10 billion industry was tottering on a fulcrum of some rather flimsy statistics. Soon afterward Nielsen reported steep, inexplicable declines in TV viewing that seemed to confirm the network's worst fears and deeply shook their faith in the company's ratings. "The thing we've always had has been this set of numbers," said Alan Wurtzel, ABC's senior research executive. "It's the foundation upon which program decisions are made, deals are made, advertising dollars are spent. When that became unreliable, inconsistent, inaccurate, unexplainable, it just threw into chaos almost everything we did, because that was the basis on which the business was built."

To make matters worse, in April 1991 the networks invited all comers to present ideas for alternate ways of measuring the U.S. audience, the television equivalent of having your spouse suddenly begin advertising for a new lover. The competition began to stir. The Arbitron Company, which competes fiercely with Nielsen to rate local TV markets, threatened to go national; it funded an effort at the Massachusetts Institute of Technology's Media Lab to develop a passive meter and announced in

November 1991 that it would begin tracking public response to the full network schedule. A French company in 1989 actually deployed a meter that approached the passive ideal; soon afterward Arbitron began testing the system for use here. Britain's AGB International, deeply gored in a past encounter with Nielsen, occasionally still hints that the U.S. market is simply too lucrative to resist.

Nielsen, therefore, found itself virtually forced to deploy its newest secret weapon—a device that may indeed be the ultimate passive meter. I met the machine in New York. It can identify viewers and even gives a rough indication of whether their heads are turned toward the TV. The system could fix a lot of the problems cited by the networks, but its deployment would have a significance far beyond simply improving the numbers. By tracking the TV audience on a second-by-second basis, Nielsen's passive meter may yield the first accurate ratings of commercials—not shows, *commercials*—and thus at last solve that great nagging mystery about the "reach" of advertising. If so, however, it will alter sharply the way consumer products are marketed in America, even the way television shows are written and produced. "The implications," said John Dimling, Nielsen Media's executive vice-president, "could be quite staggering."

But does anyone really want to know the truths that Nielsen's black box (and when I saw it, it really was a black box) may bring? What's wrong with Nielsen's numbers? Why did everyone accept them for so long? And how did television, arguably the most powerful force influencing American culture, become so dependent on such a fragile collection of digits in the first place?

At the dawn of broadcasting, before advertisers began to worry about the intimacy of radio, manufacturers doubted that radio and TV would ever be useful for wooing consumers. They needed proof, so they hired market researchers, themselves newly arrived on the commercial landscape, to conduct surveys first simply to find out how many homes in America had a radio, later to determine what programs drew the most listeners. Somewhere along the way ratings took on a power they were never meant to have, much to the chagrin even of Robert Elder, a co-inventor of Nielsen's first meter. In a 1978 letter he wrote that television "suffers greatly from the misuse of the [Nielsen Television Index], and for that reason I am not too happy about my part in getting it started."

Nielsen, founded in 1923 by Arthur C. Nielsen, Sr., acquired in 1936 the rights to the Audimeter from Elder and his partner, Louis Woodruff. The company spent six years refining the idea and in 1942 launched a national radio ratings service that directly challenged the dominant supplier of the day, C. E. Hooper Inc., whose "Hooperatings" still relied on surveys. Nielsen promised better, faster numbers and quickly left Hooper in the dust. In 1950 Nielsen launched its meter-based television index, all the while continuing a policy of aggressively patenting every conceivable audience-measurement idea—a policy that paid off in 1961 when its toughest competitor, the American Research Bureau, which had crowded one of Nielsen's meter patents, wound up having to pay Nielsen royalties on all sales associated with the technology. The ARB temporarily abandoned TV meters in 1972; it began calling itself Arbitron in 1973.

Throughout the 1950s the amount of data and the speed at which Nielsen delivered it increased sharply. At first Nielsen needed six weeks for delivery; by 1961 delivery took sixteen days. As early as 1959 Nielsen began reporting "day after" ratings from a small sample of homes (ARB did it first in 1957). Newspapers routinely reported Nielsen's rankings, a practice that strengthened the connection between ratings and creative quality first established in the 1940s when C. E. Hooper began the then novel practice of deliberately releasing to the press lists of top-rated programs. The growing influence of ratings twice drew the attention of Congress, most forcefully in 1963–1964 with a full-blown investigation that yielded 1,700 pages of testimony and, ultimately, a set of Federal Trade Commission guidelines that sternly warned broadcasters always to remember that ratings data, based as they were on statistical estimates, were "inherently imperfect."

Researchers, meanwhile, took up the hunt for the passive meter.

In 1964 a San Diego inventor named James Tanner caused a major stir at the National Association of Broadcasters meeting in Chicago, where he planned to demonstrate a ratings truck capable of capturing the tuning of televisions while passing on the street. The truck, he claimed, could monitor up to 3,500 TVs every thirty minutes at speeds of up to fifty miles per hour, giving new meaning to the notion of a ratings sweep. Tanner had to cancel his demonstration, however, because he couldn't get the truck to work. The idea died.

The next year an Oklahoma State University professor, Charles L. Allen, produced his own sensation when he published the results of his work with what may have been the first passive audience meter, his DynaScope, a stop-action movie camera that, with the help of a strategically placed mirror, took pictures every fifteen seconds of both the audience and the shows they were watching. Graduate students analyzed almost 1.5 million individual photographs from ninety-five test homes to see whether people were attentive, inattentive, or simply absent while the TV was on and discovered that 19 percent of the time the TV played to an empty room. For another 21 percent of the time a viewer was present but so involved in something else that he couldn't see the screen. The DynaScope didn't restrain anyone's behavior, apparently, for Allen's graduate students wound up poring over stop-action accounts of couples fighting and making love.

The study spurred a flurry of invention among Nielsen's engineers. They experimented with bladderlike scales hidden in couches that would identify people by weight, a concept later embodied in what employees still refer to as the "whoopee cushion" patent. The scales, however, could not tell the difference between big dogs and kids. The engineers also tried using height as an identifier. They lined doorways with electric eyes that measured each viewer who came through—high heels were its undoing.

Things took a turn toward the spooky in 1981, when David A. Kiewit became Nielsen Media's director of engineering. He had spent the previous decade building surveillance and targeting systems for submarines and bombers, a terrific background, as it happens, for anyone interested in either counting or destroying vast numbers of TV viewers. Kiewit and colleagues devised an infrared sensor that scanned rooms for "hot bodies." The system could indeed locate and count people, but it also had an unfortunate habit of counting light bulbs and toasters. One Nielsen engineer took the system home for some real-world testing and quickly got fed up. It kept reporting an extra person in his living room. "Whenever anybody upstairs took a shower," Kiewit told me, "there appeared to be a very long, thin person standing behind the couch who stood there for ten minutes or so and then slooooooowly went away." The phantom was a hot-water pipe embedded in the wall.

With a little tinkering the system could be calibrated to skip most nonhuman sources of heat, but it too proved vulnerable to the "big dog" effect. "You could pretty much set your threshold so that if a house had a small dog, you could skip him," Kiewit said, "but a big dog? You were in trouble."

Next Kiewit's group built a wall-mounted sonar set that scanned living rooms in exactly the way a ship scans New York Harbor, transmitting inaudible signals and capturing the returning echoes. The system subtracted each successive sonar image to isolate points of movement and presumed these to be members of the audience. It was sensitive enough to pick up the soft heave of a viewer's chest as he breathed—so very sensitive, however, it also picked up the soft heave of a seat cushion easing back into shape after its occupant had gotten up and left. It counted big dogs, of course, but also included ceiling fans as members of the audience. Nonetheless, it accurately sensed people about 80 percent of the time—provided, that is, they weren't wearing cashmere, which proved to have Stealth properties the air force ought to keep in mind. Still, there was reason enough to be proud. As Kiewit and a coauthor noted in a published paper: "In demonstrations of the system we called a major client representative a 'nonhuman' object only once."

As elaborate as these systems were, neither came even close to identifying viewers. A true passive meter was still a long way off, and Nielsen wasn't in any great rush to find it. Nielsen's monopoly was intact; there was no serious competition in sight.

The landscape of television, however, had fast begun to change. In the 1950s a family received three channels—well, actually 3.8 by Nielsen's count. The networks sliced the audience pie into three huge and luscious portions and didn't much worry about whether Nielsen allocated the crumbs correctly. But cable TV arrived, VCRs followed (the first hit the U.S. market in 1975), and remote controls allowed viewers to shuttle at will among the airwaves. The network's share of audience began to shrink.

A word of explanation here: Nielsen reports its ratings as two numbers, the rating and the share. The rating is a measure of average audience and is expressed as a percentage of America's total potential audience of 93.1 million TV-equipped households. On any given evening only about half of these households actually watch their TV's. Nielsen's share figures show how this active nightly audience gets divided among the various programs and stations. Suppose, for example, this Thursday night only 50 million households watch TV. Suppose too that 25 million of these active viewers watch "Cheers." The episode's rating would be 26.9 gross rating points, or 26.9 percent of all 93.1 million TV-equipped households. The share would be 50 percent, or half the 50 million viewers who really did watch TV during that portion of the evening.

Nielsen began documenting the cruel fact of the networks' declining audience in the 1978–79 season, when they still drew a robust 91 percent of the prime-time audience. This share has shrunk every year since. By 1985 the average household could get 18.8 channels; the networks' share of audience, meanwhile, had shrunk to 77 percent. By 1991 the average home got 30 channels and network share had fallen to 63 percent.

For a bit of culture shock, consider this: Seven of the fifty highest-rated programs of all time were 1964 episodes of "The Beverly Hillbillies." Each had a rating of between 41.8 and 44. In the most heavily watched of these, ol' Jed, Jethro, and Granny somehow managed to command a 65 percent share of viewers—more than the combined share of all three networks today.

By the mid-1980s the explosion in TV choice had begun to outpace Nielsen's ability to keep up. By then advertisers cared less about reaching masses of households and more about reaching narrower demographic segments of the population best suited to their products—for example, women 25–54; men 18–49; kids. Nielsen's set meters, sophisticated versions of the original Audimeter, recorded only that a TV was on and that it was receiving a particular station. Nielsen got its demographic data from viewer diaries kept by a second panel of families. Researchers believed that one member of each family, usually the already harried woman of the house, kept the diary for everyone. With so many channels, they worried, how could anyone remember exactly what a family watched, let alone the channel on which it appeared? They fretted too about the so-called halo effect caused when harried diary keepers wrote down what they *would* have watched or *should* have watched rather than what they really *did* watch.

By 1985 the networks were ready for a change, and AGB International, the British ratings giant, offered a tempting one. AGB previously had announced it wanted to wire America with a new kind of meter, one it already had deployed in Ireland, Thailand, and the Philippines, that captured both tuning and demographics simultaneously, continuously. AGB offered all this, moreover, at a lower cost.

The networks, delighted as much by the promised improvements as by the challenge to Nielsen's monopoly, helped fund an initial test of

AGB's technology in Boston. This was a tricky time for Nielsen. Even though the networks had already lost market share, they were still Nielsen's biggest customers; on a symbolic level, moreover, their continued endorsement was vital. But their contracts with Nielsen were about to expire. Nielsen had offered them a new three-year contract that would cost each $14 million.

CBS made a show of canceling its contract, ostensibly to prevent automatic renewal; in a further display of disaffection, CBS signed a one-year contract with AGB. In July 1987 David Poltrack, then and now CBS's top research official, told *The New York Times*, "It is certainly possible that we will not be a client of Nielsen come the fall." ABC also canceled but did not sign with AGB.

AGB's Boston test, which lasted a year and a half, gave Nielsen time to dust off a similar meter it had begun experimenting with nearly a decade earlier. Both were called "people" meters, in that they sought to provide an electronic measure not just of tuning, but of who was watching; both began producing ratings in September 1987 and thus gave broadcasters an opportunity to see how competing ratings systems would describe the same objective reality.

The two new systems produced radically conflicting results. The variations, moreover, occurred in a pattern that defied reduction to a mathematical constant. On the first Monday night, for example, Nielsen's people meter rated ABC's football game a 15.3; AGB gave it 11.9, a discrepancy of some three million households. Nielsen's meter-and-diary system, which Nielsen continued in order to provide stability during the transition, gave the game a 14.5. These conflicting results defined "inherent imperfection."

Nielsen flatly declared AGB's numbers were "wrong." AGB said Nielsen's were too high. Confusion reigned; advertising negotiations faltered. Ultimately the industry voted to stay with Nielsen, which was at least a known entity. AGB fled the country, trailing a reported $80 million in losses.

The new meter brought more data more quickly, including overnight demographics, but it was no friend to the networks. That first season the networks' share of audience dropped to 70 percent from 75. The networks—acting together as the Committee on Nationwide Television Audience Measurement (Contam), founded in 1963 in response to the congressional hearings—hired a respected media research firm, Statistical Research Inc., Westfield, New Jersey, to investigate the new system.

The resulting report weighed six pounds. It was 550 pages long in seven volumes and arrived in a slick, heavy-gauge gray box meant to last a century. The report, in its authors' words, "documented an erosion in the quality of the Nielsen service. . . . The vision, the actions, and the commitment of the past have been diminished."

John Dimling, Nielsen's executive vice-president, read the final and most critical volume of the report in his room in a Northbrook, Illinois, Holiday Inn. "I was about as depressed as I've ever been," he told me. "Even though I was prepared for everything they were going to say, seeing it all, just one thing after another—you think, My God, what have we done?"

As if to confirm the mournful accuracy of the network report, a few months later, in early 1990, Nielsen reported those mysterious sharp declines in audience that so troubled the networks. Viewers disappeared. Kids, in particular, failed to show up for the Saturday morning cartoons. Droves of viewers deserted the prime-time hours. The declines were so steep, so unexpected, they caused an immediate combined loss to the networks of as much as $200 million, the value of commercial time the networks had to cough up to make good on previously arranged audience guarantees.

In following months the networks launched an attack on Nielsen unprecedented for its ferocity. The assault, however, drew attention from what may have been the most significant revelation of the Contam report—how devilishly complex this business of measuring America's TV audience has become. Ronald Kessler, program director of the University of Michigan's prestigious Survey Research Center, and both a critic and closet admirer of Nielsen, thinks the fact Nielsen can produce ratings at all is something of a minor miracle. "If you look inside what Nielsen does, it is absolutely mind-boggling," he said. "Push any door and you find unbelievable detail."

At the same time he added: "Little errors mount up like crazy in a thing like this."

I don't know any Nielsen families; I have never met a member of a Nielsen family; to my knowledge there are no Nielsen families on my block. The only person I know who even comes close to having known a Nielsen family is my wife, who recalls vague feelings of childhood envy toward a family in her neighborhood that had been recruited to the cause. At any one time there are about 4,000 Nielsen families afoot in America, or one for every 23,000 of the country's television-equipped households. They are a secretive bunch, under orders to keep quiet about their Nielsen status lest someone try to coerce them into a scheme to manipulate the ratings. (They are told to report any suspicious encounters.) Together they constitute one of the most influential groups in America, for their viewing habits directly and immediately determine the allocation of roughly $10 billion of network airtime each year. A single Nielsen household accounts for about $2.5 million of that $10 billion of advertising fees. Ronald Kessler puts it another way: "It's worth a television network's time to find a $150,000 house in America that has a Nielsen meter, pay the owner $200,000 for the house, and then tune that television set to their station 100 percent of the time."

Broadcasters treat Nielsen's ratings as if they were exact numbers, not estimates. The networks sell about 70 percent of their prime-time advertising periods in what is called the "up-front" market, a time bazaar that opens every June shortly after the networks announce their schedules for the following fall. Here, advertisers buy big blocks of time in advance; in return the networks sell the time at a discount and guarantee that the advertisers' commercials will draw an agreed-on number of viewers. Deals are cut to the tenth of a ratings point; viewers become a commodity, sold on a cost-per-thousand basis. An unexpected ratings dip of a single percentage point can cost a network millions of dollars in "make goods" to satisfy the guarantees.

"As negotiations take place, deals are decided on the basis of CPM [cost-per-thousand] differences of pennies," CBS's David Poltrack said in a talk to members of the Advertising Research Foundation. Yet this, he said, ignored the fundamental error inherent in any statistical sample and the far greater error in one as fundamentally flawed as Nielsen's. A true calculation of the room for error, he said, would "tell us that even a CPM variation of a dollar or more may not be real."

Statistical theory holds that every sample, no matter how perfect— even if everyone surveyed agreed to participate—starts life with a built-in, or standard, error. If a single episode of, say, "Murphy Brown" draws a 15 rating, the standard error is six-tenths of a ratings point in either direction, according to Edward Schillmoeller, Nielsen Media's chief statistician. The episode has roughly a 68 percent chance of having a rating between 15.6 and 14.4, and a 32 percent chance of falling *outside* those limits.

This level of accuracy, however, applies only in ideal, textbook conditions, not in the rough-and-tumble world of surveying people, where the degree of error is likely to be far greater.

Nevertheless, small changes in ratings affect programming decisions. Poltrack told his audience: "Programs are canceled or shifted around the schedule after a four-week ratings trend is provided, even though differences between the points in the trend line may not be significant. In short, we have ignored the weak foundation of our television measurement system."

The classic example of a novel show battered by ratings-driven manipulation was "Frank's Place," a funky, artfully done 1980s comedy about a restaurant in New Orleans. In twelve months CBS moved the show into six different time slots on four different nights, prompting star Tim Reid and producer Hugh Wilson to complain that even their own mothers could not find the show. (A CBS executive later admitted having moved "Frank's Place" too much.)

The abuse of ratings by executives afraid to rely on good judgment and taste has turned network television into even more of a wasteland than its early critics could have imagined, creating a bleak terrain of malicious comedy—"Married . . . With Children" comes to mind, with its fixation on breasts and bowels—and "reality" shows, those first cousins of Brazilian snuff films, featuring platoons of cops gripping their nine-millimeter Berettas as they kick down the doors of countless unconvicted members of the underclass.

For one brief period, in 1990, the networks seemed ready to take some risks. Emboldened by the surprise successes of "Twin Peaks" and "The Simpsons," executives began talking about breaking new ground. "Tried and true is dead and buried," said NBC's Brandon Tartikoff, who has since left the network to try his hand at big-ticket movie production.

For the networks, however, innovation is something you try only once—even though true innovation requires the taking of risks and courts repeated failure. The history of television demonstrates that novel shows, like any new product, demand time to build acceptance. Examples abound of hit shows whose first episodes drew only lackluster ratings, including "Gunsmoke," "Bonanza," "All in the Family," "The Mary Tyler Moore Show," "Lou Grant," "M*A*S*H," "Hill Street Blues," "Murphy Brown," and "Designing Women." Network executives at least give lip service to the idea that failure is part of the game. "You just can't stop doing the unconventional," Jeff Sagansky, president of CBS Entertainment, told a *Times* writer in 1990. "Most things fail anyway." In a remark that captured the essential nature of innovation, he added: "All hits are flukes."

When ratings battered the fledgling revolution, however, executives quickly reassessed their dalliance with risk. "There was this feeling that you had to do something new and breakthrough and cutting edge, which was wrong," David Poltrack told me. "It turns out it was not what America wanted. By the time the [1990–91] season started, 'Twin Peaks' was a dead show; the 'Twin Peaks' phenomenon had pretty well died; 'America's Funniest Home Videos' settled down; and 'The Simpsons' was down as well. The shows that held up the best were the most traditional basic shows." He cited "Cheers" and CBS's own "60 Minutes," both veteran ratings performers.

Having given risk and creativity a try, the networks in 1991 scuttled to safety: to nostalgia. Nostalgia may not do much to challenge the imagination or demonstrate the creative power of television, but it pumps ratings like nobody's business.

Jeff Sagansky's CBS led the way, with specials celebrating its past glories. In February 1991 the network broadcast "The Very Best of 'The Ed Sullivan Show,'" "Mary Tyler Moore: The 20th Anniversary," and the "'All in the Family' 20th Anniversary Special." The "All in the Family" retrospective got such high ratings that CBS broadcast reruns of the show in prime time throughout the summer of 1991, and each episode ranked among the ten highest-rated shows of the week. In November 1991 all three networks again switched on their time machines. James Arness and Robert Stack both reprised their most famous crime-fighting roles for onetime TV movies. CBS launched another "Classic Weekend"; over three consecutive nights it broadcast "The 20th Anniversary of 'The Bob Newhart Show,'" "The Very Best of 'Ed Sullivan Show' II"—a sequel to a retrospective!—and "Memories of 'M*A*S*H.'"

The 'M*A*S*H' special was particularly telling. If introduced amid business conditions like those existing today, the 'M*A*S*H' series might not have survived its opening season. It was novel: it presented a wholly new TV genre, the "dramedy," and it spoke with a passionate political voice, two characteristics that ratings by their nature abhor. When the series launched its first episode in 1972, it committed what today is an unpardonable sin—it failed to become an instant hit. "The series got off to a less than promising start," wrote John J. O'Connor, a television writer for *The New York Times*, in a review of the retrospective. "Rolling off the bitingly satirical movie, the television version seemed tame and rather flat." The show needed time to gel—"time," O'Connor added, "it would not get in today's anxiety-ridden marketplace."

Daily ratings only worsen the problem. "We could probably do without daily ratings," Poltrack told me during an interview in his office at CBS's headquarters in New York. They tend, he said, to shorten the already short-range perspective of his industry. The networks, faced with shrinking audiences and rising costs, are running short on patience. " 'Murphy Brown' took three years to be a hit," he said. "This is a mentality where if you're not a hit in four weeks, we take you off and put something else on."

Having said this, however, he tipped back his chair and began flipping through a set of Nielsen overnights that had just arrived on his desk. "There's always *something* interesting," he said.

He turned to the ratings for the previous Friday and cited that night's episode of "Dallas," a CBS series. " 'Dallas' has been going up in the ratings for us, and 'Dallas' is going to have its last telecast ever in a couple of weeks. We want to see if there's any momentum building. And sure enough"—he pointed to the page—" 'Dallas' is up again in the ratings, a good sign there's some momentum."

The news about another show was less sanguine. He turned to Thursday's revised ratings. CBS had recently introduced a lackluster stopgap series called "The Antagonists" opposite NBC's top-rated comic juggernaut, "Cheers."

"The first couple of weeks it got okay ratings," Poltrack said. "We were waiting very anxiously to see what the show did when 'Cheers' went into repeats."

That previous Thursday a fresh "Antagonists" had aired against the first "Cheers" repeat of the season. "Cheers" got an 18.8 rating, or 31 share; "The Antagonists" got only an 8.1 rating, for a 13 share.

"It didn't go up at all," he said. "That's bad news, because the rating was not high enough to represent success for the show, and the fact it didn't go up at all . . ." He stopped and let the thought—and the show, as it happens—hang. "The Antagonists" didn't make it to the next season.

Ratings have attained a certain psychic precision as well. A fraction of a point can mean the difference between a producer being considered a winner or a loser, and in television the distinction matters. "It's not the reality, it's the perception" said Bonny Dore, a successful producer of such TV movies and miniseries as "Sins" and "Glory! Glory!" "If the perception is you lost—you lost," she said.

And that perception can affect negotiations for a producer's next deal—"or whether you *get* another deal."

"Does it bother you," I asked, "that Nielsen's ratings are so flawed?"

"You're simply feeding into every nightmare a producer's ever had. We work and slave and go into debt, and we do something wonderful and the numbers are, quote, 'A little disappointing.' Then to find out that maybe they're off by five share points? You just want to go kill yourself. Other than that"—she laughed—"it's fine."

•   •   •

At its very best, statistical sampling is fraught with problems. The initial response rate for the 1990 census was the lowest in history, even though all we had to do was fill out a single questionnaire and were required by law to do so. Nielsen runs a massive, continuous, partially automated survey of America 24 hours a day, 365 days a year, and intrudes on the daily lives of each recruit for two years at a stretch.

In the real world, as Nielsen has found, sampling is hell.

The process begins with the creation every ten years of a "sample frame," the population of households in America from which all Nielsen families are selected. First, using Census Bureau data, Schillmoeller's department divides the country into successively smaller hunks of territory until at last it has a collection of some five thousand "block groups," units of census geography comprising on average about 425 housing units each. Next, Nielsen sends squads of field agents into each of these block groups to count *every* housing unit, both to account for any changes in the number of homes reported by the Census Bureau and to note the addresses of potential Nielsen candidates. The crews merely count, until they reach a number selected at random by Schillmoeller's department. Assume there are indeed 425 homes in a block group. Nielsen picks a random number from 1 to 425. If the number is 125, the enumerator counts the first 124 without jotting down a single address. The next housing unit, be it in a cave, tree, or converted beer truck, is the primary target household, a "Basic" in Nielsen-speak. This is the home Nielsen most dearly wants to recruit and the one that sampling theory dictates Nielsen indeed *must* recruit. If the house is vacant, or even a vacant slab in a trailer park, Nielsen will keep coming back for five years in hopes that someone will have moved in.

In theory every household has an equal shot at becoming a Nielsen family; in practice, however, the odds for some of us are zero. Nielsen would never allow me to be a member of its panel. By Nielsen's reckoning I am "occupationally disqualified," unfit to rate, as are all my fellow journalists, every editor, producer, and advertising executive, and of course every single employee of CBS, NBC, ABC, CNN, MTV, and Arbitron. The presumption is that we could not be trusted to behave ourselves and at the first opportunity would rush out and write about the experience or tune our TVs to the stations we work for. (There is good reason for Nielsen to worry: station employees included by chance in diary panels have been known to keep quiet and "load up" the diaries with their own stations' programs.) Nielsen also builds in demographic safety valves to avoid the unlikely but statistically possible selection of an aberrant sample—say, four thousand black households. Such an occurrence might delight the networks, given that black families watch 50 percent more television than their nonblack peers, but would not do much for Nielsen's statistical credibility.

Today's people meter demands a lot of its hosts. Arthur Nielsen, Sr., wrote in 1955 that one of the beauties of the original Audimeter system was that it "operates entirely automatically and outside the collaborating family's day-to-day awareness." Today's meter is a nagging shrew, consisting of three components: a computer the size of a compact disc player known as the "home unit"; a smaller box with a numerical keypad and a face plate of red and green lights that sits atop a TV set; and a remote control, with eight numbered buttons (or sixteen, for larger households) and an "OK" button. Nielsen assigns a button to each individual in a household, even children as young as two years old. And each, even the two-year-old, is expected to comport himself in appropriate Nielsen fashion—that is, to press his button whenever he starts to watch TV and whenever he stops. Visitors pick an unoccupied button, enter their sex and age, then also report their arrival or departure. When a viewer punches in, the lights associated with his number change from red to green. Periodically the meter demands a little reassurance that someone indeed is watching and will blink a single red bulb at the far right of the set-top box. One press of the "OK" button calms the machine. The longer the prompt goes unanswered, however, the more adamant the meter becomes, blinking its bulbs in an increasingly haphazard manner until the meter is ablaze with red and green lights like a haywire streetlight. Some meters finally cry out in frustration, emitting a pained and disappointed beep.

Volunteers also subject themselves to a lot of drilling and wiring. Nielsen requires that every single TV set, VCR, and cable converter be metered and tied to the home unit. Any satellite dish has to be metered separately with an "inclinometer" that records which way, and thus at which satellite, the dish is pointing. Nielsen even takes an inventory of unused TVs kept in the attic or basement. Nielsen's agents don't simply accept a homeowner's assurance that a set won't be used. They have him swear to it in an affidavit and then attach a small plastic seal to the prongs of the plug. If on a return visit the agent finds the seal broken, he will ask permission to meter the set; if he isn't allowed to, he may eject the family from the sample.

Today's typical Nielsen home, said Larry Patterson, the company's director of field operations, has two TVs, one VCR, and one cable converter, a mélange of equipment that takes five or six hours to install. The most complex house he's come across had six TVs, five VCRs, and cable; the metering process took two full days.

In return for all this equipping and pestering, each family can pick gifts from a Nielsen catalog and gets cash payments of $2 per month for each TV and VCR in the house. A single person with one TV would get just $24 a year; the family with the complex system would get $264.

The networks worry that the burden is too great, that Nielsen families experience "button fatigue" and begin engaging in such inappropriate behaviors as failing to log in or letting a visitor *just sit there* without first registering his age and presence. Contam conducted exit interviews with families leaving the Nielsen stable and found that one out of three reported getting tired of the meter; half of these said accuracy as a result had suffered; over one in ten said they themselves "hardly ever" logged out when they finished watching a show.

The networks fear that button fatigue is especially pronounced among children. Half of the kids (or their parental spokesmen) interviewed by Contam said they did indeed get tired of pushing buttons. Nielsen takes great pains to win their cooperation. It gives them a Nielsen coloring book and shows them a video called "The Nielsen People Meter Show." Nielsen wants kids to bond to their buttons and practices some subtle human engineering. It gives them a choice of animal stickers to place next to their buttons—no commercial figures like Donald Duck or the Ninja Turtles, of course, because these might bias their viewing behavior.

Nielsen assigns the youngest child button number one, then works up from there in relation to the ages of family members. It does this to avoid button "churn," the shuffling of meter slots as people join or exit the household. Nielsen wants the oldest person on the highest button because of the cold actuarial fact that this person is likely to die first and leave a disorienting gap in the panel. "God forbid Grandmother dies," Larry Patterson said. "You don't want to leave a gap. Also, the kids may not press Grandma's button."

Who would agree to invite such an imperious guest into their homes? Far too few, as it happens. Nielsen manages to recruit only about 48 percent of the originally targeted Basics, according to Contam. Such a low rate of cooperation makes statisticians queasy; it could be an indicator of a fundamental difference between those who do cooperate and those who don't. The question is, how does this affect viewing patterns? An early Contam study, conducted in 1964 in response to the congressional investigations, found that those who cooperated watched somewhat *more* TV than noncooperators. The networks claim the people meter has reversed the pattern—that now people who don't cooperate are the heaviest users of network TV.

Nielsen's cooperation rate is actually far worse than 48 percent. In its routine disclosures Nielsen merely reports the percentage of Basics who refuse to participate and doesn't mention the number of "Alternates" it had to approach before achieving its four-thousand-household sample. In fact, Nielsen typically must contact three alternates from its second-string list before it finds a willing participant. In some cases, according to Schillmoeller, recruiters have had to contact up to thirty additional homes. Moreover, on any given day about 10 percent of Nielsen's people meter households produce faulty data that cannot be included in the daily ratings calculations. The families most likely to be excluded, Contam discovered, were the heaviest viewers, reflecting a catch-22 phenomenon literally engineered into the people meter system: the more TVs and VCRs and Nielsen equipment you have, the greater the chance something will happen to bump your data from the day's tabulations.

Fatigue causes families to drop out of the panel altogether. Other households leave for such fey motives as the fact that they just bought a slick new TV and don't want Nielsen's installers tinkering with it. Once,

Patterson lost a Nielsen household to one of the cold realities of ghetto life in New York City. He and a partner had recruited an elderly woman living in a tough housing project in the borough of Queens. Early the following week he got a call from a city homicide detective, who told him the woman had been found strangled in her bed the previous Sunday morning. He requested all the woman's viewing records for Saturday night, in case they held some clue to the timing of her murder.

She had turned off the set at 11:23 P.M. Saturday, Patterson found. But he also discovered a curious thing—someone had watched a lot of television in the woman's apartment the Sunday afternoon *after* she'd been killed.

The detective was silent a moment. "Oh, yeah," he said. "That was us. We were watching the football game."

"For him, at least," Patterson told me, "it certainly confirmed our credibility."

America's four thousand people-metered households report their findings every night from three A.M. to about seven A.M. Florida time, when the machines dutifully call home to Nielsen's Dunedin Center. It is a common misconception among us lay folk that the people meter alone produces all the information Nielsen needs for its ratings. The fact is, this nightly torrent of data is by itself utterly useless.

The meter tells only who is watching the TV set and how the set is tuned. Nielsen must merge this data with a second ocean of information, the detailed records of exactly what programs appeared on thousands upon thousands of TV stations and cable "head ends" around the country—not what the stations planned to broadcast, but what they actually did broadcast and the exact times at which they did so.

On any day the task is monumental: the networks supply Nielsen with their daily lineups, but typically these succumb to special reports, late-running baseball games, natural disasters, and so forth, regional events that might cause an affiliate to interrupt the network "feed." Nielsen keeps track of all this by stationing robotic TV watchers in all the TV markets where Nielsen families reside and assigning them the mind-vaporizing task of watching television twenty-four hours a day, *forever.* They watch for a basic network signal hidden to us viewers that indicates when the network "feed" is being broadcast by an affiliate. If the signal arrives at its scheduled time, Nielsen assumes all is well. Any discrepancy is called a "conflict." In a typical week Nielsen's program records department in Dunedin will resolve between 12,000 and 15,000 such conflicts, often by calling stations to find out just exactly what did air. During the first week of the 1991 Gulf War, Nielsen confronted 50,000 conflicts and in the process exposed a bit of affiliate treachery. A few stations had dumped their network feeds to broadcast CNN instead.

Contam factored together all the forces tending to reduce cooperation and the supply of usable data and determined that Nielsen's people meter panel had a final, *net* response rate of only 35 percent, meaning that only 35 percent of Nielsen's originally targeted "Basics" produced usable data on any given day—a rate, Contam reported, "below all industry or government standards for high-quality operations. The rate has declined steadily over recent years, and indications are that unless a different effort is introduced, it will continue to do so. At some point . . . a totally different measurement approach will have to be considered."

"As you can see, this is your typical living room," said Christopher Lubniewski, a Nielsen client-service representative. The room was a barren, windowless office in Nielsen Media's executive headquarters in New York. Nielsen's new passive people meter, a squat black box the size of a videocassette recorder, was perched before me on the shelf of an incongruous breakfront, the only thing even remotely living room–like.

The machine and I had already had been introduced—that is, it had scanned me and then stored four images of my face—three head-on portraits and a quarter profile. It was ready now to try matching the real me to these digital mug shots.

If it succeeded, it would display on a nearby video screen my name and a number indicating how confident it was about the identification. A number and no name would mean it had failed. I did not want a zero. A zero would be a pretty good indicator that I had died or at least stopped breathing. Anything between sixty and eighty-three would mean I was a person, although not someone the meter knew; anything higher, that it knew me well enough to display my name.

The meter scans the room every two seconds, looking for signs of life. It compares each fresh image to its predecessor to capture any portion of the image that has changed. The difference between the two is the digital representation of movement, the hallmark of human-ness. A life-size photograph brought into the room might fool the system for a moment, Lubniewski told me, but over the next few scans its lack of movement would cause the meter to ignore it.

The system next locates the mélange of digits most resembling a human head, a search program that may at last help Nielsen separate men from dogs. "If a cat or a big dog jumped up here," Lubniewski said, "the system would scan it and try to find the head, and during the match-off would give it a score of zero to sixty"—a nonhuman moving object. The machine would notice every departure and return. Its reliance on head-on or nearly head-on views, moreover, means it would not count people who were present but were involved in other activities, like reading the newspaper or making love on the floor.

The machine gets good but deeply qualified reviews.

"It's very accurate," said Robert A. Warrens, senior vice-president and director of media resources and research for J. Walter Thompson USA. "I sat in a room in different positions, and overall it was able to pick me up 100 percent." But many who have seen the meter worry that it could degrade Nielsen's already poor cooperation rate, especially given today's heightened concern for privacy.

"We know that one out of every two households has a TV in one or more bedrooms," said Nicholas P. Schiavone, NBC's vice-president of media and marketing research. "Now I come to your home and tell you I'm going to set up a recognition meter in every room of your household where there's a TV. Will people allow a device that can recognize—that can *see*—into those rooms?"

Nielsen wondered the same thing and installed a nonfunctioning version in a group of Nielsen homes to see if their occupants, led to believe the system really worked, would indeed accept a cameralike device into their living rooms, bedrooms, even bathrooms (where 1 percent of American households currently park a TV). The answer, apparently, was a qualified "yes."

Nielsen expected to deploy the machine fairly soon. In a 1991 interview Willliam G. Jacobi, Nielsen Media's president and chief operating officer, told me he would "be disappointed if the passive meter were not playing a role in the rating system within the next three years."

If the meter works, it will solve Nielsen's problem of button fatigue. One school of thought holds the passive meter could even improve initial cooperation rates by eliminating the workload now associated with the current generation of people meter. It would do nothing, however, to help Nielsen keep up with the proliferation of miniature portable TVs and track the ranks of so-called out-of-home viewers, the great uncounted masses who watch television while on vacation, in hotels, away at college, or on the job. To help meet these challenges, Nielsen's Dunedin researchers began experimenting with a pocket-size electronic "diary" that panelists would, in theory, whip out to record the shows they watch in bars and elsewhere. They also began testing ways by which various pieces of Nielsen equipment could communicate with each other through the ordinary plugs and circuits of a house, thereby reducing the need to run so many wires through homes. Moreover, Nielsen hired its first chief research officer, a kind of research cop, to study Nielsen's existing ratings methods and look for simple ways to improve them.

The passive meter, however, is the thing Nielsen most likes to show off.

"Try moving your chair backward and forward," Chris Lubniewski suggested. The meter registered my identity with manly scores of about ninety.

Lubniewski took a seat on an adjacent chair, and together we kicked our way throughout the meter's field of vision. It named us both. I tried covering the top half of my head with a legal pad, something I often do when I watch TV. The machine hesitated. I was a person all right, but it couldn't say who.

Changes in hairstyle won't throw the meter, Lubniewski said— although he did mention a recent exception. "One woman came in here wearing her hair very tight," he said. "She let it go and it fell in front of her face, and the system *did* get confused."

This could be forgiven, I decided: in a similar situation I'd have felt likewise—but what about shaving a mustache? Someone tried it, Lubniewski said; the machine wasn't fazed. I quickly asked Nielsen's public relations man, sitting nearby, if I could borrow his glasses. The machine named me with its highest score yet.

It was time to get serious. Man to machine. I stuck out my tongue, yanked back the corners of my mouth, and closed one eye, a little maneuver I picked up from my three-year-old daughter. Lubniewski smiled, but the smile looked thin to me; it masked, I was certain, the kind of ennui that can come only from watching armies of otherwise sober people suddenly let down their hair or flourish surprise pairs of glasses.

"A lot of people try to fool the system," Lubniewski said. "You have to remember, it scans the room every one or two seconds. You could fool it, but chances are if it misses you—if you sneeze or make a face—we'll still know you're there."

I smiled past my fingers but held the pose a bit longer just to make sure the system got it. It identified me as human but otherwise didn't know me from Adam. Satisfied, I tucked in my tongue.

An instant later the monitor displayed my name with a pouty score of eighty-five.

A true passive meter is almost certain to appear before the end of the century. Barring the unexpected arrival of a new challenger, that meter will function like the one I saw demonstrated in Nielsen's offices. In the past, fundamental advances in ratings technology have brought far-reaching change to the business and culture of television. What changes will this meter bring? What revelations about the audience-holding power of commercials? Of TV itself?

History is full of broad hints about the awful truth—plunging water pressure in Toledo, the DynaScopic chronicles of TV sex in Oklahoma. The best indications of what lies ahead, however, come from the actual deployment of near passive meters here and in France. In 1987 R. D. Percy & Company, a now defunct ratings concern, installed an infrared body sensor in 609 homes and demonstrated that television sets played to empty rooms about 13 percent of their operating time. This proportion climbed sharply for certain categories of shows. Golf commentators, for example, spent 20 percent of their time whispering stroke-by-strokes to unoccupied couches and chairs. Viewers abandoned "Good Morning America" and "Today" for roughly twelve minutes out of every hour; commercials as much as doubled the absentee rate.

French advertisers recently got a real-time look at commercial avoidance. In France Mediametrie holds a virtual monopoly over TV ratings. In 1989, however, a challenger, Telemetric, deployed a form of passive meter called "Motivac" that detects the presence of people by sensing motion, just as Nielsen's meter does. Its ability to identify viewers, however, depends on the fact that the French watch TV the way Americans did back in the 1960s—that is, with the whole family gathered on favorite seats around a single TV. Viewers must provide Motivac with detailed information about their TV-watching habits, including where they most like to sit. If Motivac finds a person on that *chaise favorite*, it checks its memory for the likely occupant.

Motivac provides Telemetric's clients with a moment-by-moment "spike graph" of the nation's viewing; it proved with dismaying immediacy that vast numbers of viewers flee prime-time shows during the final credits and commercials. It found, for example, that a collection of commercials broadcast during a World Cup soccer match in 1990 triggered a virtual stampede from the living rooms of France, with the TV audience suddenly shrinking to 3.5 million from 9 million. Telemetric also discovered that high ratings garnered by French news shows during the Gulf War were illusions. Viewers gathered only at the beginnings of each broadcast to catch the headlines, then left the TV on and went about their business elsewhere in the home.

Such grim news here could trigger an immediate restructuring of the pricing of advertising time. No advertiser believes everyone stays for the commercials, of course, but a second-by-second measure of audience would at long last document the rate of desertion. Advertisers will discover that some shows hold their audiences more tenaciously during commercial breaks than others. For most of my friends, the Super Bowl is a big beer and popcorn event, but the half-life of beer in the male body is known to be brief. Suppose advertisers discover that most of America flees to the john during those ultraexpensive Super Bowl spots? Suppose, in contrast, they discover that nearly everyone who watches those sober Sunday morning talk shows stays put? I'd like to think commercial ratings would bring an element of justice to television. At last advertising agencies would find themselves subject to the same ratings tyranny that producers and TV writers have had to endure all these years. Suddenly agencies too would find their Nielsen rank published in *Variety* and the *L.A. Times*. Think of the implications—now *commercials* could be canceled!

Second-by-second ratings, however, could lash the creative content of shows even more tightly to the numbers. Real-time ratings would provide programming executives with an unprecedented ability to tinker with the content and structure of television shows. "It is conceivable," John Dimling told me, "that if you literally had second-by-second or minute-by-minute ratings, you'd know what people in a given demographic group tend to leave the program at what point in time. The use of that information in making programs could be kind of mind-boggling. You could do a content analysis of the program, and relate the content to when people tend to leave, or when they come back. Or if they come back. It may turn out that a certain point in the story or a certain production technique tends to interest people or not interest people."

Suppressing a shiver, I asked: "You mean one could rate individual characters? Even subplots?"

"Sure, sure," he said without an instant's hesitation.

If Nielsen stands now on a threshold, so too does television itself. Ratings began simply as a way for advertisers to prove to themselves that radio and television could indeed help them reach masses of consumers. The numbers soon took on a life all their own and an authority they were never meant to have; they became the soul of television. But when is enough enough? How much information is too much information? Does TV now risk snuffing the last ember of creativity under a yet more massive cascade of deceptively precise numbers? Before Nielsen takes that next great technological leap, I'd like to invoke that old FTC warning. Even at their best, Nielsen's ratings will always be estimates; they will always be "inherently imperfect."

Another surveillance technology, however, already has seized the marketing imagination and merged its own cascade of imperfect data with the ratings produced by Nielsen and Arbitron—a coalescence of data that threatens to ensnare human creativity in an even more restrictive skein of false precision.

Now companies can know not only that you watched the Super Bowl, but that you suffered from hemorrhoid itch while doing so.

8

THE THIN RED LINE

There is nothing wrong with your television set. Do not attempt to adjust the picture. We are controlling transmission. We will control the horizontal, we will control the vertical. We can change the focus to a soft blur, or sharpen it to crystal clarity. For the next hour, sit quietly and we will control all that you see and hear. You are about to participate in a great adventure. You are about to experience the awe and mystery which reaches from the inner mind to the outer limits.

—"The Outer Limits," TV series, 1963

By now we have all become accustomed to supermarket scanners and the shimmery red filament they cast over our soups, toothpastes, and cereals. Some of us watch the light, even peer deep inside the glass to observe its glowing helium-neon source, but most of us long ago tucked the scanner into that bleak and fast-expanding cupboard of commonplace technologies we don't understand and have no desire to understand, like TVs, telephones, fiber optics, VCRs, compact discs, and digital radio. The novelty has worn off. Get on with it, please, get me out of this store before my children erupt.

To the marketers of America, however, that plate of glass embedded at the end of the cashier's conveyor belt has become a window onto our consuming souls. Grocers embraced the technology in the 1970s because scanners gave them a chance to know for the first time just how much of each grocery item they sold on a daily basis and allowed them to automate the checkout process and thus to boost the productivity of their cashiers (not, mind you, to speed our passage through the lines; that was a dividend). But marketers soon realized there was a lot more power stored in scanner records than grocers had imagined. Scanners brought to the phenomenon of mass consumption the power of an electron microscope. They revealed the nuclear structure of consumption: the individual and his purchases. The marketers, driven by their insatiable need for information, now peer directly into the pantries of millions of consumers across America. Look back into that scanner and what you really see is the red-rimmed gaze of Betty Crocker, Aunt Jemima, Mrs. Paul, Mrs. Smith, Sara Lee, and the Pillsbury Doughboy watching your every purchase. You may as well get up on the glass and dance there stark naked. Your secrets are known: you have hemorrhoids, arthritis, and a nasty case of hay fever every spring; your twelve-year-old son just bought a package of condoms; you suspect you are pregnant.

The marketers have discovered things about consumers they never could have known before. Patterns materialized, phenomena emerged. Some scanner studies turned up bits of tantalizing minutiae. Consider, for example, what Information Resources Inc., the grand vizier of scanner intelligence, discovered through an analysis of sales of condoms. Sales reach their second-highest velocity on New Year's Eve. No surprise there—it's a time when we shed our regrets and stoke our hopes. Anything can happen! But the night comes and goes, and our lives remain the same. As we settle into the new year and face the gray January dawn, love's ardor wanes. Condom sales take a dizzy fall. Where has love gone? Sales rise ever so slightly toward Valentine's Day but fall again, plummeting now. A mark of embarrassment, perhaps, at having wooed our targets and won, only to realize it was all so very wrong—sales sink deeply to their lowest point of all.

But what are we to make of what happens next? Sales begin to climb, slowly, inexorably, rising, dipping, rising yet higher, dipping again, then higher still (yes, like the act itself!), climaxing at last on July 25.

July 25?

For the year in question, that was a Monday.

A Monday?

Of course. Midsummer, and Puck afoot. The point where summer romance reaches critical mass. With youthful abandon we buy condoms by the case, only to have them stew in the far reaches of our wallets (and purses!) for the rest of the year, envelopes of lost hope.

IRI's spokesman, Bob Bregenzer, took a rather less romantic view. "Aside from New Year's," he wrote in a note attached to the jagged graph that captured this mystery, "condoms appear to be a warm-weather category."

Not to be outdone, Nielsen Marketing Research, IRI's arch competitor and cousin to Nielsen Media, told me the peak day for condom sales in Indianapolis is the day before the Indianapolis 500 auto race. "And if you've been to the Indy 500, you'll know why," one Nielsen researcher said, laughing. Nielsen noted too that scanner data allowed it to quantify a truth parents have known since the invention of the fold-down seat in a shopping cart: If you bring the kids with you to the grocery store, you will spend a lot more money than if you go alone. To be precise, if you are a woman, you will spend 29 percent more, if a man, 66 percent.

Such discoveries are just icing, however. Knowledge mined from scanners has given marketers new powers of manipulation. I don't mean the vague and indirect power conferred through the deft kneading of image and sexual desire. That's old stuff. I mean directly.

Pull the lever, the dog bites.

It all began with a boxcar problem: how to keep track of thousands of railroad cars during their travels through the sinewy rail yards of America. The problem had harried railroads since their earliest days. In 1959 Sylvania Electric assigned a new employee, David J. Collins, fresh out of MIT's Sloan School of Management with a degree in industrial engineering, to scour the company's laboratories for technology that might solve the problem. He found it.

Collins developed a way of representing the identification codes of each freight car by combinations of red, white, and blue lines that, when illuminated with a concentrated beam of light, cast a reflection distinctive enough to be captured by an optical sensor mounted beside the tracks. By 1967 the technique became the standard for rail-car tracking. Collins left Sylvania in 1968 to found his own company, Computer Identics, where he and colleagues devised tiny black-on-white versions of the railroad symbols and were the first to adopt lasers as the scanning light source. It is Collins, more than any of the other parties involved in scanner technology—among them IBM, MIT, the Battelle Institute, and RCA—who bears the most responsibility for the proliferation of bar codes and their appearance on virtually everything worth counting and cataloging, including at last count the backs of live honeybees, the wristbands of hospital patients, the identity cards of Palestinians, the number tags pinned to runners in the New York Marathon, and, in one pilot program, the back molars of U.S. soldiers.

In 1969 a group of supermarket chains formed a committee to look for more efficient, more precise ways to track sales of groceries from their shelves. Until then they had only oblique measures, such as reports produced every two months by the A. C. Nielsen Co. By 1971 the committee decided to endorse a special numerical code, the Universal Product Code, or UPC, that could be used to identify every grocery item. The next year the committee formed the Uniform Code Council, Dayton, Ohio, a nonprofit company that would manage the distribution of UPC codes to manufacturers. In 1972 the council made bar code the official symbolic language of the grocery industry.

Bar code is an ingenious architecture, its structure far more complex than is visible to the casual observer. Look closely, say, at the bar code on a can of Campbell's cream of broccoli soup. (I just happened to have one at my desk.) Notice, first, that a series of twelve numbers runs along the base of the bars. This is the UPC code. The first number merely identifies the broad class of item being scanned. The number on my broccoli soup, as on most groceries, is 0. The Uniform Code Council assigns the next five numbers, which identify the manufacturer. The manufacturer, however, decides what the next five numbers will be, in accordance with his own method of identifying the brand, size, and flavor of each of his products. Bar code represents each coded number with seven invisible spatial fragments called "modules," each to be filled in or left open depending on the numeral. The code says nothing about price; rather, the code links each product to a price stored in the grocer's computer, where it can readily be changed.

The final number of the twelve-digit UPC code is the "modulo check digit," arrived at through an equation involving the preceding numbers of the code. A scanner quickly runs the same calculations. If the solutions match, the scan is a success.

Scanners read bar codes by running a low-power laser, typically a helium-neon laser, or "hee-nee" (from the chemical symbols for helium and neon, He-Ne), across the bars and spaces. The dark bars absorb light, the white bars reflect it. An optical sensor collects the returning light and converts it into a pattern of high and low voltages, an electronic reflection that can be read by computer.

The Marsh supermarket in Troy, Ohio, made history in 1974 when it became the first supermarket to scan UPC bar codes. The automation of America's grocery stores occurred thereafter with breathtaking speed. Consider the experience of Giant Food Inc., a 153-store chain based in Landover, Maryland, an early leader in adopting scanner technology. In 1975 Giant estimated that scanners would save the company $5,529 a month per store, mainly by reducing labor costs at checkout. The company estimated it could save another $2,745 per month per store if it stopped stamping prices on each individual item, as was then universal practice. At first the installation of all that new equipment seemed daunting. An internal memo estimated the company would be able to convert only six stores a year to scanners. Soon, however, Giant was converting two stores a week and by the end of 1979 had equipped every supermarket in its empire.

But scanners proved controversial. Consumer advocates worried that once grocers stopped marking prices on each item, they'd be able to raise prices without consumers being aware they were doing so. The Senate Consumer Subcommittee, drawn to the fray partly because Giant's principal market includes Washington, D.C., where the senators did their shopping, held a round of hearings to investigate how scanners would affect food prices. The country's major food chains, worried that controversy would snuff out this promising new technology, agreed among themselves to continue stamping prices until scanners had proven their worth and consumer worries had subsided. Today prices are listed only on tags attached to the shelves on which products are stocked.

Giant began exploring new uses for the information, providing another proof of my second law of data dynamics, that information collected for one purpose will be used for purposes other than those originally intended.

Giant put scanners to work in full-time remote surveillance of its employees. It programmed its computers to watch for subtle diversions from normal sales patterns at each checkout lane, having found that by the end of each day the pattern of sales from any one lane should mirror the pattern of other comparable lanes. Any major departure gets flagged in a daily "exception log." The system is subtle enough to raise a warning about a scam known as "sweethearting," when checkers deliberately fail to scan high-ticket items brought to the checkout counter by their friends, family, and, of course, sweethearts. The computer notes which checkout line runs abnormally "light" on such items as steaks and roasts. "It's not an indictment," Robert W. Schoening, Giant's senior vice-president for data processing, told me. "It only says there's something strange going on here."

Giant also has begun using scanner data to tailor the mix of products in its stores to the demographics of customers living around them. Bulk sizes of ketchup, for example, sell better in family neighborhoods than in neighborhoods dominated by singles. "Some products are high movers in a Jewish neighborhood or black neighborhood or Italian neighborhood, or whatever," Schoening told me. "There *are* ethnic-based products."

K Mart Corporation, which installed its first scanner in 1984—O portentous year!—and completed installation in all its stores in November 1990, sets its headquarters computer to watch for sales of any item that exceed the national average for that item and to signal such anomalies in so-called peak week reports. The company discovered that in March sales of confetti boomed at its stores in the Southwest. No one knew why.

K Mart investigated and discovered a longtime practice among Mexican-Americans of stuffing Easter eggs with confetti. K Mart then made sure that stores in the region stocked enough confetti to have it available even on the day before Easter, thus increasing sales even further.

"Essentially the scanner becomes the eyes of the merchant," said David M. Carlson, K Mart's senior vice-president, information systems. "It wasn't until we got scanners in all twenty-two hundred stores that we had what S. S. Kresge had when he had only one store. We jumped from not knowing much at all about what was selling to literally knowing *everything* about what was selling."

But scanners offered another power denied managers in the age of the big store. Now, like their ancestral corner shopkeepers, they could also know who their customers were and what they liked to buy.

In the late 1980s and early 1990s retail chains and third-party consumer intelligence companies began experimenting with programs designed to connect anonymous scanner data collected at the checkout counter with flesh-and-blood consumers. Often described as "frequent shopper" programs, they typically require that shoppers fill out a detailed demographic questionnaire and then carry a special plastic card with an ID number represented in bar code or embedded in a magnetic strip. Shoppers present their cards each time they make a purchase and in return receive discounts, coupons, or points toward a free gift. There is a grand paradox here: we consumers bridle at the thought of carrying a national identity card yet for the promise of a few cents off our food bills gladly carry an ID card assigned by our grocers.

Retailers lure customers into their programs by offering an array of incentives. Shoppers at Wegmans Food Markets Inc., a chain based in Rochester, New York, can take advantage of the store's advertised weekly specials only if they are members of its Wegman's Shoppers Club. When they buy any of the advertised products, they automatically receive a credit at the cash register, provided they present their ID cards. The card can double as a debit card, check-clearance card, or even Visa charge card, a function Wegmans offers through an affiliate of Chase Manhattan Bank.

Waldenbooks, a K Mart subsidiary, heightened the paradox when it required that consumers in its "preferred reader" program *pay* for the privilege of letting the company track their book purchases. For a $10 annual fee members receive a card with a bar-coded number that automatically entitles them to a 10 percent discount on almost everything in the stores, even books already discounted. Members—there were four million active members in 1991—present their cards to cashiers who scan both the card and the bar code printed on the cover of each book. For every $100 a member spends at Waldenbooks, he gets a $5 coupon.

He also gets mail. He gets it from Waldenbooks and from other companies to whom Waldenbooks reveals his purchasing secrets. For its part, Waldenbooks sends a collection of special mailings geared to each member's taste in books. Buyers of Tony Hillerman's latest Navajo crime novel, for example, may get a brochure on mysteries. Within ten days of the start of the 1991 Gulf War, the company launched a special flier on books about the Middle East to readers whose past reading habits indicated an interest in the region.

Retail-based programs are small potatoes compared to the scanner intelligence systems now operated by the largest collectors of scanner data: Citicorp, Information Resources Inc., Nielsen Marketing Research, and Arbitron. They've been racing to wire the consumers of America, in the process filling vast electronic aquifers with billions upon billions of bits of information about the things we buy.

- Citicorp's scanner intelligence unit, called Citicorp/POS, collects information on 3 million households through "frequent shopper" programs and shopper ID programs at some 700 stores nationwide. Unlike the other third-party scanner intelligence companies, Citicorp allows outside marketers to tap its vast data banks to find new customers and send them more junk mail.

- Information Resources Inc., based in Chicago, operates a service called InfoScan through which it collects all purchase information from 2,700 grocery stores, 500 drug stores, 150 mass-merchandise stores (like K Mart), and 60,000 individual households whose members must present an ID card each time they shop. IRI has formed data-sharing alliances with both Arbitron and Citicorp.
- Nielsen Marketing monitors 3,000 stores. In 1991 Nielsen collected specific purchase information on 15,000 households but planned to increase the number to 40,000 by 1992. Members of these panels use a hand-held scanner to scan everything they buy as soon as they get it home; 4,500 households also are equipped with TV tuning meters that allow Nielsen to link TV viewing directly to shopping behavior. Nielsen Marketing plans to incorporate Nielsen Media's passive TV meter once it is deployed.
- Arbitron expected to have 18,500 households enrolled in its program, called ScanAmerica, by 1995. In November 1991 it began providing network ratings using a national ScanAmerica panel of 1,000 households. These shoppers not only scan their groceries at home, but have the added pleasure of having to punch buttons on an Arbitron people meter, akin to Nielsen's much criticized meter, each time they watch TV.

The torrents of data spilling from this intelligence network are now required reading for any brand manager who hopes to compete in the big leagues. Marketers and retailers don't even like to discuss how they use scanner technology, for fear of inadvertently leaking some precious corporate secret to the competition or for piquing some malcontent's concerns about privacy. "There are some things we're doing that we just don't want everyone to know about," said a spokeswoman for Vons, a grocery chain based in southern California and an active member of Citicorp's network. Pillsbury, whose cute doughboy seems the picture of openness, likewise demurred. "It's not a subject we would warm to," Pillsbury's head spokesman told me. "All it would do is alert our competition as to how we view the technology."

The national third-party intelligence gatherers, not surprisingly, were far more open about their technologies and the data they harvest. Competition in the industry is brisk, and they miss no chance to strut their stuff and—especially in the case of IRI and Nielsen—often drop catty little remarks about each other's grievous flaws. Only Citicorp kept mum, responding to my repeated requests for interviews by sending a couple of pages of press releases describing the program. But then Citicorp's swelling data base and its practice of peddling names to outside marketers are also the most likely to raise the blood pressure of America's privacy gladiators.

The attraction of scanner technology is powerful. It lets companies observe market phenomena they previously couldn't have seen. It advanced the marketers far along in their century-long drive to turn their art into a science. The most striking power conferred by scanners, however, was the power to turn entire communities into real-life consumption laboratories where the shopping behavior of real people using real money could be tweaked, tuned, and monitored without anyone in town knowing the tests were under way.

As a kid I developed a passion for science-fiction and horror films. Maybe this had something to do with growing up at a time when men were launching themselves into space and threatening each other with intercontinental ballistic missiles. Ants, Gila monsters, spiders, you name it, were continually being distorted by fallout from atmospheric nuclear tests, growing to immense size, then venting their anger on the unsuspecting populace of the nearest town, usually some isolated place that found itself unaccountably cut off from the tanks, fighters, and tactical nukes that could have reduced even the largest ant to a pool of formic acid. Lots of uninvited visitors arrived, too, invariably in flying saucers. They crash-landed in outlying places and, in one notorious case, ate sled dogs for lunch. What I liked most about all these horror films were the first twenty minutes or so when all the strange things happened and no one on camera knew the cause. I must have watched a thousand small-town sheriffs turn to their deputies and say, "I ain't never seen nothin' could do *that*, 'leastwise nothin' human."

Of all those horror movies, one had the most lasting impact on my imagination and, incidentally, forever made me wary of putting plants in bedrooms. The star was Kevin McCarthy, who played a small-town doctor just returning to town after an extended absence occasioned, apparently, by a bout of nervous exhaustion. He begins to notice the town has changed but can't quite put his finger on how. People he once knew so well now seemed devoid of affect and passion, as if someone had dumped a truckload of Thorazine into the city's water supply. Soon the doctor realizes the problem: seedpods. Big ones from outer space that take over your body while you sleep. The movie, the original *Invasion of the Body Snatchers*, so colored my imagination that scenes came back to me in 1991 as I drove the last few miles of interstate from Chicago to Eau Claire, Wisconsin, a town I had visited a quarter of a century before on a family trip out west.

Eau Claire had changed. I'm not talking about the arrival of the Ship Shape Car Wash, built for some reason to resemble a cruise liner. No, something *strange* had happened here. Thanks to Information Resources Inc., of Chicago, the citizens of Eau Claire had begun seeing things no one else could.

Information Resources was the first company to recognize how scanner technology would allow the study of consumers under controlled conditions. By collecting scanner data and simultaneously monitoring the many promotional forces that bombard shoppers, IRI saw a way to tease apart the many threads influencing our shopping behavior and see which ones tugged hardest at our wallets. The company moved quickly. By 1979, just five years after the first deployment of a supermarket scanner, IRI had wired its first town.

Until then, if an advertiser wanted to test his TV commercials, the best he could do was grab a few thousand people from malls around the country, have them watch a commercial, then ask how much they liked it and how much of it they remembered. The shoppers' responses served only as an index, a suggestion of how the commercial might work in boosting sales. In the end advertisers simply had to let their TV ads fly and hope for the best, a vast and costly gamble so lush it produced three national networks and hundreds of cable TV and independent stations. Through it all, however, advertisers smiled ruefully and quoted a remark attributed to various market-minded souls, among them Philadelphia retailer John Wanamaker: half of all advertising money is wasted; the trouble is, no one knows which half.

IRI was after the same kinds of towns the Martians always chose. Isolated towns. If you lived there, you shopped there. Towns with one newspaper and one cable supplier, but with enough stores to generate levels of competition typical of the country as a whole. IRI installed scanners in each store and persuaded the cable operators to feed their cables first to an IRI studio in each town so the company could tinker with incoming commercials. It sent its own agents—"retail test coordinators"—to all the stores to keep track of newspaper ads, in-store displays, and anything else that might tend to influence shopping patterns. IRI named the new service BehaviorScan and invited companies to try out their new commercials, products, and tactics on real people. The company wired six cities. As of 1989 they were Pittsfield, Massachusetts; Marion, Indiana; Midland, Texas; Grand Junction, Colorado; Cedar Rapids, Iowa; and Eau Claire.

Kathy Jo Brihn, IRI's spy master in Eau Claire, promised to tell me all about it, provided I agreed not to identify any company or product involved in any of the tests being conducted in the town.

I met Brihn in the lobby of the Holiday Inn. Except for a brief stint in Arizona, Brihn had lived her entire life in Eau Claire. She liked Eau Claire; it was comfortable but also gave her a taste of life in the big city. She wore a simple dress, drove a simple Toyota—albeit a red one—and spoke softly with that Midwest tendency to caress the hearts of certain words as if each vowel were a puppy to be stroked. Brihn would have looked at home behind the counter of a bakery that specialized in fresh apple pies—espionage was a job.

"I'll take you first to one of our markets," she said. "Then I'll give you a little tour, and take you to the studio."

She took me to Duke's, a spanking new supermarket and one of fifteen Eau Claire stores—eight grocery, seven drug—wired into "B-scan," as Brihn liked to call the system. Fifteen tests were under way that Wednesday morning in Duke's, she told me. These were not one-day affairs. Most BehaviorScan tests last about a year, she said, although one Eau Claire test took only four weeks. The longest in Eau Claire took two years. The cost of a typical test ranges from $250,000 to $350,000 but can run as high as a cool million, depending on the amount of time and number of wired towns involved. IRI has run over six hundred BehaviorScan studies; in 1990 BehaviorScan alone contributed $23.4 million to IRI's total revenue of $166.7 million.

We stood near Duke's "Wall of Values." Four IRI agents routinely visit the BehaviorScan stores, Brihn told me. They record the Universal Product Code numbers of every item mentioned in store fliers and newspaper ads, or pyramided in the "end caps" at the end of each aisle, or showcased in special promotional bins and displays, like the Wall of Values. This attention to detail allows IRI's analysts to keep track of the various forces tending to boost or depress sales of products and thus to know, for example, whether a new commercial alone accounted for a change or whether some other force also played a role.

As we strolled through the store, we passed some unusual caramel-and-chocolate cookies stacked in an end cap. I hadn't seen them in my local Giant.

"These look good," I said. "Are these one of yours?"

Brihn smiled. "I can't tell you that," she said. "We don't really want to make our presence known in the stores except at the checkout lines, and that's so they show their cards. We don't want to do anything that's going to attract them to any of our products."

The residents of Eau Claire know BehaviorScan by its less ominous *nom d'épicier*, "Shopper's Hotline." Members of the 3,500 households enrolled in the program begin their careers as laboratory mice by filling out a detailed demographic questionnaire. Hotline shoppers must show their ID cards each time they shop. As an incentive they receive an annual $10 gift certificate. Each time they use their cards IRI enters them in a monthly contest, dangling a grand prize of a "dream" vacation or $500 cash and many lesser prizes.

"How about these?" I asked.

We had returned to the front of the store and stood now adjacent to a big bin filled with blazing orange packages of peanut-butter M&M's, another product new to me at the time.

"Try harder," Brihn said.

I picked up a bag. "I've never seen them before," I said.

"They *are* good," she said mildly, then changed the subject.

Brihn moved closer to the checkout line and described how the checkers even collect and bag all the coupons presented by BehaviorScan shoppers. The checker marks each bag with the shopper's ID number; at the BehaviorScan field office in Eau Claire, employees call up each shopper's records and enter the code numbers from each coupon. The computer then checks the shopping list for the couponed items.

I wanted to hear more about the test products. "Have you had some real—"

"Real *dogs?*" Brihn laughed, anticipating the exact wording of my question. "Oh, yes."

"Well, like what?"

"There's *no way* I'm going to tell you what those are. I respect what the companies are trying to do. I also want some business."

We left Duke's and headed for higher ground, the place where IRI controls the vertical.

The air was rich with the scent of hot, freshly cut grass. Crickets chirped from deep shade under two big satellite dishes. Brihn led me to the door of a small building, one of those austere little hovels you see throughout America suckling the bases of giant red-and-white antennas.

Inside, all was cool dark video sophistication. A train of sixteen pairs of five-inch TV monitors gleamed from high on the rearmost wall, one pair for each incoming signal, among them the alphabets: CNN, TNT, TNN, USA, ESPN, ABC, CBS, NBC. There were triple-color monitors, intermediate-frequency monitors, Sony videotape drives. Action played on every screen. A body, rendered in black and white, flew through the air propelled by the concussion of a Japanese hand grenade. A woman leapt about and clapped her hands. A talk show host said something to his female co-host, who clearly thought him brilliant.

It was midmorning—TV limbo.

A young woman sat at the BehaviorScan control console in deep concentration as she tried to track the progress of the body, the woman, the two hosts. She was about to stage what IRI calls a "commercial event," a bit of electronic legerdemain through which she substitutes a test commercial for the regularly scheduled commercial, leaving the audience—she hopes—none the wiser.

For this era of advanced automation, the process is surprisingly manual. To know exactly when to seize control of the air, she had to keep precise track of each show and each commercial. Her event log told her the target commercial was supposed to appear during the 11:58 break in "The Match Game," in the B position, meaning it was to be the second commercial in the break. She would have to load the substitute commercial, cue it, and check it on the cue monitor to make sure the tape itself was in good physical condition. A single second of black air would separate the A and B commercials. At that instant she would have to hit the play button and hope for the best.

The studio is allowed to intercept only those commercials made by the clients who order the tests. Once the operator cuts in, she still must watch the originally scheduled commercial to make sure it is the correct target. She needs quick reflexes. If the commercial is not the one she expected—as is all too often the case—she must immediately hit another button that kills her cut-in and allows the original commercial to run. She must limit "contamination" of the original as much as possible.

It was now about 11:50.

The big occupational hazard for newcomers to the job is getting distracted by the bodies and hosts on the screen, said David Gorton, manager of the studio. Gorton is a big, bearded man, who would look very much at home in a sleeveless T-shirt astride a Harley-Davidson motorcycle. "You have to learn you're watching commercials, you're not watching programs," he told me. "You gotta be able to *not* pay so much attention to the show that you miss the commercials."

IRI has gotten better at this over time. In the early days the cut-ins caused a lot of contamination. "You could always tell when they put on a commercial for 'Shopper's Hotline' people," one early member said. "The screen got all screwed up. This herringbone pattern came on, like they were broadcasting from Mars."

Gorton said his studio avoids miscues and other sources of contamination about 90 percent of the time, although now and then, particularly in times of national turmoil when network lineups shift rapidly, the rate drops to 75 percent. The Gulf War caused a good deal of consternation on this hilltop. Baseball games are a routine summer trial. A game can have thirty commercial breaks, each to be watched and counted. Operators in other IRI markets running the same test in the same game may check in with each other just to make sure everyone has counted the same number of breaks.

The studio can do two broad kinds of interceptions. In the first, called an "on-channel cut-in," IRI broadcasts a new substitute commercial to every cable subscriber in Eau Claire, regardless of whether or not these households are members of IRI's "Shopper's Hotline." The second technique allows IRI to send substitute commercials into specially targeted groups of homes that meet specific demographic criteria. To reach these panels, IRI creates in effect a parallel channel. Just when the target commercial appears, the operator can switch all the converters in the homes of the target group of hotline members to the IRI channel, then return them to the regular broadcast when the commercial is done. IRI operates two such ghost channels and can send two different substitute commercials to two distinct groups of converter-equipped households at the same time.

On any given night, therefore, viewers in four houses side by side could find themselves watching four different commercials at exactly the same time and while watching the same program. "Let's say three of them have cable, two of them are converter panelists, and the fourth just has an antenna," Gorton explained. "The person with the antenna is going to see the air commercial no matter what we do because he's not on the cable system. The person who's got cable but who isn't one of our converter panelists is going to see the on-channel cut-in. The other two could see two different commercials, depending on what panel group they're in."

It was almost 11:57.

The operator glanced quickly at a monitor awash with purplish light. The picture was stable, no squiggly lines or jolts of light. This meant the tape's physical condition was good enough for broadcast.

The tape was a public-service announcement aimed at recruiting teachers and was to be broadcast to converter households in place of the client company's regularly scheduled commercial. The test was designed to see whether reducing the number of times the commercial was shown would decrease sales. If not, the client could cut back on its advertising and save millions of dollars.

The commercial break began. The operator watched and timed the A commercial.

She hit a button.

The new public-service advertisement appeared in the outgoing monitor, headed for a group of converter households identified only as "panel 16."

"The power of teaching," the announcer said. "The power to wake up young minds. The power to wake up the world. Teachers have that power. . . ."

BehaviorScan helped give companies the confidence to introduce dozens of new products, including Velveeta slices, Frito-Lay's Sun Chips, Equal (a sugar substitute), General Mills Fruit Roll-Ups, Dole Fruit 'N Juice, and Ivory Liquid Hand Soap.

The B-scan network also produced some unexpected troubling news for the marketers of America.

"People would rather forget about me now," Gerald J. Tellis told me, chuckling a bit at his newfound notoriety. Tellis, associate professor of marketing at the University of Southern California, analyzed a year's worth of BehaviorScan data on toilet paper sales and corresponding TV advertising in Eau Claire and found that TV advertising didn't work— or, if it worked, had very limited effects.

His results, first published in the *Journal of Marketing Research* in 1988 but reported widely in the business press, caused a furor in the advertising world. Tellis repeated his analysis, this time using laundry detergents and yogurt, and came up with an even clearer conclusion. Television advertising in those two product categories, he told me, has "no impact. *Period.*"

Tellis first reached his Avenue-shaking conclusions after he studied fifty-two weeks' worth of sales of twelve brands of toilet paper sold through Eau Claire's BehaviorScan stores and correlated those sales to patterns of TV advertising for each brand. Tellis found that advertising had only a tiny effect on sales. Within this narrow band, he found, advertising worked best when used to introduce spanking new products. Otherwise it helped to encourage already loyal buyers of name-brand toilet paper to keep buying their favorite model.

Tellis conceded, however, that certain individual ad campaigns do have a powerful effect. "If you have an innovative product or an innovative campaign, it will work," Tellis said. "But if you're going out advertising for the umpteenth time for the same product at the usual times, it won't."

IRI weighed in with its own study, a huge three-volume affair called *How Advertising Works*, based on an analysis of 389 BehaviorScan tests conducted from 1984 through 1988. The report concluded that an advertiser's attempts to build sales by increasing advertising weight (to "heavy up," in market-speak) would indeed have a measureable effect on sales . . . roughly *half* the time.

John Wanamaker would have smiled.

Data harvested by IRI and its sister intelligence companies have given marketers new ways to find untargeted market niches among the vast, amorphous masses of America's TV watchers. By combining TV ratings and scanner data, the independent intelligence companies can now show advertisers not just who watches a show, but what those people tend to buy. The combined data, besides providing another dandy proof of the Law of Data Coalescence, show that conventional ratings mask wide variations in brand preferences even among virtually identical products.

Consider diet Coke and diet Pepsi.

On any given weeknight, Arbitron's ScanAmerica tells us, roughly 9 percent of America's twelve- to thirty-four-year-olds watch late night television. As described by conventional ratings, the late night audience would look the same to brand managers for both soft drinks.

But combined ratings, which Arbitron has dubbed "Buyer-Graphics," show a rather different landscape.

ScanAmerica first breaks the broad group of twelve- to thirty-four-year-olds into two groups, the people who buy diet Coke and those who buy diet Pepsi. At this degree of resolution, late night seems to draw roughly the same amount of attention from both groups. But ScanAmerica can narrow the focus still further, by dividing the two camps into even smaller groups, the heavy and light users of each product. Suddenly a fundamental, if inexplicable, difference materializes. ScanAmerica data indicate that 11.2 percent of all heavy users of diet Pepsi watch late night TV, while only 6.4 percent of heavy users of diet Coke do likewise, a difference of 4.8 percentage points—a point spread as vast in the eyes of media buyers as the Mojave.

ScanAmerica promises also to alter advertisers' perceptions of individual shows. In Denver during one ratings period CBS's "60 Minutes" had an overall rating of 17, meaning that 17 percent of Denver's TV-equipped households watched the show. The BuyerGraphic analysis, however, estimated that 37.4 percent of all Denver residents who drank Miller beer watched the show, while only 12.9 percent of the city's Budweiser drinkers did likewise. Anheuser-Busch, which makes Budweiser, might see in this the chance to advertise heavily to woo Miller loyalists. Miller might see "60 Minutes" as a nice forum for introducing new Miller variations to its constituents or for commercials aimed at further cementing their loyalty.

Combined ratings and scanner data will markedly alter the buying and selling of TV time. Such data already have shown that some overlooked broadcast periods, known as "dayparts," may be more cost-effective for advertisers than prime time, which traditionally has been the most coveted daypart and therefore the most expensive. Such data may also alter the shows themselves. If a TV series is proven to draw a disproportionate number of Coke drinkers, will we soon see a disproportionate number of Coke cans in the hands of the show's stars during the episodes themselves? Will scanner-based ratings drive a return to the sponsorship system that governed the early years of TV, where a given sponsor not only bought all the airtime for a show, but also produced the show itself or at least exercised broad control over its production? Remember: Procter & Gamble already produces the soap opera "Guiding Light."

Imagine the possibilities—"Late Night with Diet Pepsi"! Coke, its competitive passions enflamed, might work a deal where every table in the on-camera set of "The Arsenio Hall Show" would sport a can of diet Coke, casually at hand as if it were indeed the drink of choice for Arsenio and his guests. Mazda might wade in with a remake of "Route 66," featuring a couple of likable guys—maybe even James Garner, a past Mazda spokesman—tooling around the country in a cute red Miata!

All this, however, presupposes that those crisp, handsome numbers generated by the scanner panels of Arbitron, Nielsen, and IRI reflect real-world phenomena. Many of the criticisms that Contam aimed at Nielsen's people meters apply here even more strongly, given the workload scanners impose on consumers.

Consider the issue of bias as reflected in the initial response rates— the percentage of people who, when first approached to join the panel, agree to do so.

Critics of Nielsen's people meters were appalled that only half of the originally designated sample of households agreed to cooperate. Yet response rates for the scanner panels are far lower. A survey by the Advertising Research Foundation found that the initial cooperation rate for the Nielsen in-home scanner program was only 10 percent. The rate for IRI, which requires only that shoppers present an ID card when they shop, was 40 percent. Arbitron's current service was not included in the survey, but its predecessor, formed by SAMI/Burke and later absorbed by Arbitron, had an initial response rate for its in-home panels of only 11 percent.

Gale D. Metzger, president of Statistical Research Inc. and the architect of the massive Contam report that reviewed Nielsen's people meter system, argues a 10 percent response rate is clear evidence of glaring bias in the sample. "No matter what you do later," he wrote in the December 1990 issue of *Marketing Research*, "no matter how you weight or adjust or modify, you are analyzing a very select group of people who are willing to be analyzed. They are unique in that they are willing to subject themselves to this single source task. They represent nothing besides themselves. The actions or reactions do not apply to any other group. One cannot evaluate marketing strategies for the total population on the basis of volunteers. They stand alone."

Alice Sylvester, senior associate media research director for J. Walter Thompson, put it a bit more succinctly in her remarks to a 1990 conference on behavioral research in New York. "At 10 percent response," she said, "we stand a pretty good chance of having marvelously integrated product purchase and media consumption data on the lunatic fringe!"

One need only consider the joys of shopping to see the kind of bias these household panels must exhibit. Imagine for a moment you are the mother of two small children—better yet, you are the *working* mother of two small children. You have just done your weekly megashop to fill the pantry so that the food won't run out next week while you and your husband are away at work.

Suppose, now, you were foolish enough to enroll in Nielsen's household panel. You return home with one hundred items. Your children are hungry. Each has a death grip on your thigh, as if for the moment they can derive sustenance from your loins alone—in the place of those Circus O's and fudge-covered Oreo cookies they *know* you've got hidden in one of those bags because *they* picked them off the shelf.

Here's what Nielsen now commands you to do (as demonstrated to me by Nielsen's Connie Latson, in Nielsen's product demonstration room at Northbrook, Illinois):

1. First, pick up your personal scanner.

   It's a serious-looking hunk of electronics packaged in a battleship gray box with a small display screen and lots of tiny buttons. Punch in the identity of the store. The scanner will ask, Who did the shopping? Did you shop alone? If not, who went with you? Name, age, and sex, please.

2. Begin scanning.

   You bought 100 items, you must scan all 100. With each pass the gray box asks how many of each item you bought and whether the product was included in some kind of promotion. God forbid you should shop at a store not enrolled in the Nielsen network. If so, you'd be expected to punch in the price of each of your 100 items by hand.

3. At the end of each week, you must report back to Nielsen.

First, dial an 800 number, hold the scanner to the line. The machine will fire a burst of sound into the phone. Now listen. The computer at the other end will tell you if it received the transmission intact.

4. Your personal scanner now asks you what the computer said. Was the transmission indeed okay?

You enter a "Yes."

Like some earnest lover who will not be denied, the scanner comes back with one last query:
"Just checking. Are you sure?"

Where scanner technology really proves its ability to target the untargetable is the supermarket, the primary battleground in the war for the hearts, minds, and paychecks of shoppers. In particular, scanners injected new power into an old and weary marketer's tool: the coupon.

My wife likes coupons. To say she would kill for them is an exaggeration, but only a slight one. She considers coupons bits of treasure sprinkled over the landscape by benevolent companies anxious to give us all a break. She sifts carefully through the dozens of slick sheets of advertising that come each Sunday shoved in the folds of the *Baltimore Sun*, my local newspaper. She and my brother-in-law, a real estate lawyer, once spent an otherwise pleasant evening debating the best way of sorting and storing all the coupons they amassed. My wife delights in discovering coupons for products our family would buy anyway. Occasionally she practices a mild form of coupon abuse called "misredemption," where she hands the cashier a coupon even though she hasn't bought *exactly* the product specified in the coupon. After every shopping trip she makes a point of taking me aside and listing just how many coupons she used—eighteen in one trip alone!—and how much money she shaved off the final bill. To my wife the marketers are a bunch of pretty nice guys with deep pockets.

To the marketers, my wife is the enemy.

Scanner data proved vividly to marketers that coupons and other short-term promotions could trigger instant if short-lived bursts in the sales of their products. Such data, the crack cocaine of marketing research, give brand managers the heady immediate thrill of grabbing large chunks of market share from their competitors. "It was very seductive," Gian Fulgoni, chief executive officer of IRI, told me. "People started spending more and more money on promotion and taking money out of advertising."

Advertisers in 1990 spent an estimated 60 percent of their total marketing budgets on coupons and other quick bang promotions, only 40 percent on traditional advertising—exactly the reverse of the spending ratio in 1980.

But scanner data exposed the dark side of coupons. Studies proved conclusively that coupons often wind up in the hands of the wrong people, people like my wife who use them to get a break on products they would have bought anyway, and demonstrated vividly the costs of misredemption. IRI found that 8 percent of redeemed coupons were misredemptions. This is big money. In 1990 America's consumer products companies issued 306.8 billion coupons. Consumers redeemed only 4 percent of these, at a cost to the issuing companies of $4.8 billion. Eight percent, or $384 million, was paid to consumers who never even bought the products to begin with—a $4 bonus per household.

Scanners can provide a ready solution to the misredemption problem. Now stores like my local Giant simply scan the bar code on the coupon and look for a match among the codes scanned from the groceries in each shopper's cart. No match, no discount. More important, scanner technology at last gave marketers a way to insure that their coupons reached the right consumers to begin with.

Some four thousand stores in fifty-three major grocery chains, including Giant, Safeway, Foodtown, Alpha Beta, Dominick's, Schnuck's, and Tom Thumb, have installed a system called Checkout Coupon, built by Catalina Marketing of Anaheim, California. You've seen it— it's that insolent little cream-colored box that spits out coupons matched to items you already bought.

The Catalina system (first tested, of course, in 1984) seeks to modify your shopping behavior. It watches the codes that flow through the store's checkout computer as the cashier scans each product from your cart. When the system spots a given code, the so-called trigger product, it prints a coupon as if by autonomic reflex. When you buy hot dogs, for example, you get a coupon for mustard. During one of my wife's shopping trips, she bought me a Sensor razor made by Gillette, which caused the Catalina machine to print a $1.25 coupon for a can of Edge shaving gel. The coupon said, "For best results use Edge gel with your Sensor razor."

Catalina's clients spent $32 million on the service for 1991, mostly for the privilege of ambushing their competitors. When they spot a shopper who has bought something from the competitor, they leap from the Catalina machine brandishing a coupon for their own products.

On one trip to my Giant I bought a package of Sun Chips, a new snack chip made by Frito-Lay. It triggered a coupon for Nabisco Harvest Crisps.

I bought Gorton's fish sticks for my kids; an incensed Mrs. Paul snapped off a coupon for her fish.

I bought Cascade dishwashing detergent; Palmolive offered to take a buck off the price of its liquid gel model.

I bought Stouffer's microwave French bread pizzas, and the Pillsbury Doughboy shot me a seventy-five-cent chit for Oven Lovin's, his microwave pizzas.

Catalina's coupons seem to be more effective than standard coupons in winning the attention of consumers. Giant Food found that between 8 percent and 12 percent of the Catalina coupons get redeemed, compared to the 4 percent redemption rate for coupons as a whole.

Catalina sells access to Checkout Coupon in 13 four-week cycles. Its clients, among them Coke, Pepsi, Campbell Soup, Borden, M&M Mars, J. M. Smucker, Procter & Gamble, and Heinz, buy exclusive control over coupons for a given category or subcategory of product for one or more cycles. Arch competitors like Coke and Pepsi can even be clients in the same cycle, although Catalina enforces a set of rules designed to avoid the kind of unbridled coupon warfare in which Coke would blurt coupons at Pepsi buyers and Pepsi would spit them at Coke buyers until both companies quit from sheer competitive exhaustion.

Catalina has surprised some shoppers with its offerings. For a time, women who were breast-feeding and who bought breast pads received coupons urging them to try prepared baby formula. A condom maker offered coupons to anyone who picked up a tube of Ortho-Gynol spermicide. The same company also issued condom coupons to shoppers who bought baby diapers, as if in a mechanized rebuke for some previous moment of passion and abandon.

"It ran for one day," said Daniel D. Granger, Catalina's senior vice-president for marketing, in a telephone call direct from the U.S. Open, which he was attending. "If we have something in like that, we get an *immediate* reaction. You have to be careful."

The system, however, leaves a lot to chance. Catalina distributes its coupons at the checkout line *after* the shopper has shopped. This means the shopper has to remember to take the coupon out of the bag once she gets it home. Second, she has to save it. (The invention of the refrigerator magnet was a vital precursor technology.) Finally, she has to remember to bring it with her on her next trip to the store.

The marketers want to get much closer to the action. And they know precisely where the action is. They know, from studies conducted by the Point-of-Purchase Advertising Institute (POPAI, pronounced "Popeye"), that grocery shoppers make two-thirds of all their purchase decisions after they enter the store, a ratio that has held more or less constant since 1965, when POPAI first conducted its studies. The institute breaks these in-store decisions into three categories: "generally planned" purchases, where a shopper planned on buying a soft drink but hadn't decided in advance which brand; "substitute" purchases, where the shopper planned to buy, say, Coke, but for whatever reason bought Pepsi; and "unplanned," where the shopper had absolutely no intention of buying a soft drink and, on a mad and reckless whim, picked up a six-pack of Hires root beer. In 1986, when POPAI did its latest study, mad and reckless whims accounted for 52.6 percent of all in-store decisions. We are growing more impulsive, apparently, for this total was 12 percent higher than in 1977. Our most impulsive purchases, according to the 1986 study, were newspapers and magazines—we bought them without any prior intent 84 percent of the time, a statistic that no doubt testifies to our passion for keeping up with the posthumous travels of Elvis and the birth of the latest two-hundred-pound baby.

These numbers describe a vast national reservoir of impulsiveness, a last frontier in the age of mass-market decay. If only, the marketers lament—if *only* we would be there just at that point of consumptive climax, stroking each shopper's cheek, wheedling, cajoling, twisting. "Go on, girl! You'll never get a better chance to buy Jif at this price. *Carpe diem*, babe!"

The fact is, in a few advanced supermarkets, marketers can do exactly this—metaphorically speaking, that is.

■ ■ ■

In 1991 VideOcart Inc., a Chicago company spun off from IRI, began testing a system that promised to give marketers a chance to influence consumers while they shopped. The centerpiece of the technology was a shopping cart, one I first encountered at the Giant Food market in Frederick, Maryland.

This was no ordinary cart, certainly not the garden variety I often found upended in the creek bed next to my childhood home. Called VideOcart, this one was an electronic frigate. It had a steel-encased battery pack welded under the bottom rack. A computer monitor, roughly the dimensions of a kid's Etch-A-Sketch, was cantilevered off the specially extended handle. The monitor had a light blue liquid-crystal display screen; five red buttons studded each side of the surrounding black plastic case.

A long phalanx of VideOcarts was "nested" outside the store, each recharging itself discreetly through a metal shoe that extended down into a low-power charging rail. I picked a comely cart and shoved it inside. A signal from an infrared trigger mounted overhead—one of 148 such triggers dangling from the ceiling throughout the store—told the monitor to turn itself on. The screen glowed a pretty liquid blue. I took the cart for a spin.

At each trigger point—I counted roughly three per aisle—the overhead devices told the monitor what to display, thus providing the illusion that the cart was my Columbus, navigating its way from star to infrared star, always aware of its exact position in the store.

The blue in the screen dissolved, suddenly, then reconstituted itself with a command: "Pick up Some Fannie May Candy!"

Sure enough, just three feet away stood a small, clear-glass counter packed with Fannie May truffles, butter creams, fruit fudge, almond clusters, pink ladies, and milk fluffy mash.

The bologna hailed me next, a siren call of price cuts amid the cold cuts. Sixteen ounces of Kitchen Queen Bologna, only $1.19.

I entered aisle two, the juice aisle.

VideOcart tugged on my sleeve. Tropicana Twister fruit drink was on sale today in the forty-six-ounce orange cranberry or orange peach flavors. VideOcart showed me the usual price, $1.97, with a line through it. Today's price was $1.49.

I hurried on. Specials cried out to me.

Aisle 3. Kidney beans. Canned tomatoes.

Aisle 5. Ninety-nine cents off on a twenty-ounce package of Kellogg's Frosted Flakes!

At aisle 6, the condiments aisle, something very strange began to happen. An animated commercial appeared on my screen. VideOcart's programmers created the illusion of action by juxtaposing screen after screen of graphic images, each blending into the next.

Two Rolls-Royces traveled toward me, side by side.

Words appeared.

"Pardon me, but do you happen to have any Grey Poupon?"

Dazed, I pressed a button, this one for the store map, then another button for my own location. Blue concentric squares came hurtling in from all sides of the screen, pinpointing my location just opposite the prune juice. (The same feature may soon allow VideOcarts to cry out when they are being kidnapped from the grounds of a store. Interestingly, in VideOcart's first three years of operation only one cart was stolen, this from a Pathmark in Garden City, Long Island, an upscale suburb of New York City. One cart was shot, however; this incident too occurred at the Garden City Pathmark.)

Nabisco flashed an ad for its new Zings. "Lightning strikes the world of snacking!" Pepsi launched a windsurfer across my screen.

Aisle 12. Witch hazel, only $1.29.

Aisle 20. Giant's own nacho chips, only $.86.

Aisle 21. Klondike ice-cream bars, $1.68.

The screen cleared, shifted, images arrived and faded frame by frame, tracking the downward trajectory of two Tylenol "Gelcaps" falling end over end into an open palm.

"The POWER," the screen told me, "is in your hands!"

In 1991 VideOcart added a link to store scanning systems that allowed each cart to flash an electronic coupon at a shopper just as she found herself adjacent to the product being promoted. A shopper, for example, might see a screen offering fifty cents off on a purchase of Bold detergent. If she wants the discount, she hits a button, thereby transmitting a message by FM radio to a VideOcart computer in the store. That computer, in turn, tells the store's own computer to note the moment when the shopper's cart, identified with an electronic ID code, enters a checkout line. The store computer then watches the flow of UPC codes from the shopper's basket to see if she has indeed purchased Bold.

"As soon as the scanner scans it," exulted Robert McCann, Jr., executive vice-president of VideOcart, "bingo! You get fifty cents off your bill!"

He called it a boon to consumers. "There's no paper. You don't have to walk around with an envelope filled with coupons. You don't have to bother clipping all this stuff out of newspapers and magazines and so forth, and having all the aggravation of saving it someplace in the house."

Most important, you don't have to think. Press the button: instant reward.

For the marketers there is an instant reward, too. With the electronic coupons of VideOcart, they no longer have to wait for the redemption lag associated with conventional coupons or even Catalina's reflex coupons. They can know the impact of a new promotion virtually in real time.

All this promotional warfare has taken its toll on consumers. The proliferation of coupons and deals appears to have caused a fundamental change in consumer behavior certain to bedevil marketers and complicate their efforts to survive the shift to micromarketing. Researchers working with scanner data argue that we consumers have become so accustomed to the heavy volume of coupons and promotions that we simply swing like Pavlovian chimps from deal to deal, unmindful of the true or imagined distinctions among the brands we buy.

"The thing that brand managers were *aghast* to discover was the low degree of brand loyalty," IRI's chief executive, Gian Fulgoni, told me. "That was a revelation. Even in cigarettes, which probably had the highest loyalty levels of any category—even there we're now beginning to see that individual smokers are not just smoking one brand." Randall S. Smith, president of IRI's testing services and data-base divisions, cited an IRI soft-drink study that found that heavy users of Coca-Cola were also heavy users of Pepsi. "They were just switching back and forth depending on which two-liter bottle was on special that week."

On the one hand, therefore, companies are spending billions to make their look-alike products *seem* different. On the other, they are spending billions on promotional warfare that has conditioned consumers to view the products as interchangeable.

The companies can't help themselves. Hooked on immediacy, they are trapped in an escalating data race. "The manufacturers are painfully aware of the fact that promotions have short-term effects, that if the competition begins promoting next week, they may lose what they gained this week," Smith told me. "They recognize there's a trend toward lower loyalty. But when everyone's dealing heavily they can't stop. Because once you've started the cycle, you *can't* stop."

David Curry, a marketing professor at the University of Cincinnati who studies the impact of scanner technology on corporate practices and culture, argues that scanners, while indeed bringing new powers of market vision, have also brought new and damaging pressures to the already intensely competitive consumer products game. "Right now," he said, "there are forty-one different shades of pink lipstick. We've got twenty-six varieties of *cat food*! What we also have thanks to scanner data is sales information on every one of those damn things." Managers can get the information broken down by individual store, even by individual household. "There are thirty thousand scanner stores in the country. So instead of one national marketing policy, or ten regional policies, suddenly you've got thirty thousand. Managers can now ask questions like 'Are my sales any different when I sell my stuff through Wal-Mart versus when I sell it through Kroger versus when I sell it through Safeway?' Or they can ask 'When I sell it through Kroger stores in Cincinnati, is it different from when I sell it through Kroger stores in Seattle?' This begins to drive these guys nuts."

The detail and speed of scanner data feed our national obsession with short-term gain. Managers already face great pressure to produce immediate big-score profits. The pressure forces them to emphasize short-run tactics. One result, Curry said, is the destructive proliferation of coupons. "We've trained people to be deal prone. The housewife who used to be loyal to a given store and loyal to a given brand now is certainly not loyal to that brand. You realize that X is as good as Y, and you just wait until you see which one goes on price deal. Maybe you buy it at your usual store, but there's a whole segment of consumers out there now that not only switch brands on the basis of deals, they switch stores."

The question is, how much data is too much data? In such a still imprecise art as marketing, does all this data merely confound understanding?

"If you're a hydraulic engineer and you're interested in the volume of water that flows over a particular dam, you're not going to be interested in how each molecule of water finds its way over," Curry said. "Brand managers used to be interested in very macroscopic things like market share, a nice concept. Simple. What's our market share for the whole nation? It's like asking what's the total volume of water flowing over the dam. The problem with scanner data is that now we've got little tags on every molecule. Each of those molecules is a person or a household. We know exactly the path every one of these little guys takes. The question is, do we want to care? In some cases, maybe we do. That's the point. You can't simply ignore it."

Judging by technology under development, the pressure on managers will only grow. Information Resources Inc. and Nielsen are refining software that rapidly pinpoints promotional sorties by competitors. Such software greatly improves managers' ability to sort through the vast seas of data but promises to accelerate the pace of promotional warfare and perhaps distract managers from long-term research and planning.

In an August 1991 visit to Nielsen's Northbrook headquarters, I got a look at an early version of a program that would greet a manager each morning with a map of the United States on which warning lights would indicate a promotional incursion by one or more competitors. Rudolph W. Struse III, Nielsen's vice-president of marketing, has even suggested that in the future promotional warfare will be waged automatically, by "knowbots," expert systems trained to do battle between the Cheese Whiz and Velveeta with little human intervention.

Indeed, within the next few years companies will have to cope with even more immediate flows of data.

Columns of numbers jolted slowly down the screen of a computer monitor as Connie Latson continued her demonstration of Nielsen's intelligence-gathering prowess. The numbers, generated through a service Nielsen calls ScanQuick, constituted the ultimate demonstration of the power of scanner technology to speed the collection of sales information. Five hundred miles away at a grocery store in Kansas City, shoppers were moving through the checkout line. I watched their every purchase the instant it was registered in the store's computer. I felt I'd been let in on a monumental secret.

The left-most column contained the numbers that identified each checkout line. Next across were the twelve-digit UPC numbers of each item being purchased and, just beyond this, an abbreviated description of the product. The prices came next, then the quantity, and then the exact time of the purchase, in hours, minutes, and seconds.

In aisle 9, at exactly 11:41:40 A.M., someone bought Sanka coffee packaged as a collection of single, one-cup servings. Did the buyer have a sleeping problem? High blood pressure? Was the buyer single, as the packaging might indicate?

The same shopper also became the owner of Royal gelatin (11:41:47), chicken breasts (11:41:48), fresh liver (11:41:49), a greeting card (11:42:28), plums (11:42:33), hot-dog buns (11:42:37), and—how predictable—Ballpark Franks (11:42:49).

What possible benefit could this real-time data provide, other than to serve as a Barnum-like teaser to pack 'em into Nielsen's client roster? Edward Tunstall, a Nielsen vice-president and director of the Nielsen Advanced Information Technology Center in Bannockburn, Illinois, had some ideas.

Tunstall, a man of pronounced military bearing and an avid fan of Tom Clancy's technowarfare novels, came to Nielsen in July 1989 after twenty-seven years as a civilian researcher for the U.S. Navy. Like David Kiewit, who aided Nielsen's quest for a passive meter, Tunstall was an expert in remote electronic surveillance and from 1988 until he joined Nielsen was director of Navy Laboratories at the Space and Naval Warfare Command. He spent a good deal of time chasing down submarines off Japan and in the Mediterranean.

One use of real-time data, he told me, might be to set off an alarm in the store that a "stockout" had occurred—that is, that the store had run out of a particular item. The store's point-of-sale computer system would notice when a particular product that had been selling well all day had suddenly stopped moving. "You just quit selling Coke," Tunstall said, describing the kind of warning such a system might deliver. "Better go check your stock."

Also, data showing exactly what products people bought on a given trip could provide a clearer glimpse at the demographics of each store's territory. "You can start to infer behavior from what's in the market basket," Tunstall said. "If it's around Passover and you're in Chicago and someone goes in and buys matzo balls and Pampers, you've probably got yourself a young Jewish family. If you're down in New Mexico and people buy Pampers and beans, they're almost certainly Hispanic. If they're in Chicago and they buy Pampers and pickled pigs' feet, they're almost certainly black."

Moreover, he said, such finely grained data could be used to prospect for patterns among different products. How often do Coke buyers also buy Doritos? Do Pepsi buyers tend to buy potato chips instead? What products do mothers buy when they pick up a package of disposable diapers? He cited one real-world example of this effect, discovered by Nielsen in Britain during an analysis at a British pharmacy chain. The chain sold a large array of products, including dog food, which it sold at a slight loss as a lure. Through market-basket analysis, Nielsen discovered that the dog fanciers of Britain came to the chain and bought only the dog food, nothing else. The chain removed dog food from ten stores and discovered overall store profits did not fall. Next it removed dog food from all its stores. Chainwide profits rose .2 percent, not bad for a business that usually, according to Tunstall, had a profit margin of only 2 percent.

Tunstall let his imagination run free. He envisioned a day when real-time scanner data might lead companies to change their prices to reflect changes in shopping patterns over the course of a day. The prices could be adjusted instantly at any shelf through the use of electronic price labels, which by 1991 had begun to appear in some advanced supermarkets. The labels display each price in a tiny liquid-crystal display monitor mounted on the shelf. "Here's a sexist example," Tunstall said. "It's ten o'clock in the morning and Mrs. Housewife goes in to do her shopping for the day. The reason she chose ten o'clock is the babies are up from their morning naps and they haven't gone down for their afternoon naps. So the price of Pampers is a dollar lower.

"At five o'clock in the afternoon, Dad's on his way home. His wife called him and told him to bring home some Pampers. The price of Pampers is up, but the price of a six-pack of beer is down. So he's going to buy the Pampers *and* a six-pack of beer and go home.

"The use of the information inherent in the data collected by scanning devices has not been scratched," Edward Tunstall said. "It just hasn't been touched."

But what about us? When companies do begin scratching the surface, will we be left naked and shivering, our last secrets exposed?

In January 1991, during the behavioral research component of that Miami Beach conference I described earlier, Gerald Saltzgaber, then still head of Citicorp's scanner intelligence unit, told the audience it was his goal to build a "census" data base containing the names and purchase histories of shoppers from forty million households. With a lopsided smile he glibly dismissed privacy as a worthy issue: "We just don't think consumers are all that concerned about their groceries."

The audience laughed in warm agreement.

Saltzgaber was right, of course. We don't worry about our groceries. We don't even think about our groceries, beyond their ability to satisfy a current nutritional need. Scanner technology—its power to collect so much minute detail about each of us and over long periods of time—has imbued our lowly purchases with descriptive powers no one ever intended them to have. Moreover, today's products by themselves are much more likely to reflect some aspect of our personalities and phases of life. In the pursuit of new markets—in trying to escape the lethal contraction and fragmentation of the mass market—marketers have introduced an astounding array of products geared to every mood, taste, and physical condition. At the same time, our grocery stores have swollen in size to accommodate this crush of precisely targeted products, to the point where they provide a little of everything from French tickler condoms to motor oil. In 1985 the average supermarket stocked 11,036 distinct products. By 1990 the number had increased almost 50 percent to 16,486. Safeway alone stocks 25,000 items per store. In 1991 manufacturers tried force-fitting another 12,000 *new* products, or roughly 33 new products a day, into the mix. The narrower the market niche a product fits, the more precisely it describes the buyer. Increasingly, products function like shards of mirrored glass, each capturing a glint of identity.

One summer afternoon I took a walk through my local Giant with the express purpose of looking for products that might betray some *concrete* clue about the people who buy them. I tried seeing the shelves through the eyes of the next generation of scanning system, programmed to track individuals through their lives.

Produce came first. Clearly most of the products here had no inherent descriptive power. Grapes? Tomatoes? Iceberg lettuce? Potatoes? What could a sack of Idahos possibly say about you or your family?

Ah. But suppose you just bought fresh ginger, fresh basil, a handful of deadly hot serrano peppers, a little radicchio, arugula, jicama, some ugli fruit—now we're starting to get a hint of personality. You're an adventurer. You like to cook. You've got bucks—who else pays that kind of money for basil? Maybe we'll just pass your name to Williams-Sonoma. Or ship you a brochure on cookbooks. Or offer you a gastronomic tour of Europe.

Dairy and meat

Well, well, Mr. Grumbach! So what's going on? Suddenly you go from buying butter and bacon once a week to buying margarine once a month? You buy chicken without the skin, you buy fish, and unsalted peanuts, when before you got yourself a nice juicy porterhouse steak, a pound of butter, and a container of sour cream at least once a week? Do we detect a brush with mortality, Mr. Grumbach? High cholesterol? Heart attack? The death of a friend? Perhaps we'll send you a subscription to *Health* magazine. Or—now this is just a suggestion, Mr. Grumbach—perhaps you'd like to start planning now for Eternity. We have just the place: Skylawn! Just think of it, hee, hee, as a layaway plan!

Diapers

We see, Mr. Morton, that you just bought a package of Huggies, small, "For Him." First time anyone's bought diapers in your household. Congratulations, Mr. Morton. You're a new, first-time parent, and you have a son. And what's this—a container of Nursoy? What's-a-matter, Mr. Morton, kid got colic?

Cat litter

Oh, I give up. Let me guess! You have a cat, don't you, Mrs. Schmedling?

Hamster litter

(Yes, my Giant sells it. It's green.)

Condoms

Yo, Janet! Second batch in a month, babe. Things getting just a tad more exciting in *your* life, we can see. Rattle those timbers, girl!

Condoms and roses!

Why, Mr. Williams! Someone just might think little ol' you was having an affair.

Tampons, Motrin

Say no more, Mary. We know how it is.

EPT home pregnancy test

Tsk, tsk, Janet. With all those condoms we just knew you were headed for trouble! Sounds like *you* could use a little mail from Planned Parenthood, sweetie.

Extreme examples? Well, yes and no.

We have already seen, for instance, that IRI tracks sales of condoms. Even Gerald Saltzgaber, in his Miami Beach talk, noted how Citicorp's scanner data could identify which households were health conscious and could be used to track a family's progress from one life phase to the next, from formula, to cereal, to teen magazines. Indeed, in 1991 Citicorp became the first company to begin peddling mailing lists derived from a frequent shopper program. Among the selections: a list of 511,227 "weight-conscious" consumers.

A few companies already have begun trying to harness the power of our grocery histories.

In 1991, for example, Catalina tested a new wrinkle in its Checkout Coupon idea in fifty stores. The new system, operated in conjunction with a store's existing frequent shopper program, prints coupons tailored to the purchase history of each member. A coffee company might use the system to provide loyal users with a special deep discount designed to shore up that loyalty. A soft-drink maker, interested in luring the competition's customers, might request that the new Catalina system spit coupons at shoppers whose histories betray a marked tendency to switch from brand to brand.

Another company, Advanced Promotion Technologies of Deerfield Beach, Florida, founded by Procter & Gamble, A. C. Nielsen Co., and CheckRobot Inc., launched a system that reads special "smart cards" that store each shopper's history on a microcomputer chip and can be read at the grocery store by a smart-card reader. The system, called Vision Value Club, allows manufacturers to identify individual shoppers whose histories match a given customer profile and to offer those shoppers discounts, coupons, and other promotions, even to send them direct-mail offers. By formal agreement Procter & Gamble and its products get first dibs on the available space in the system "during all promotion cycles for all participating stores in all market areas" and for up to nine years. The system extends Procter & Gamble's reach directly into the lives of consumers.

The intelligence technologies are merging. Soon, through the coalescence of direct-mail and scanner networks, marketers may be able to target us by our immediate, daily needs, even our moods. A man buys Preparation H, probably he is not happy. Ditto the woman who buys Monostat cream, now available off the shelf. We buy infant-size disposable diapers at midnight; we get a letter from our local cloth-diaper service telling us the benefits of front-door delivery. We buy a pregnancy test; we hear from the big obstetrics practice up the street. We buy a gross of condoms; we get an angry letter from the Vatican.

We will see such "real-time" campaigns within the next decade. There is motive, certainly, and in the merger of intelligence technologies, there is opportunity. The coalescence of these technologies is already transforming the relationship between consumer and marketer. The marketers say it could lead to a closer, more responsive relationship, yielding better, perhaps even cheaper products tailored to our needs.

Certainly some shoppers see it that way. In Eau Claire I stopped by the home of Fred and Cheryl Poss, members of IRI's BehaviorScan panel for well over a decade. They are smart consumers. They both teach school. Fred now and then devotes one of his high school English classes to decoding the symbolic imagery of TV commercials. The Posses' two young children, Nick and Cheri, can recite the family's Shopper's Hotline number at will; their dog, I have no doubt, could have pawed the digits in the carpet.

The hotline, Fred and Cheryl agree, gives them a chance to express their opinions about the products turning up in their stores. "Hopefully," Cheryl told me, "if I buy a product repeatedly, the manufacturers will know it's a good one and that maybe they should put some energy into it." In the 1950s, she said, her mother would complain in person to her grocer when a product failed to satisfy. "There was a more direct link.

Now I go to a great big supermarket. I don't even know the owner anymore. The checkers keep changing. It's very impersonal. And I'm busy. I don't take the time to write a letter and say 'This soap is lousy, it fell apart in the shower.' This is kind of a modern way of complaining."

But how did they feel about being watched all the time?

Fred considered this a moment. "I think it's a good thing," he said. "The name 'BehaviorScan' naturally conjures up some bad, awful thing. Big Brother watching you. But keeping track of what people approve of—that I think is very positive. I can see this kind of thing growing, as kind of our future. America right now seems to be struggling competitively. For us to keep track of what was successful and what works and what doesn't work—any system that makes hard data that you can study and analyze and gather instantly and retrieve instantly probably is what will help keep people paying attention to being competitive."

A nice vision.

But the marketers have demonstrated a less lofty inclination. Instead of refining the products they sell, they have concentrated on refining the tools of selling. The coalescence of the mass surveillance technologies does indeed promise to erase the last barriers between consumer and marketer, but it may create in its place a seamless Pavlovian realm in which companies possess unprecedented power to know us—and therefore to know precisely the moment to make us rise from our chairs, go forth, and shop.

The marketers need more from us, however. At best, and despite the robust flow of data, scanners and other remote mass surveillance methods still provide only a bloodless sketch of consumer behavior, just as records of weapons purchases tell the Central Intelligence Agency only part of what it needs to know about the intentions of unfriendly nations. For the CIA, the next step is to send in the flesh-and-blood spies. The marketers do likewise in an attempt to solve the last mysteries of consumption: *How* do we shop? Once we are rolling down the aisles at Piggly Wiggly, how do we behave? And how do we really use the things we take home?

PART FOUR

THE HIDDEN

OBSERVERS

A Few Spy Stories

9

THE HIDDEN OBSERVERS

*We look in the refrigerator, the kitchen cabinets, and the
closets. We ask people to show us their favorite things. We
learn a lot more by looking around than we'd ever find out just
asking people about their homes. Nothing is hidden from us.*

—Margaret Mark, director of research
Young & Rubicam, 1989

Tannersville, Pennsylvania, is an important gateway to the natural
wonders of the Pocono Mountains, but the town makes it clear from the
start where its real interests lie. Shortly after I took the Tannersville exit
off Interstate 80, which bisects the Poconos, I passed a man and woman
selling homemade cider from the fence of a graveyard. A few dozen
yards farther along, a sign as high and broad as a barn wall welcomed me
to Tannersville and listed the area's major attractions: Mark's Sub Shack,
Skip's Western Wear, Ribs & More, PocoWear, the Mt. Pocono Bee Hive
Flea Market, the Taste Bud Restaurant, Crazy Frank's, and a dozen other
commercial establishments, including two candle shops and two
McDonald's, one eight miles to the left, the other six and a half miles to
the right. I went left and immediately came to a newly built, treeless
complex of factory outlet stores, The Crossings, sprawled in a clear-cut
vale. Each building was low, austere, a ware*haus* style of textured,
cream-colored cinder block. Perky red signs identified each outlet.
Dansk was there, of course. So were Pierre Cardin, Corning Revere,
Harvé Benard, L'eggs, Lanes, Bali, American Tourister, London Fog,
Izod/Gant, Carole Little, Socks Galore, Perfumania, the Home Store,
and my destination, Pfaltzgraff, the quintessential factory outlet store,

selling china, stoneware, porcelain animals, folk-art mugs, Christmas decorations, oven mits, blue glassware, and even airline meal trays (only $.39 each!).

I had an appointment to meet Paco Underhill at the store and found him waiting on a bench outside, doing what he does best and, incidentally, what he does for a living. Watching. Observing. Mentally cataloging and sorting.

Spying.

Underhill stands six feet four inches tall and weighs roughly two hundred pounds. The Day-Glo pink baseball cap he brought with him from Manhattan, where he lives and works, tended to make him look even taller, as if it drew some auroral charge directly from the heavens. The edges of the cap shuddered with refracted light. His size, the confidence it conferred, helped him fight off a lifelong stutter that still forces him to navigate carefully the plosive reefs of conversation but also gives him a kind of wide-eyed charm when he speaks, in particular when he pauses before an especially treacherous passage. As he arranges the mechanisms of speech, his warm brown eyes open wide to express mirth, surprise, or intrigue well ahead of the joke, trick, or revelation itself. Invariably the words come just right, even the name "Pfaltzgraff," a name from hell for a man who stutters—but also the name of Underhill's client.

In the 1970s, as a student of urban geography at Columbia University, Underhill became fascinated with the techniques of urban analysis pioneered by William "Holly" Whyte, the noted critic of cityscapes who used cameras to analyze how well public spaces served the public. Underhill adapted Whyte's techniques to the commercial landscape and founded Envirosell Inc., a Manhattan company that specializes in the surreptitious filming and tracking of consumers in retail stores and malls throughout the world. The company's client list includes AT&T, CBS Records, Hallmark Cards, Philip Morris, Quaker Oats, Citicorp, Wells Fargo Bank, Bloomingdale's, Brentano's, Kinney Shoes, Revco, Woolworth, Waldenbooks, Burger King, and Noxell Corporation, a cosmetics unit of Procter & Gamble.

Underhill got permission from Pfaltzgraff Company, the largest U.S. manufacturer of stoneware, to allow me to observe how he conducted his store surveillance. Underhill told me his agents—his fieldwork specialists—were conducting a simultaneous study of Pfaltzgraff stores both here in Tannersville and in Birch Run, Michigan. Pfaltzgraff was preparing a new design for its outlet stores and wanted Underhill to study, in particular, how the company could get people to buy more items per visit and not lose patience with the long lines that build because so many fragile items need to be wrapped.

Envirosell conducted its study of the two Pfaltzgraff stores on the weekend of September 28–29, 1991. If you shopped at either store, you were captured on film. Moreover, one of Underhill's agents probably followed your every step through the store, noting on a layout map the exact moment at which you entered, the direction you traveled, where you paused, what items you touched, what you bought, and the exact moment of your departure. If you grumbled and groused about long lines, they noted that, too.

At no time, however, did you know you were under surveillance.

The point of all this, Underhill told me, is to give retailers a vivid look at how people really do behave in their stores and to show how even subtle changes—altering the angle of a display, for example—can markedly improve a store's sales. His background, he said, suited him ideally for the task. His stutter and the frequent moves his family made as his diplomat father changed posts worked together to make him a career outsider. "Because I grew up as a stutterer, I often had to rely on what I could see, rather than what I could ask," he said. By the age of twenty-one he had lived in ten countries, including South Korea, the Philippines, Poland, Malaysia, and Indonesia. "I just remember the painful experiences I went through trying to figure out what was going on and what the rules were, so that I wouldn't be teased or tortured or laughed at. In retrospect, I've simply made a business out of what was a very highly personal surviving in society."

It isn't enough for companies to know precisely what we buy, what we watch, and how many advertisements we encounter. They want to know *how* we consume: How do we comport ourselves in the aisles of our grocery stores? How do we bake our cakes and prepare our dinners? How do we do our wash, *really*? The pressures of today's marketplace drive companies in the pursuit of the most subtle nuances of consumer behavior, things that people meters and scanners cannot pick up. And once again they run into that most daunting of obstacles: the consumer. We consumers simply cannot tell the whole truth about anything, it seems. We dodge, duck, and mislead even when we don't intend to.

When surveyed, when grabbed in a supermarket by an agent from Procter & Gamble, we don't disclose the real truth but respond instead with answers meant to please the interviewer, to conform to some cultural standard of correct behavior or to fit some wishful dream of our own.

The dialogue goes something like this:

Surveyor: "Hello, ma'am. I see you have your son with you. Could you list for me exactly what you served him for lunch yesterday?"

Consumer: "Why, yes. Let's see. A banana. And some homemade chicken soup. No salt, of course. Then I made him a tuna-salad sandwich. For a dash of color I gave him a sliced tomato from my own garden." [She pats child on head.]

The Inner Consumer: "What did I serve? What did I *serve?* I'll tell you what I served. I opened a can of Chef Boyardee ravioli. I poured the ravioli in a bowl and stuck the bowl in the microwave. Then I popped open one of those little boxes of Ninja Turtle juice. I took the bowl of ravioli out of the microwave, but it was too hot, so I stuck it in the freezer. To make it fit in the freezer I had to rearrange the fish sticks, microwave pizzas, Eskimo pies, and TV dinners. The little angel threw a hunger tantrum, so while I waited for the ravioli to cool I gave him a couple of Oreo cookies. Okay? *Okay?*"

To counter this natural tendency to dissemble, marketers deploy anthropologists, archaeologists, and psychologists to observe us at work and play, film us from hidden cameras, even live with us and keep detailed notes on our daily behavior, always without revealing the true reasons for their missions—all this in the hope they will capture us in naked acts of consumption that reveal some subtle new truth about the way we shop now. Their tactics show how far today's marketers are willing to go—how far they feel compelled to go—to find new ways of squeezing the last good dollars from their markets.

This brand of surveillance goes by many labels, among them such neutered terms as "observational research," "unobtrusive research," and even "account planning." A better term would be behavioral espionage. The practice will become more and more important to companies as their marketing departments struggle to interpret the strange new consumer phenomena captured by optical scanners and to cope with the dangerous market forces the marketers themselves created, such as declining brand loyalty, promotional excess, and the numbing proliferation of advertising and look-alike products. "There's been a growing awareness, a sensitivity to the fact that much of the consumer behavior that takes place operates under a set of rules we don't understand very well," said Langbourne Rust, a leading commercial observer of children.

Marketers always assumed consumption was a "high involvement" act—that is, that shoppers really did think about their purchase decisions, examine ingredient lists, and notice even subtle changes in packaging. The marketers tricked themselves into this belief. Traditional research techniques forced consumers to devote a lot more attention to products and advertisements than they ever would have given them in the real world. The fact is, Rust said, "there's not a whole lot of ratiocination about purchasing."

To see firsthand what really happens in the consumer jungle, the marketers dispatch their spies. Rust and his peers spend a lot of time loitering in malls, stores, and restaurants and hanging out behind one-way mirrors, watching consumers react to products and to each other. Researchers study how changes in "atmospherics" affect the pace and profit of consumption. One study found that when a restaurant played slow music, each group of diners drank 3.04 more alcoholic drinks than when it played fast music, boosting the gross profit per group by $7. Ogilvy & Mather, the big New York advertising agency, sends agents to five "bellwether" cities, New York, Los Angeles, Chicago, Seattle, and Miami, to look for signs of cultural shifts. They photograph store mannequins and abduct restaurant menus, which the agency later subjects to a detailed content analysis. "The menus, of course, are invaluable for us," said Jane Fitzgibbon, group director of the agency's TrendSights division. She discovered, for example, a pronounced turn toward the traditional. "If I see meat loaf on one more menu," she said, "I'm going to throw up."

Allison Cohen, an account planner with the New York agency Ally & Gargano, invites herself into the homes of consumers and films their most mundane behaviors. Once, in trying to woo Toblerone chocolate to her firm, she asked a select sample of chocoholic consumers to reveal to her and her camera operator where they hid their secret stashes of chocolate bars and bon-bons. Women do most of the hiding, by the way; men are more open and tend to stockpile their chocolate in the freezer, where it is known to be off-limits to everyone else.

One of Cohen's clients wanted to learn what home cooking really meant today. "The best way to find out was to go watch it," Cohen told me. A recruiter found her a sample of willing housewives. Cohen, adopting the enthusiastically inquisitive manner of a new neighbor—and paying $75 to $100 to each of her hosts—filmed their cupboards and pantries and their preparations for dinner. Her hosts soon forgot she was there. One woman burst into tears as she discovered that her microwave oven had broken down. Cohen described the home cooking of another woman: "She was making her family's favorite Friday night dinner— chicken nuggets, potato puffs, and fried onion rings. She made a salad and served Mrs. Smith's apple pie for dessert. Now to her that was a home-cooked meal. She *cooked* it because she stuck the chicken nuggets in the oven, she stuck the pie in the oven, and she made the salad from scratch. That personalized it enough so that it became her meal."

Cohen's conclusion: "Women are now more engineers than they are artists. They assemble meals. They don't cook them. They put meals together out of components."

The corporate snoops tail us through stores without our knowledge. They film us from hidden cameras and eavesdrop as we battle with our kids over whether to buy Kellogg's Frosted Flakes or Product 19.

Why do companies feel the need to snoop so deeply into our private affairs? Have they become so estranged from the ebb and flow of consumer life that they must film us making dinner? What are they after? What have they learned? Where is the line between research and invasion?

Who are these people?

Paco Underhill led me inside the Pfaltzgraff store. Eight cameras stared down from the tops of display partitions, like shiny black crows eyeing rodents on the forest floor. The cameras recorded the travels of shoppers continuously on videotape or jaggedly at two-second intervals on Super-8 film. Three fieldwork specialists, Craig, Tony, and Carole, tracked the progress of target shoppers on 8½-by-11 maps attached to clipboards. Each female shopper was an O, each male an X. The agents guessed their ages. Typically the agents marked one map for each customer, charting each path with a colored pen. Arrowheads noted the direction of travel. An O marked on the path itself indicated where the shopper had paused, an X where he or she had touched something.

Underhill's agents moved stealthily. They masked their true interest by pretending to take inventory of store merchandise. Heads bowed, eyes sliding ever so discreetly, they tracked their targets no matter how long they stayed, no matter how many times they returned to the same displays.

In this and other studies, Underhill has captured on film shopping phenomena no one previously had noticed or at least been able to quantify. It has long been an axiom of retailing, for example, that shoppers approach stores from the right and tend to turn right once they enter. Underhill's films captured this right-leaning tendency in irrefutable detail—although the Pfaltzgraff store proved to be an exception. Underhill also knows that a shopper entering a shoe store will make a purchase 20 percent of the time, but that if the sales staff can get him or her to sit down, the likelihood of a sale rises to 50 percent. Long lines at a cashier counter—known in the retail game as the "cash-wrap"—will discourage shoppers from coming into a store; yet a certain level of crowding, which Underhill has dubbed "laudable crowding," can actually attract shoppers. He knows too that promotional cigarette displays set up at the cash-wrap will most attract young men and elderly women: "the young men based on image, the Marlboro macho stuff; the older women based on price."

Often Underhill's cameras and spies expose obvious flaws that somehow no one else caught.

In a study of telephone stores for AT&T, Envirosell discovered that about 20 percent of the people who entered the stores were kids. His films vividly showed how much valuable time the sales staff wasted simply protecting phones displayed too close to the floor. A film shot in a Starbucks coffee boutique captured a toddler grabbing a teapot worth several hundred dollars from a low display—"a perfect height for a three-year-old to mess around with"—and gleefully slamming it against the floor.

A little grabbing can be good, sometimes. "We know that kids are powerful motivators," Underhill said. They grab things from promotional displays, bring them to their parents, and, as Underhill puts it, "introduce" the parents to the product. "We've captured kids climbing into the racks to pull things off—literally climbing the shelving!"

Retailers can harness this power, he said.

He proposed, for example, a way that a grocery store could improve its chances of selling a kid's cereal emblazoned with a popular cartoon celebrity. Place the box or promotional display so the child can see it from far enough away to build up a good and powerful demand whine. Put it in the middle of the aisle, he said, not the end. Have it jut a bit into the child's range of vision. "Now you get 'Daddy, Daddy, Daddy, Daddy, Daddy, Daddy, Daddy, Daddy!' " Underhill whined, mimicking exactly my eldest daughter. "If you put it closer to the head of the aisle, you might get only three 'Daddies.' "

Underhill bristled at the idea that he helps marketers exploit consumers. "There's nothing I've done as a company that I don't feel quite proud of," he said. He called himself a "savvy consumer advocate" who had "positioned that advocacy in a way that business buys into it and makes it work."

He does not invade anyone's privacy, he told me. First, he does not record sound with his cameras, although his cameras do have the capability. "When you start to record sound *and* visuals, that may be an invasion of privacy," he said. "I don't want to walk away from any scene knowing what someone's name is." Second, he said, he doesn't care about the details of individual lives. "I'm not interested in what Mrs. Jones does, I'm not intruding on Mrs. Jones's privacy. What I am interested in is whether Mrs. Jones, Mrs. Smith, and Mrs. Brown all do the same thing. And if they do, what can I learn from it, and how can I apply that learning?"

Craig Childress drifted among the shoppers in Pfaltzgraff, carefully tracing one consumer's path on his map. He took a break, and we walked until we found a bench that wasn't already packed with young and old shoppers with large merchandise bags clamped between their knees. The uniform of choice was sneakers, loose pants, and windbreakers, usually blue or maroon, often with the names of fraternal associations stamped on back. The mall teemed with people. The parking lots were nearly full. Everyone on the benches looked exhausted. The fresh troops streaming from the parking lot walked briskly, eyes bright, stepping high.

"The film is really good at picking up some things, but I learn a lot by overhearing," Childress told me. He considered eavesdropping his specialty, a way to capture details and motives the camera misses. "When I look at film, sometimes I can't tell when a customer is frustrated. But if you're right down there with them, you can really see, my

God, they are really upset because the cash-wrap line wraps around the display they want to go to and they can't get through. I can *see* that."

Childress teaches creative writing at St. John's University in New York and holds three degrees: a bachelor's in psychology and two master's of fine arts, one in English from the University of California, the second in playwriting from the University of Iowa. One of his plays, *Animal Games*, was produced in Los Angeles. He described it as a tragicomic look at child abuse. The *Los Angeles Times* hated it. Underhill likes to hire employees with a background in drama—his stable of fieldwork specialists includes an Obie award–winning puppeteer—because they take direction well, are excellent observers, and can immerse themselves in the role of spy.

Childress arranged his teaching schedule so that he taught only on Mondays, thus leaving the rest of the week open for espionage.

"It's fascinating," he said. "You come to different parts of the country and just get dropped in to overhear things." He shook his head at the wonder of it.

"I'll tell you what I love," he said, suddenly animated. "I love to see quarrels in stores. I just love it. To see if they get so caught up in a fight that they forget where they really are."

He gets close to his targets. He counts on the mental oblivion that seems to accompany consumption. "It's amazing how close you can get to people without their realizing you're tracking them," he said, chuckling. "I haven't gotten caught once in this job—and probably won't. I've tracked hundreds of people. If you stay to the side of them, they don't notice you. They're so caught up with what they're doing and where they're going and where their kids are. It's like you fade into the background. It's amazing."

Underhill slipped on his pink baseball cap and we stepped out for lunch. We drove a few hundred yards to Billy's Pocono Diner, adjacent to the outlet complex, where a hamburger cost $1.85 even in 1991 dollars. We drove because no one walks at this crowded synapse of consumption, other than to and from a car. In fact, pedestrian traffic is expressly forbidden. Signs at the main intersection below the "Tannersville Welcomes You" billboard show a silhouette of a man in midstride, his body circled and slashed under the ubiquitous red symbol of prohibition. This was good advice. The main artery, Pennsylvania State Route 611, was built for a two-lane era, before Frank went Crazy and when Subs were but a twinkle in Mack's eye. Now the two lanes carried four lanes' worth of fast head-on traffic. This was air bag country, the stuff of Chrysler ads.

We took a table in Billy's back room, where an unsmiling waitress in sneakers and a blue windbreaker took our order, then sauntered away.

Underhill opened a manila file and showed me a quarter-inch-thick stack of maps his three agents had made in the two hours since the Pfaltzgraff store had opened. He expected to have roughly eighty maps by the end of the day.

The first sheet described a brief visit, in and out, mapped with a pink pen. Underhill referred to the shopper as "the lady in pink."

He traced her route with a finger. "This suggests she's been in the store before," Underhill said. The pink line went directly to a display of bowls at the back of the store, then to the cash-wrap, where she bought two bowls. "She walks in the door, knows exactly what she wants, then walks out."

The next map told a markedly different story. Pink ganglia choked two displays; pink sinews looped endlessly between them. It was an abstract portrait of indecision.

"They were in the store thirty minutes, shopping with a cart," Underhill said. "Two O-3's. Women, twenty-six to forty. I would think they are probably trying to buy a present of some kind. The choice is obviously between this pattern, and glassware, and this pattern. They've wandered all through the store, and they're bouncing back and forth among these three areas. This is *classic*. They came in and turned to the right. They've obviously looked at this display"— he pointed to one display thickly surrounded by pink—"then they came back and looped back around. They touched something. They ended up buying four folk-art mugs and twelve clear glasses. It took them thirty minutes to make up their minds."

The tracker had stayed with them all thirty minutes and had not been detected.

In the heat of consumption, we shoppers notice little of what is happening around us. Underhill's crews often even see people shoplifting. One tracker saw a middle-aged woman pick up three books, stick one in her purse, then pay for the other two. Underhill's cameras captured a man in a hardware store hiding tools in his baby's diaper. Craig Childress tracked a woman who pulled an expensive jogging suit from a rack, took it right to the cashier, and said, "I'd like to return this."

"But who in his right mind," I asked Underhill, "would steal in full view of half a dozen cameras and with someone holding a clipboard standing right nearby?"

Underhill shrugged. "People are oblivious."

The Pfaltzgraff store needed more chairs, Underhill told me. Chairs allow weary shoppers to rest while their more enthusiastic companions continue scouring the store. It is another axiom of retailing that the longer a shopper stays in the store, the more likely it is that he or she will buy something and spend more money than if driven out by a moaning spouse. The two chairs at the front of the Pfaltzgraff store were occupied most of the time.

Long lines were a problem. Underhill's trackers tailed shoppers who became so frustrated with the long wait at the cash-wrap that they simply put down the items they planned to buy and left.

"We forget," said Howard Freedman, the Pfaltzgraff vice-president who hired Underhill, "that the last impression shoppers get is the cash register, and we've always treated that as a stepchild. On a busy day, on a Saturday, the lines really become an obstacle. Plus, they become an annoyance to customers."

Underhill's study also provided concrete evidence of what Freedman had always thought to be true: that women shopping alone or in the company of other women buy more than when they shop with their husbands. Underhill suggested working out ways to separate women from their men, perhaps by establishing a special sitting area.

His study captured one subtle problem Freedman had never even considered. The store had not set out an obvious cart return area, and often shoppers who no longer needed their carts simply left them in place, adding to the congestion. "The next four or five people think that's where the carts go," Freedman said. "Very obvious. We should have known about it, but nobody ever thought of it."

One of Underhill's findings, however, went directly against the weight of retail lore, even his own previous research. At Pfaltzgraff, he found, customers turned left and right in equal numbers. "We were surprised it was equal," Freedman told me. One possible explanation: Pfaltzgraff's top-selling "Yorktowne" pattern, which draws collectors from hundreds of miles away, was displayed on the left.

The Envirosell trackers also observed a phenomenon Underhill had seen elsewhere and that has become one of the central findings in a growing body of information he refers to collectively as "aisle theory." He first described it to me at his offices in New York when he showed me a few surveillance films his company had made for Waldenbooks, Revco, Bloomingdale's, Champs, Target Stores, and The Broadway chain of California department stores.

"As I was looking at this clip," Underhill said, "I saw something that was probably one of the major pieces of our research."

The projector clattered and roared just like the old Bell & Howell Super-8 projector on which my family had shown so many films from our summer journeys west. Granted, this projector was a bit more sophisticated—it wound the film all by itself, and when Underhill froze the picture at a particular frame the film didn't melt—but it still chattered mercilessly, noise I found oddly reassuring in this age of silent digital technology.

The shoppers on the screen were moving quickly in Chaplinesque fashion through a Revco drugstore. Underhill had filmed them with a stop-action movie camera and was now playing back the film at regular speed.

I saw shoppers staggering up and down the aisles, products accumulating mysteriously in their arms, but nothing else struck me as unusual.

"See that guy?" Underhill said. "He's got a shopping basket."

In the industry, shopping baskets and carts are known more formally as "shopping aids."

The man and his basket were the stuff of revelation, apparently, but I still couldn't see why.

Underhill stopped the film. "I'll demonstrate this on you," he said. "Stand up."

I stood, and he began piling things from the surrounding table and bookshelf into my arms.

"Here you go," he said, adding a book. "And here you go. Here, and here."

Soon everything began tumbling from my arms.

Underhill grinned. "The point is, less than five percent of people walking into the drugstore pick up any form of shopping aid." He pointed at the film. "So here is a drugstore frantically merchandising, promoting, and pricing for the impulse purchase, and what we discovered was that if somebody's hands are full, they ain't going to buy it."

Pfaltzgraff had the same problem, Underhill said. It offered baskets at the front of the store, but few people used them. "One of the things we're going to tell them here is that one of the ways of getting people to increase the average casual purchase is by taking those baskets and sticking them throughout the store and training the employees to hand them to people. Say 'Here, would this make things easier?' "

"Ass-brush factor" is another of Underhill's discoveries. Underhill showed me a film clip shot at the southeast entrance to Bloomingdale's in Manhattan, using a time-lapse camera mounted over the doorway. Shoppers entered, dispersed, some quickly riffling the men's ties in a display, most rushing past toward the depths of the store.

He stopped the projector.

"Once more. Stand up."

Once more I stood.

"Okay, you are standing at the counter. You are looking at ties. The most sensitive part of your anatomy is your tail."

He began brushing my tail with his hand, back and forth.

"Ass-brush factor is simply the idea that the more likely you are to be brushed from the rear while you shop, the less likely you'll be converted from browser to buyer."

In retail-speak, the "conversion ratio" of that display or counter will be low.

We watched a man examine a tie on a tie rack.

"The effectiveness of that fixture diminishes markedly by ass-brush factor. Men seem to tolerate it better. Women are *very* sensitive to it."

He showed another clip, also from Bloomingdale's, but this time of the Clinique cosmetics counter. He found that shoppers who stood on the side of the counter that faced the main traffic aisle—the "driveway" or "power aisle"—tended to browse but not buy. Here the conversion ratio was low; on the other side, sheltered from the crowds, the ratio was far higher.

A young mother browsing the windward side of the counter came up with a defense against ass-brush factor. She placed her stroller so that it formed a barrier against onrushing shoppers. "No one is going to brush her here," Underhill said. "Note, as she moves down the counter she moves the stroller carefully with her, positioning it."

The Maginot stroller worked. She leisurely studied the cosmetics as shoppers streamed past, flowing away from her barrier.

"Did she do it deliberately?" I wondered.

"If you asked her whether she was doing it for that reason or not, I don't know whether she could answer," he said. "But when you observe the phenomenon over and over and over again, with different people, different strollers . . ." He shrugged.

"It seems to me," I said, "that so many of the things you've observed are, well, obvious."

"They seem obvious," he agreed. "And yet you wonder then how people could do business for generations and somehow what's obvious hasn't come up before."

Most of Underhill's clients would survive without him. He captures nuance and fine-tunes the performance of going concerns. "I'm not sure I buy into all this stuff," Pfaltzgraff's Howard Freedman said, referring specifically to the ass-brush factor. "I take some of it with a grain of thought." Nonetheless, he considers the $24,000 he paid Envirosell to be money well spent. "If we get one or two good ideas out of it and pick up some extra business, what I paid him will be peanuts."

In certain situations, marketers argue, observation becomes a necessity. Figuring out kids, for instance.

Kids don't function like adults. "Don't think of children as small adults," one researcher advised at the Miami Beach marketers conference. "Think of them as big Martians." Kids stymie researchers who approach them with traditional adult tactics. Kids have minimal powers of discrimination. They like virtually everything they see. They lack the ability to report on their own behavior. They try desperately to please their elders, especially strange elders with clipboards. And they have a disturbing knack for giving detailed reactions to products they never even tried. Once, for example, Langbourne Rust asked a group of second-graders what they thought of Big Bird toothpaste. They liked it. They liked the way it looked. It tasted good. There was one problem: the product did not exist.

Rust has spent over twenty years observing kids, often from behind one-way glass and for such clients as ABC, CBS, NBC, Children's Television Workshop (makers of *Sesame Street*), Quaker Oats, General Foods, Procter & Gamble, Lipton, McDonald's, Hasbro, Matchbox, and Lego. Every fall from 1977 to 1985 Rust conducted his syndicated Saturday Morning Attention Study of new children's TV shows, for which he sat eighty or so kids in ten different rooms to watch the new programs. Video cameras behind one-way mirrors recorded where their faces turned during each program to provide a measure of which shows most held their attention.

Rust attributes his interest in observation to his being raised a country boy and spending a lot of time "sitting on a stump" watching wildlife pass by. "I've always been a critter watcher," he said. "Now I just watch different critters."

Recently he spent a lot of time standing discreetly in store aisles, secretly observing critters and their parents to help marketers figure out how best to take advantage of the ways kids and parents interact when they shop together. The project, commissioned by the Advertising Research Foundation, exposed an important secret that I, as a father who takes my kids shopping, would have preferred the marketers not discover.

Rust and co-observers loitered in toy stores and in the candy and cereal aisles of supermarkets. As part of their mission, according to an ARF progress report, they were to capture "as much of the actual dialogue as possible, including the tone of the dialogue and the existence of verbal and nonverbal behavior or interactions."

In little grocery stores, like those in Manhattan, Rust first identified himself to the managers. In larger supermarkets he simply took up a position and waited. "I may have been a little lax there about getting permission," he told me. He tried to stay out of sight of store employees who might wonder why a man would spend two hours in a single aisle.

Originally Rust planned on disguising each observer's note sheet to resemble a shopping list. He quickly realized the camouflage was unnecessary.

"No one ever notices. Ever." Consumers, Rust told me, tend to shop in a trancelike state, like "idly grazing pasture animals," as he put it. Nonetheless, there are certain rules a retail spy must follow. The main rule: "*Never* turn your face toward the person you're looking at. People have an extraordinary ability to notice from their peripheral vision that someone's looking at them."

Preliminary findings from Rust's study captured behaviors that marketers would be foolish not to pounce on.

For example:

- Girls get more involved in grocery shopping and choosing brands than boys and thus, Rust said in a talk to the ARF, "may perhaps be more productive targets for advertising."
- Parents control the intensity of their kids' product demands through

deft navigation of store aisles, "thereby avoiding the dangers lurking around certain retail corners."

- The youngest children do most of the asking for products when they shop with parents, but older kids are more cunning—"more skilled negotiators," as an ARF progress report put it.

Here, however, is the revelation every mother has always known and every father with an ounce of integrity will concede to be true. The ARF report trod this ground gingerly: "Fathers are often less skilled at negotiation than their usually more seasoned female counterparts."

In short, dads are suckers.

Imagine the marketing potential! Father-and-son days at the local Piggly Wiggly. Candy racks in hardware stores. Discount motor oil at Toys "R" Us. Action figurines on sale at the beer display!

There is reason, however, to take heart. The process of getting suckered is less painful than suggested by the common wisdom, with its lurid tales of tantrums among the Goobers and episodes of rapid oxygen depletion. "In general," Rust told me, "the parent-child interactions in grocery stores are a very positive, upbeat social time between parent and child that both seem to enjoy a lot."

Such observations, clearly, do little to explain the deep meanings of consumption. As Ernest Dichter, the founder of motivation research, well understood, consumers of all ages are notoriously inept at explaining the real motivations behind their purchase decisions and the symbolic importance of products to their lives. Ever since Dichter discovered the prune was an undersexed witch, symbolism has been important to American marketers. It will become far more important in coming years, however, as companies rely more and more on carefully crafted symbolic allusions to differentiate their products from those of the competition.

But who do you call when you need a few good symbols?

The two anthropologists took the leopard-covered chairs. Their mission had been to venture into the wilds of America and observe men in their natural habitats—in gyms, bowling alleys, and bars; at baseball games; on campus and the fairway, even on a Boy Scout camping trip—and to report back on the state of manhood in America. How did men see themselves? How did they define masculinity? How did they behave in the company of other men? Who were their role models? What products symbolized manhood today?

They had returned now for a "debriefing," to be delivered to Penelope Queen, executive vice-president of Saatchi & Saatchi Advertising, New York, and three female colleagues in Queen's spacious office overlooking the Hudson River. Queen believes strongly in the value of observational research and often dispatches anthropologists on expeditions to hunt the symbolic meanings of consumption. She invited me to attend.

The anthropologists were John Lowe and Tim Malefyt, both from the "cultural analysis division" of Holen North America, a New York–based consulting firm that specializes in behavioral research and whose clients have included such diverse companies as Hyatt Hotels, Sara Lee, Illinois Power, and Campbell Soup. In a brochure intended to woo clients, Holen proclaims that "marketers and managers will be the heroes of the nineties" for their ability "to unlock the secrets of human striving and forecast the next turn of human needs, wants, and desires."

These two heroes brought bleak news.

There was indeed a problem "out there," Lowe said. His direct, dark gaze and slightly pointed beard gave him the look of an angst-ridden Russian writer. "The prevailing sense is one of malaise," he told us through a wan smile. "As one of our respondents said, 'It's hard to think of a man who's really happy.' "

He let that thought drift a moment, then nodded at the tragic weight of it. The four Saatchi women watched him with sober-faced attention. Queen sighed. "Oh, my God," she said, her voice breathy and girlish but freighted with sympathy.

She wore red shoes and a short white dress, the hem etched permanently along the top eighth of her long freckled legs. Often she reached up, bracelet clanking, to dust her hair back in place, then down to align her skirt, a pitcher's ritual of physical adjustment. Brush, align, clank.

She stared at Lowe over a pair of half-glasses, the kind that give old men such a cantankerous cast.

Lowe was enjoying this.

"There is no clear model of what it means to be a man today," he said, his voice cool and even. "Mostly out there is a sense of confusion and a vague sense of loss. And the reasons are fairly clear. Traditionally men have tended to define themselves by what they do, and frankly that's no longer very distinctive. You have women fire fighters, you have women police officers, you have women bosses. It's hard for men to find many activities that are inherently masculine anymore."

"What also came through and kind of surprised me a little bit was this underlying feeling of failure as the sole family breadwinner," Lowe said. "Many men expressed a kind of shame that they can't do what their fathers had done."

Sole providers no longer, men now felt inadequate. They had been demoted from family CEO to mere partner. They would never achieve what their parents achieved. Life was harder. The fifties were better. Even sex, the last arena for unequivocal displays of masculinity, was getting confusing. Women had become more "demanding" in the sack, Lowe said. "To put it succinctly, quantity is no longer the be all and end all of male sexuality. Now there's this quality thing. As one of the men put it, 'You have to be a provider and James Bond in bed, too.' "

I shifted a bit on my chair. The room seemed to be getting warmer. Where was the Marlboro man when you needed him? Instead of galloping over the prairie, men were thrashing about trying to find masculine role models for today's society. Lowe ticked off a list of traits and conditions that men believed described masculinity: strong, rugged, hard, self-assured, forceful. And violent.

Violence was a tricky category. Men disavowed it, of course. But then again . . .

"One of our respondents said one of his role models was James Cagney because he could squash a grapefruit in a woman's face," Lowe said.

"Hmmmmmmm," Queen murmured. She gave Roz, one of her colleagues, a long slow look over the tops of her glasses, dropped her voice, and purred, "Very interesting."

Women had it easy, Lowe reported. Femininity came naturally to them. They had breasts, lactation, periods. If they ever forgot they were women, this triad would remind them. But men, Lowe said, "don't think of themselves primarily in terms of biological characteristics. Masculinity tends to be more culturally confirmed."

One new shift was evident: men had begun seeing fatherhood as an important element of masculinity, and they appreciated being given more cultural leeway to get involved with their kids.

Whom did men look to as models? A few celebrities seemed to embody today's masculinity, although in no consistent pattern. All had a strong, well-defined "masculine core" but also other attributes that took them beyond Dirty Harry. The list included

Bo Jackson, for his versatility;
Nolan Ryan, Jack Nicklaus, and, yes, Abraham Lincoln, for their integrity;
Norman Schwarzkopf, for authenticity, for being "real";
Magic Johnson, for his intelligence (although this study was conducted before he disclosed his sexual exploits and the fact that he was HIV-positive);
Harrison Ford and William Hurt, for being sensitive but not being yucky about it;
Frank Gifford, for his family orientation;
Arnold Schwarzenegger, for being tough but embodying "parental" attributes, a dividend from his starring role in *Kindergarten Cop*.

The men who just didn't "work" anymore were

Alan Alda. *Too* sensitive! "Sensitivity is always said with a sneer by men," Lowe reported.
Sylvester Stallone. Too Rambo, too Rocky.
Clint Eastwood. No one really knew where he stood anymore on the macho/wimp continuum.
George Bush. He could wage war, but could he pick up chicks?

Lowe's observations of men at play taught him that men seek the company of other men for relief from sexual confusion. "Pickup basketball is a beautiful example," Lowe said, flashing a smile that verged on beatific. "You go out onto the court typically with strangers. The team is made up of five players or less. There's not much strategic thinking, it's all individual peformance. It's typically an 'in your face' kind of game with no referees. The net result is to establish with a bunch of strangers that you are effective. When you can do that, you come away feeling real good about yourself as a man. Little things, like who passes to whom during the game, become a really powerful statement of recognition and respect. By giving that ball to somebody else, you're telling him, 'You can make the play; I believe you can do something with this ball.'"

In bars he observed men playing at taking charge. They bought rounds of beer. They told stories and jokes. What they were really doing, of course, was seizing control, *commanding* the attention of others. The jokes tended to be crude, derogatory, sexist, horrific—like jokes about accused cannibal and murderer Jeffrey Dahmer of Milwaukee—and offered men "a safe way to talk about deep terrors and anxiety."

What did all this mean for products? For advertising strategy?

Men, Lowe reported, sought "markers" of manhood, products that helped them look and feel like men. Jeeps, for example; real men drove Jeeps, real Jeeps. The manly Jeep, was the CJ-7. "It obviously has characteristics of ruggedness, solidity; of sturdiness, being able to go anywhere; and it also relates to typically male situations of being out in the wilderness," Lowe said. "So you put those two together and you create a more masculine object, that 'double' marker."

Basketball shoes like the Nike Air and Converse Magic Johnson models were even more effective at helping men be men. They were triple markers: in a single product they packed all the symbolic associations of the namesake athletes, of the sport, and of the shoe's masculine design. "They're kind of clunky, they're kind of solid, and they're performance-oriented," Lowe said.

The result was a kind of supermarker—a psychoactive sneaker. "These men clomp around in their basketball shoes and feel better about themselves. It lets them deal a little better with all these other changes that are going on in their lives."

Queen tried summarizing what she had learned so far about men, slowly counting off the traits. "A great deal of ambivalence . . . anxiety . . . anger . . ."

The room was indeed getting warm. I felt so . . . pathetic.

"A harkening back . . . a dependence on older symbols of masculinity . . . less valuing of women in general. . . ."

Something was missing. Queen was dissatisfied. "Where are the women, John?" she asked.

She wanted to know more about how men saw women, how women fit into their lives. As she fanned the pages of Lowe's written report, titled "Rebound from Androgyny," she said, "There's no *section*, John."

Where, she also wondered, did men stand in relation to the changing values of society as a whole? She understood that men seemed to need a traditional masculine core, but hadn't that always been the case?

"I'm very confused," she said. Brush, align, clank. "I'm so confused I don't know how to unconfuse myself."

The conversation got murky. There was much talk of gender specificity, maleness, cores of being, even of hunters and gatherers: how the great change men were undergoing now was just as significant as the shift from a hunter-gatherer society to an agricultural society, from preindustrial to industrial.

Brush, align, clank.

Queen was frowning. Lowe rested his chin on his fist, two fingers supporting the side of his face. "I guess there's something missing," he said, looking pained. "If I could . . ."

He let the thought trail off.

What struck me most about the debriefing, however, was a remark Roz made early on. She laughed and joked to John Lowe, "I can't believe you get paid to do this."

"True enough," he said, laughing. But the look on his face said he would not have minded if in that instant a jet from nearby Newark Airport had dropped an engine in her lap.

In fact, cultural spies like Lowe and Malefyt may find themselves in great demand in coming years, according to Steve Barnett, a leading corporate anthropologist. Barnett taught cultural anthropology at Princeton, Brown, and MIT, founded Holen, and more recently worked as director of research for Nissan North America, before resigning in 1991. The hunt for symbols will become the next corporate battleground, he told me. "More and more products are essentially equivalent," he said. "The nature of technological improvement and manufacturing improvement is such that, for example, there is relatively little difference among a Honda, a Toyota, and a Nissan, at the level of just the hard parts of the vehicle. And that's becoming more true for things like TVs, like stereos, and a wide range of other products. If products are by some objective way becoming more equivalent, more like commodities, then their symbolic function becomes more important because that's what differentiates them."

His mission as a consultant is to help companies find the symbolic link between consumers and products, "precisely that function that people can't tell you about in a survey." Already, he said, the smartest companies have begun forging powerful symbolic associations for their products. "Look at Nike and Reebok," he said. "They're entirely focused on creating strong symbols, in part using athletes, in part using other advertising techniques. In fact, the shoes are exactly the same."

Symbols will become so important, so much in demand, Barnett predicts, that soon America's consumers will have to cope with a symbol shortage.

Consumers use symbols to define themselves, he explained, but consumers today have gone from pursuing a single life-style to pursuing two or more at once. Thus a stockbroker by day becomes a blues musician at night. A factory foreman becomes an independent film-maker. Each life-style requires its own set of symbolic products or props that help people play out these multiple roles. The stockbroker drives his Buick to work; when he drives to the Dirty Dawg Saloon that night, however, he wears his Levi Strauss denim jacket and drives the midnight blue El Camino he restored in his spare time. Each person, therefore, will need more symbols, Barnett said. There simply won't be enough to go around. "People are going to want to represent themselves in more ways than there are going to be products that can be used to represent them," he said, "and there is going to be a big fight for the control of symbols."

A devastating symbol famine could leave millions of us looking for definition. The symbolless would clog our cities. Semioticians would become tycoons. Bumper stickers would appear: "He Who Dies with the Most Symbols Wins!"

We'd have no choice but to call in the heroes of the nineties, the men from Holen.

The marketing imagination leaves no means of surveillance untested. Even garbage, the marketers have found, can reveal the secrets of consumers. How else could one find out what cat owners *really* read? Or learn the truth about what they really feed their cats without falling prey to the dissembling caused by "guilty dry syndrome"?

Physical artifacts have long provided rich clues about human behavior. Researchers have tried to estimate the income of consumers by analyzing the decorations on their front lawns (the study was called "The Variability of Non-Living Objects Found on the Front Property of Households"); to establish a link between bathroom decoration and the use of hallucinogenic drugs ("Individual Bathroom Decoration Correlated with Educational Level and Drug Use"); and to estimate sexist attitudes by the size and grandeur of tombstones on the graves of men and women ("The War Between the Sexes: Do They Fight It to the Grave?"). One researcher used the presence and number of cigarette butts as a leading indicator of anxiety among psychiatric patients.

There is no lusher, richer repository of physical clues to our behavior than the garbage we dispose of every day. You say you practice safe sex? Then where are the condom wrappers? You quit drinking for keeps? Well, where'd these empty bottles of Mad Dog come from? Archaeologists and other professional snoops have long acknowledged the descriptive powers of garbage. The archaeologists study ancient garbage pits to learn how our ancestors lived. Reporters and police root through contemporary Dumpsters for clues about the people they investigate. From 1975 to 1979 federal agents probed the garbage of mobster Joseph C. Bonano, Sr., for clues of mob activities. In 1991 private detectives hired by Avon Products Inc. made three secret trips to the Dumpster outside the Dallas headquarters of Mary Kay Corporation, looking for evidence that Mary Kay might have destroyed evidence important to a legal dispute between the two companies. They even filmed the Dumpster with a video camera. "If you want to win," said one private detective interviewed about the dispute by *Business Week*, "you'll resort to anything. Winners go for the garbage."

By that standard, William Rathje is a winner. Rathje is an archaeologist with the University of Arizona and an expert on Mayan culture. In 1973 he began applying the principles of archaeology to the study of contemporary America and founded the now celebrated Garbage Project—*Le Projet du Garbage,* as he dubbed it initially—to analyze systematically the garbage of Tucson, often without the knowledge of the households being studied. Rathje went on to conduct "garbology" studies in neighborhoods and landfills throughout the country, puncturing myths of human consumption along the way.

"As you might suspect," he wrote in *Garbage* magazine, "people are an utterly unreliable source of information. What people claim in interviews to have purchased and used, eaten and drunk, recycled and wasted, almost never corresponds directly to the packaging and debris in their garbage bags."

People overreport such positive behaviors as eating healthy foods but underreport the negative, like eating big fat steaks and drinking bourbon. For one of Rathje's studies, interviewers first surveyed a sample of households to ask how much beer their members drank in a week.

Eighty-five percent claimed they drank no beer at all. The remaining 15 percent reported they only consumed eight cans or less per week. Rathje and his student sorters then analyzed the garbage produced by these households and exposed a somewhat different pattern. Beer cans turned up in 75 percent of the garbage sampled. Fifty-four percent contained more than eight cans. "In fact," Rathje reported in the journal *Early Man*, "many households averaged 2½ six-packs (15 cans) every seven days."

Our society, so geared to consumption and disposability, provides particularly lush ground for the practice of garbology. Rathje and his disciples have studied candy consumption for candy companies, package disposal for packaging trade associations, and "food-management behavior" for Frito-Lay. Two marketing professors, Melanie Wallendorf and Michael Reilly, used the Garbage Project data base to study consumption by Mexican-American households and found they consumed far more soft drinks, caffeine products, packaged pastries, and convenience foods (prepared soups, canned vegetables, frozen vegetables) than their "Anglo" peers, observations of clear value to the many companies now turning their attention to the nation's vast Hispanic market.

Reilly, now a marketing professor at Montana State University, later analyzed the Tucson data specifically to hunt for ways that companies could use the information to better understand their markets and products, especially those classes of products that escape the checkout-scanner network, such as cat food sold through convenience stores.

Cat food, Reilly argued, offered a prime example of how pet-food makers could use garbage to get a truer picture of what people feed their cats than they would get from interviews. Cat owners, it seems, suffer what Reilly calls "guilty dry syndrome"—that is, they feed their cats dry food, feel guilty about it, and then lie to market research interviewers, telling them they serve only the finest canned and moist feline cuisine. Their garbage doesn't lie, however. Thirty percent of cat owners brutally fed their dear little bunchkins *only* dry food, Reilly found; a mere 9.9 percent served only the moist variety.

Reilly also demonstrated how Rathje's garbage data base could be used to study brand-switching behaviors. Cat owners who served only dry food tended to switch brands less often than others who served either moist food only or a combination of both dry and moist foods. People who bought 9-Lives cat food in both its dry and canned forms "tended to be less brand loyal than users of other brands" of each category. "Accordingly," Reilly wrote, "a cat food marketer would find it an easier task to switch 9-Lives users than to switch users of comparable products."

Reilly also found clear evidence of unfair species discrimination among pet owners. "In houses where there were both cats and dogs," he reported, "the cats invariably got a better grade of food than the dogs." Dogs did not lead lives of Dickensian oppression, however. They got three times more table scraps!

Reilly deduced this scrap factor from data showing exactly how many grams of food waste each household discarded. Garbage Project sorters wielding scales and wearing gloves weighed each and every hunk of gristle, bone, and crust extracted from each load of garbage. Over the five-week study period, families who owned neither cats nor dogs threw out 1,713 grams of food; cats-only families tossed 1,495 grams; cat-and-dog families, 1,360 grams; dogs-only, 1,140 grams. The presumption was that Fido's stomach accounted for the debris shortfall in dogs-only households.

Garbage can also be used to gauge media penetration and expose hidden correlations between products and magazines. Cat owners read more than dog owners, Reilly found, basing his judgment on how often publications turned up in their garbage.

I can see the cat owners of America pursing their lips and nodding— "Yes, it's true. We do read more, darling, because we are smarter than the rest of you, especially those of you who seem to need the loutish, dripping, and slavish attentions of a mere *hound* before you can feel good about yourselves. It does take a rather high intellect to appreciate a cat."

Ah, but what publications do those cat owners read? *The New Yorker*, surely, or *The Atlantic*. Perhaps even *Foreign Affairs*?

No—the *National Enquirer*. The tabloid turned up in the garbage of cat owners more often than any publication found in the garbage of households where dogs drip and howl.

This is not to say, however, that dog owners read *Le Monde* to their kids at breakfast. Dog owners, it seems, read *TV Guide*.

Sifting, scanning, spying, filming—it's a lot of effort to take for the information one gets in return. Isn't there a more direct way? An implant again comes to mind, a little something to be injected into the bodies of consumers to monitor every purchase they make, every show they watch, every commercial and advertisement they encounter. Consumers could then spy on themselves, electronically and objectively, forever. The idea conjures an engaging vision: a team of neatly suited researchers from Procter & Gamble speeds through downtown Manhattan in a zebra-striped Land Rover, firing tranquilizer guns at predesignated consumers as they bolt for cover. "That's Quigley all right!" Thump! "He's down!" they cry. They tie his legs and feet together. Quickly, deftly, they inject the device under the skin of his upper arm. He begins to wake. Tenderly the men from P&G place a steaming cup of coffee (Folgers, of course) beside his twitching fingers. Then—away!

There is a wishfulness in such jokey schemes that is at once charming and spooky and that speaks worlds about the marketers' appetite for our consuming secrets. The heroes from Holen might describe such ideas as the marketers' way of dealing with their deepest terror, their fear of not knowing enough. Implants, of course, are pure fantasy.

Or are they?

FRAGMENTS OF AN IDEA

I. *The Transmitter* (From a flier describing the TX1400L Injectable Transponder, made by Destron Inc., Boulder, Colorado):

> "The transponder consists of an electromagnetic coil, tuning capacitor, and microchip sealed in a tubular glass enclosure. . . . Although specifically designed for injecting in animals, this transponder can be used for other applications requiring a microsize identification tag."

II. *The Receiver* (From U.S. patent 4,726,771, issued to Lee S. Weinblatt):

> "Seiko . . . markets a system including the UC 2000 wrist terminal with 2K bytes of memory, a chronograph, a four-line display, and a partitioned memory. . . . Such a unit can be readily modified for this invention by attaching it to an antenna of a suitable size and type and a microchip that functions as a receiver."

III. *The Underlying Concept* (From "Cow 54, Where Are You?" in *Beef Today*, February 1991):

"Cows would be implanted at the tailhead with a tiny cylindrical transponder. As the bull breeds the cow, the number, the date, and the time would be recorded by gear strapped to the bull. The [bull's] unit would also contain a transmitter that would pipe the data to the office. . . .

"In a multisire herd we can find out which bull bred which cow and when. . . . That will let us calculate calving dates, find out which bull is working, and keep track of the calf's genetics."

"I'm not worried," Lee Weinblatt said. "It'll work."

Weinblatt was leaning over a long table in a conference room at his PreTesting Company headquarters in Englewood, New Jersey, a few minutes from the George Washington Bridge. He held a "handwand scanner" made by Destron Inc. of Boulder, Colorado. The scanner, shaped like a miniature version of those metal detectors you see deployed at beaches by optimistic men in search of loose change, was designed to pick up very faint electronic signals broadcast by tiny transmitter chips known as transponders. Destron makes these, too, in an array of sizes. The TX1400L described in the excerpt above can be injected under the skin using a special syringe. One Destron transponder lay on Weinblatt's table. Roughly the size of a grain of cooked rice, it comprised half the technology Weinblatt figured he would need to build the ultimate consumer intelligence weapon—a system capable of transforming consumers into automated sensors and providing a lush second-by-second record of their every contact with the commercial world.

The fundamental technology worked, I knew. Chips like the one on Weinblatt's table had been injected into baby salmon to track their travels through the rivers of the northwestern United States. The Dutch government wanted to implant every pig in the Netherlands, all twenty-two million of them, with transponders by 1991, to help keep track of swine diseases. The Dogs Home Battersea, in London, implanted transponders in thousands of dogs so that if any alumni ever got lost again and wound up back at the home, the staff could simply scan them with a handwand to learn their identities. "Having become accustomed to having the information, we should feel deprived without it," wrote a Dogs Home official in a July 1990 report on the technique. "To discontinue implanting would be a retrograde step."

"It's Murphy's law," Weinblatt said, holding the handwand scanner a millimeter above the chip. "When something is supposed to work, it doesn't."

He pulled the trigger. Nothing happened. "NO ID FOUND," appeared in the scanner display screen. What made this especially maddening was that the handwand had worked on the very first pass of the morning, beeping pertly and displaying an ID number broadcast by the chip, one of thirty-four billion possible codes.

Weinblatt, the Thomas Edison of marketing research, a man to whom every market research problem had a technological solution, stared glumly at the scanner. His glasses, dark-framed and heavy, had slipped a bit down his nose.

He knew machines. He liked machines. Plaques describing a couple dozen of his many patents cover most of the west wall of his office. One describes a means of counting how many people really look at billboards. The solution: Beam a laser—a harmless one—into the eyes of passing drivers, then capture the light reflected by their retinas. Weinblatt was good with machines—this was betrayal.

He pushed his glasses back into place. Once more he passed the scanner over the chip.

"NO ID FOUND," it said.

He shrugged, opened a box, and unveiled the other half of his technology.

"We're not talking high-tech," he said. "This is technology available right this second."

Weinblatt prides himself on puncturing treasured marketing beliefs by capturing the real-world behavior of consumers. He began his career as a hospital-based psychologist, then quit to become a market researcher. Along the way he founded Telcom Research, a company that specialized in showing consumers advertisements and package designs and using cameras to track the movements of their eyes. (Unlike "pupilmetrics," which measured the dilation of pupils, this system monitored where the pupils actually pointed.) In its heyday Telcom maintained a fleet of four mobile test laboratories that could park anywhere and allow Telcom researchers to nab passing consumers on a truly random basis. The vans even rose on hydraulic jacks to reduce the potential for distortion caused when people climbed aboard. But Weinblatt became disenchanted with such forced-attention studies. "The problem was that on almost any study we did, people knew they were being tested." If he showed consumers a single package, of course they would pay attention to its details. "But," he asks, "who says anyone's ever going to get that close to your package?"

In 1983 and, yes, in 1984, Weinblatt first set out to test ways of capturing real-world behavior. A photography enthusiast, Weinblatt began hiding cameras in ceilings, boxes, shelves, and lamps to study such phenomena as how people really read magazines. At an American Marketing Association meeting in New York he showed a video clip of a woman thumbing through a magazine while riding the Long Island Railroad. The railroad wouldn't allow him to install a camera in the car, Weinblatt told me later, so he mounted a tiny camera in the shoulder pad of an employee's suit and assigned him to ride among the commuters.

He also hid cameras in the ceilings of doctors' waiting rooms to observe how people read magazines while waiting. One seminal revelation of his magazine studies: Weinblatt found that 40 percent of us read magazines from back to front, or begin in the middle, important news for advertisers who had always paid a premium to place their ads in the first few pages of magazines.

"You want to see the 'toys'?" Weinblatt asked me during a visit to his headquarters.

He walked to his desk, rummaged through a drawer, and pulled out the tattered remains of a wrapper for a bar of Ivory soap; once it had contained a camera. He showed me a Sony tabletop radio in which he had hidden a video camera used to capture people in their own living rooms as they watched TV. He showed me a sleek black Italian lamp that he uses to study how much attention people give to advertisements in magazines. Hidden near the bulb is a camera that films the magazine; another camera hidden in the base watches the reader's eyes. The readers never know they are on camera.

Next Weinblatt led me to a small office across the corridor and challenged me to find a camera disguised somewhere inside. I scanned the office. There were too many possibilities. Books? The desk? The lamp?

I gave up.

Weinblatt smiled like a schoolboy who had just glued his teacher to a chair.

"The sprinkler," he said.

Two fire sprinklers jutted from the ceiling—too many for such a tiny office. We positioned ourselves under the shiniest of the two. Weinblatt pointed to a tiny mirror jutting from the sprinkler's base, led me into a neighboring office, and switched on the camera. By remote control he rotated the mirror to scan the room. The image was crisp and clean, far better in quality than the surveillance tapes federal spies seem able to produce.

"I had to promise everyone who works here this would be the only camera I'd hide," he said. "Otherwise no one would ever go to the bathroom again."

Weinblatt has secured cameras to shelves to watch how people react to products. In a study of frozen food displays, he discovered that shoppers spend one-third less time examining frozen foods displayed in new vertical freezer cases (the kind with the glass doors) than when the foods are set out in the old open horizontal cases. The old cases, nicknamed "coffins," encouraged browsing and increased the odds that shoppers would notice new products. Now, however, shoppers march directly to the door they want, open it, reach in with icy precision, then close it fast.

The reason?

"We were all taught well by our mothers to close the refrigerator door," Weinblatt said. "I can't remember, though—was it to keep the cold air in or the warm air out?"

During one of Weinblatt's shelf studies, a hapless shopper picked up a camera-loaded cereal box and, oblivious both of its unusual weight and of the video cable that ran from its rear, pulled it toward his cart. The cable stretched. Boxes erupted along a forty-foot length of shelf and tumbled to the floor. The man looked to see if anyone had noticed, gently replaced the box, and walked briskly away.

Another study demonstrated beyond a doubt just how little attention we consumers devote to shopping for groceries. Weinblatt hid a camera in a box of Cheer detergent, then stuck labels on the box and its neighbors that read "NEW AND IMPROVED" to test whether anyone paid attention to those weary but ubiquitous adjectives.

"No one looked," he said. "No one even saw it."

He got bolder. This time he pasted a three-inch disk on each box that read, "NOW SWEETENED WITH NUTRASWEET!"

Again no one noticed. "Not even people who picked them up and put them in their shopping carts! We had an interviewer meet them at the end and ask 'Did you notice anything new about this?' They said 'No.' "

Okay. So maybe some people didn't know what NutraSweet was; maybe they didn't know it had no business being in a laundry soap.

Weinblatt took off the gloves. This time he placed labels that exclaimed "NEW IMPROVED TASTE!"

"Finally people noticed," he told me. "When we asked them what it meant, they said 'I don't know. Maybe it works better?' "

The second half of Lee Weinblatt's proposed spy system is a wristwatch.

Weinblatt pulled a sophisticated digital Seiko watch and pager from a box. The watch already had many of the features he would need to make his vision a reality, he said. It was proof, too, of how much digital apparatus could be crammed into a small space. He proposed to build a miniature version of the balky handwand scanner on the table and to disguise it as a wristwatch to be worn by a select sample of consumers. The watch would be available in an array of pleasing styles to suit the tastes of fashion-conscious subjects, both male and female. It would capture special electronic signals broadcast every time each volunteer opened a magazine or was close enough to a radio or television to hear a commercial.

Each commercial would be branded with its own unique code number, the electronic equivalent of the Universal Product Code (this in itself is not a new idea; a Nielsen engineer told me he liked to think of it as a Universal *Broadcast* Code). The code would be transmitted through unused carrier frequencies just as captions are now transmitted for interception by special adaptors placed on the televisions of deaf viewers. Each magazine would have its own code number, too, the number stored in a tiny transponder implanted in the binding of each or in advertising inserts similar to the perfume ads we encounter all too often. The magazines would broadcast their signal each time they were opened and engulf us not with fragrance, but with inaudible electronic signals. Magazines would cry out to us as we passed, *The New Yorker*, no doubt, with the digital equivalent of a Gregorian hum; *Elle*, something seductive; *Cosmo*, an orgasmic roar.

The watch would even identify the wearer to the optical scanners in supermarkets, which in turn would collect all the Universal Product

Code numbers of the wearer's purchases for later analysis to see just what impact all those media encounters had on his or her behavior.

Response rates would be high, Weinblatt claims. Subjects wouldn't have to do a thing except strap it on each morning. Recruiting costs would be low, installation a breeze. No wires, no buttons, no on-screen prompts. A motion detector, like the sensors already built into watches that count the miles you walk, would tell whether the subject actually wore the watch or had set it aside.

Clearly there are a great many obstacles to Weinblatt's plan. First, how *do* you get the various devices consolidated in a chip that small— and who does it for you, and who pays for the work? Second, how do you reduce the price of the transponders to the point that magazines, already sorely pressed to make a profit, could be persuaded to implant them in their issues?

All valid objections, Weinblatt agreed, but he claims he is in no hurry. He has patented all aspects of the idea. Nielsen and Arbitron declined to fund its development, but as of the summer of 1991 two Japanese companies were considering the idea. "Right now I have no pressure," Weinblatt told me. "Patents are good for seventeen years. Technology is moving toward me, not away from me."

Now, if only the handwand scanner on Weinblatt's table would work. He could not resist another try.

"NO ID FOUND."

"The weird thing is," Weinblatt said, "it did this yesterday and frustrated me no end, and just as I was about to throw it against the wall, it worked, it did chip after chip. It's like it knew I was getting frustrated. . . ."

He tried again.

"NO ID FOUND."

"Well," he said, "you saw it work once."

"Can I smack it for you?" I said.

Weinblatt considered the idea. He struck the machine himself with the base of his fist. He held the handwand low over the chip. He pressed the trigger.

"NO ID FOUND."

It is not for nothing that the license plate on Weinblatt's Lincoln reads "Emuna." The Hebrew word, by his translation, means "keep the faith."

THE CULTURE OF

THE SECOND GUESS

What It All Means and Should Anyone Care?

INVADED!

You had to live—did live, from habit that became instinct—
in the assumption that every sound you made was overheard,
and, except in darkness, every movement scrutinized.

—George Orwell, *1984,*
1949

As the marketers plunge ahead with more creative and widely inter-meshed efforts to capture our secrets, the rest of us find ourselves in the position of feeling that something about their pursuit is not quite right yet not being able to express our concerns without seeming, well, silly. On first glance the consumer intelligence system looks utterly mundane, generating only letters and phone calls. You don't want any, no problem. Throw them out or hang up.

Why then does all this probing and snooping give so many of us the creeps?

Journalists wrestle with the same question, although as a rule we do not handle it very well. Most of us simply drop the word *privacy* somewhere in the first three paragraphs of the story and quickly conjure one of the privacy gladiators who, as a result of our attentions, are fast becoming the new celebrities of the information age. We can always count them for a few scary thoughts, which we jot down with a collective sigh of relief. If the advocates are not available for interviews— if they have gone home to count the number of times they were quoted that week; if they have been so inflated by calls from *The Wall Street Journal* and *The New York Times* that they will not stoop to return calls to the *Podunk Daily Orange*—there is always the Orwell option. All we need do is slip in a reference to George Orwell, Big Brother, or *1984,* and we fulfill the minimum professional requirement of tossing to the masses a little perspective. Once done with the "nut graf," as I was taught to call it, we proceed with our stories.

To conjure a generic, one-paragraph notion of privacy, however, is to underestimate the power of the marketing surveillance technologies to cause a wide range of changes in our daily culture: to annoy us, disrupt our thoughts, break our hearts, erode the bounds of self, even, as I hope to show in the next chapter, to short-circuit the checks and balances of government.

Every afternoon after the kids have retired for their naps I tiptoe down the stairs past their rooms to check for the day's mail. It comes, typically, through the slot by my front door and spreads in an alluring fan of colors. I can see the mail from the last bend in the stairs, and each time, whatever the day, regardless of what mail came the day before, my heart pounds just a little bit harder. I doubt there is a man or woman alive who can pass a freshly delivered load of mail without taking a look.

These inherent powers of distraction give direct-marketers an advantage over advertisers peddling their wares through traditional media. They know that consumers will at least look at their mail, if only to cull it for the trash; that we will pick up our phones, if only to slam them down again. The intimacy of radio that so worried advertisers in the 1920s was nothing by comparison.

Attention alone does not make a sale, of course, but the techniques of mass surveillance now allow marketers to find our vulnerabilities more efficiently—to fashion messages we *cannot* ignore—and to use the disruptive powers of post and phone to make sure we receive them. Targeting has given them the power to worry us when we are not worried, to make us aware of our flaws when otherwise we might be content, to make us feel sorrow when moments before we felt only happiness.

One can argue, certainly, that advertisers have always had the power to alter our moods. We have all seen starving Third World babies staring out from clouds of flies in the charity ads of glossy magazines. Those AT&T commercials that let us eavesdrop on long-distance conversations always caused my wife's eyes to well with tears. The difference lies in what we expect from the various media. We expect to encounter voluminous advertising in our magazines and newspapers and have learned to ignore it. We anticipate the TV commercials that bombard us each evening: when the ads appear we head for the john, grab a beer, converse with our spouses, read our newspapers, tally our taxes, or simply skip to the nearest cable station for a quick hit of news or the latest Madonna striptease. If the mood is right, we make love.

When the phone rings, however, we stop whatever we are doing. First we stare, like deer caught in the lights of an onrushing car; then we rise.

Most of us have the luxury of walking leisurely to the telephone; those of us who leave our answering machines perpetually engaged must sprint to the phone in the three rings allotted, leaping kids, Tonka bulldozers, and our half-naked helpmates staring at us in disbelief as we pass overhead in a flesh-tone blur.

No matter how much junk mail and how many junk calls we receive, we keep going back to our boxes and phones. For some consumers—first-time mothers, pregnant women on bedrest, the elderly, the handicapped, the thousands of men and women incapacitated by AIDS—the phone and mailbox become still more compelling.

All too often there's a huckster on the line, and thanks to the miracle of mass surveillance he may know enough about you to cause a fundamental change in your mood. The question is, who gave him the right to know? "Granted, there are stores that sell products to short, fat people, but you don't want to get a catalog from them," said Mary Culnan, Georgetown University's privacy advocate. "Just because someone looked at your motor vehicle records and found out you're five feet two and weigh 250 pounds, does that give them the right to target you?"

Anyone who buys a new house, especially a first-time home buyer, can expect to encounter a common example of this psychoactive targeting. Buying a house is at best one of the most angst-ridden experiences a man or woman can endure, second only to open-heart surgery. The popular description of how you feel is "housing remorse." You wonder if you did the right thing. Can you really afford the house? What if the economy takes a dive and you lose your job? What if *you* take a dive and can't go back to work?

Housing remorse is no secret to the direct-marketers of America. Soon after you buy a house you *will* receive a flurry of letters pitching mortgage insurance (which you most likely don't need) and hinting broadly that death or at the very least dismemberment lurks just around the corner. My wife and I received a dozen such letters in 1990 after we bought our latest Baltimore house. My favorite came from Midland National Life Insurance Company of Sioux Falls, South Dakota (Midland provided the bold print; I provided the ellipses):

COULD THE MORTGAGE MONSTER TURN YOUR AMERICAN DREAM INTO A NIGHTMARE?

This is a very exciting time in your life. . . . But it can also be a little frightening. After all, it's probably the largest investment you've made thus far, and there may be a monster in your contract. . . .

The monster, of course, was death or, more precisely, the havoc death tends to wreak on one's ability to make monthly payments. My wife and I were reasonably certain that our existing life and disability policies would protect us against such future mayhem. Nonetheless, each of these letters somehow managed to darken my day and shunt my thoughts to severed limbs, car wrecks, and the diffuse terror inherent in signing on for thirty years of payments totaling the cost of a small corporate jet.

Psychoactive junk mail affects moods and thoughts a lot more than one might think, mostly in minor ways but sometimes dramatically. Suppose you are overweight and not happy about it, and suddenly out of the blue you receive a catalog showing clothes for the "full-figured" woman or a letter pitching the latest wonder diet? Now suppose you are a man who is impotent. Worse, it's your fortieth birthday, a day freighted with angst and regret regardless of your circumstances. Seeded among the real birthday cards is that fortieth birthday greeting telling you all about the sexual dysfunctions that await you in years ahead.

One privacy researcher told me he spent months intercepting the mail delivered to his home so that his wife, who had just endured a miscarriage, would not see all the baby-oriented offers cramming their mailbox. In August 1990 Heloise, the helpful hints czar at *Good Housekeeping* magazine, asked readers to tell her about the misleading ads they received in the mail. Their responses described more than mere deception. Heloise wrote: "Your letters poured in, and I can report that *the heartbreak—the sadness, shattered feelings, family rifts, grief, doubt, and devastation—caused by the ads is beyond imagination.*" The emphasis was hers.

I called Heloise—that's her legal name, by the way—and she told me she received as many as ten thousand letters, most of them the same format: a clipping of a full-page newspaper advertisement describing antiaging tablets and creams and diet pills with an apparently handwritten suggestion that the recipient give the stuff a try. A single initial served as the sender's signature.

One ad, for an antiaging cream made by NDI Inc. of Chatsworth, California, showed "before" and "after" photographs of the faces of two women, one obviously old, the other young and smooth. (The caption never actually says the photographs depict the same woman, but their side-by-side position on the page certainly is intended to convey that impression.) A note scrawled in blue at the top reads:

Jeanette—
Order it. It's Great.
J.

In many other variations of the same approach, the personal note is written on one of those little yellow Post-it notes and stuck to the newspaper advertisement. A letter from Vita Industries Inc., Sparks, Nevada, peddling Gero-Vital antiaging pills (from a "famous Romanian clinic used by movie stars!") had this note attached:

Kathy—
Try it. This works.
R.

Thousands of elderly and overweight Americans received these letters; thousands believed the letters were sent by friends or family and felt crushed that their age or weight had advanced to the point where people would send them such oblique advice. Some wept. Some grew depressed. Some ordered the products—only to receive a subsequent torrent of sucker-seeking mail. Many broke off relationships with the people they suspected of mailing the notes. For one recently divorced woman, according to a published report, a note like this was the last straw; convinced it had been sent by her ex-husband's new wife, she killed them both.

The recipients realized the letters were junk only when they read Heloise's column. Interestingly, many had saved the letters for a year or more.

"I will have to admit," Heloise told me, "it's a damn smart marketing ploy."

Isolated heartbreak still does not constitute a national crisis, at least not on a par, say, with the killing of children by urban gunfire. Indeed, a poll conducted in 1991 by Louis Harris & Co. for Equifax found that a majority of Americans saw direct marketing as "primarily a nuisance." Why worry so much about a mere national nuisance?

Junk mail and junk calls are only superficial manifestations of the most troubling aspect of mass surveillance—the fact of the surveillance itself. The surreptitious collection and coalescence of personal information constitutes nothing less than an assault on human dignity and the sanctity of self. If mass surveillance gives us the creeps, it is because the techniques intrude on ground we know to be sacred.

"At an instinctive level," Alan Westin wrote in his introduction to an earlier, 1990 Harris-Equifax survey, "many consumers feel that for a commercial entity to collect names, addresses, and consumer characteristics and store it in a computer data base, without the consumer's knowledge or agreement, appropriates some uniqueness from the consumer. It's a modern counterpart of the tribal native's belief that being photographed by the anthropologist captures and transfers some of the individual's essence to the photo taker and could be used to manipulate him."

You can never predict who among your daily acquaintances will become a fast and loyal friend, nor can you predict whether the introductions you arrange for others will lead to love or warfare. You can, however, measure the strength of your own existing relationships. You do so on a subconscious level every time an important event occurs in your life. That is, you figure out whom to tell first. To measure a social bond, you count the depth and quantity of secrets the bond enables you to disclose. Our personal secrets are the control rods that slow or hasten the social reactor.

To test this, go through your address book and draw a little house next to the names of everyone to whom you have disclosed the purchase price of your home. (Does your boss know? Your nanny? Your impoverished brother? Your millionaire sister? That competitive friend who's beat you at everything since the math test in sixth grade?) Next, draw a baby carriage (or, if you prefer, a dollar sign) next to the names of every friend you would call the moment you discovered that you or your wife was pregnant. Now draw a court gavel next to every friend to whom you would confess that you had just been stopped for drunk driving. Finally, draw the symbol of your choice opposite the name of everyone who knows what kind of birth control device you use.

"The makers of the Constitution undertook to secure conditions favorable to the pursuit of happiness," Louis Brandeis wrote in 1928. "They recognized the significance of man's spiritual nature, of his feeling and of his intellect. . . . They sought to protect Americans in their beliefs, their thoughts, their emotions, and their sensations." Brandeis called the right of privacy the right to an "inviolate personality."

In 1964 Edward J. Bloustein, a law professor at New York University, analyzed Brandeis's views on privacy in an influential article published in the *New York University Law Review.* Bloustein wrote: "I take the principle of 'inviolate personality' to posit the individual's independence, dignity, and integrity; it defines man's essence as a unique and self-determining being."

Control over one's "personal isolation" and the ability to limit unwarranted intrusion is central to Western man's definition of freedom and dignity, Bloustein argued. He wrote: "A man whose home may be entered at the will of another, whose conversation may be overheard at the will of another, whose marital and familial intimacies may be overseen at the will of another, is less of a man, has less human dignity, on that account. He who may intrude upon another at will is the master of the other, and, in fact, intrusion is a primary weapon of the tyrant."

In 1967 Alan Westin fashioned an often cited definition of privacy that later became the core concept of the Privacy Act of 1974, which sought to regulate the handling of personal information by government agencies. The right to privacy, Westin argued, is "the claim of individuals, groups, or institutions to determine for themselves when, how, and to what extent information about them is communicated to others." When Vincent Barabba, director of marketing at General Motors, was still director of the Census Bureau, he defined privacy as "the right of the individual, to the extent possible, to control what information about himself he releases, to whom he releases it, and under what conditions."

By that standard, the 1990 Harris-Equifax poll indicates, our right to privacy has been trampled. Seventy-one percent of American adults— about 130 million people—agreed that "consumers have lost all control over how personal information about them is circulated and used by companies."

Harris presented the same statement to the executives of the privacy-intensive industries. Their answers do little to restore confidence in the sanctity of private records. Of the direct-marketers, over half agreed that consumers had indeed lost all control over their information. Of the credit grantors, 40 percent felt likewise.

The poll, moreover, found disconcertingly low levels of trust among executives for the information-handling practices of their own industries. The executives were asked to rank their degree of trust from one to ten, with one meaning "you do not trust them at all."

Among direct-marketers, 28 percent said they had little trust that direct-mail and telemarketing companies would collect and use personal information about them "in a responsible way." Most enlightening— and a bit unsettling—was that 73 percent of credit executives, presumably aware of the coalescence of credit and marketing information, likewise said they had little trust for the way their direct-marketing brethren handled personal information.

What would Brandeis have to say about today's obsession with collecting and merging masses of personal records about tens of millions of Americans at a time?

The fact is, the technologies and techniques of mass surveillance allow companies to learn details we never would have told them if asked directly—details, even, that the law in other contexts prohibits companies from collecting, such as information on race, age, religion, and sexual orientation. The technology gives companies unprecedented power to muscle in on the "sacred" corners of our lives, those personal events we treasure as ours alone, and to transform them into commodities for subsequent sale, rent, or barter, a process consumer theorists call "commoditization."

American Baby applauds every conception. First Foto invites itself to every birth. Metromail leaps to the fore to toast every marriage, graduation, and new driver's license. I can be impressed that American Baby managed to send a first-birthday greeting, the Trojan teddy, to my home, but that doesn't alter my feeling that my kid's birthday was none of the magazine's business and that its superheated commercial interest cheapened the experience.

All this snooping is taking its toll.

National surveys suggest that a kind of creeping paranoia has begun to color our daily interactions with corporations and with each other. The most striking evidence came, again, from the 1990 Harris-Equifax survey. By 1990 concern had risen to the point where 79 percent of Americans said they were "somewhat" or "very concerned" about threats to their personal privacy, up from 64 percent in 1978.

This concern was refreshingly bipartisan, with conservatives, middle-of-the-roaders, and liberals all expressing about the same amount of angst. Blacks were more concerned than whites, however, with 64 percent choosing the highest level of concern compared with 43 percent of whites. Even executives in the privacy-intensive industries were concerned about their own privacy, with 66 percent of direct-marketers and 56 percent of credit executives expressing moderate to high levels of concern.

Moreover, a 1991 follow-up study by Harris found that America's privacy angst increased in the span of a single year. Harris found that the percentage of the public who were "very" concerned increased to 48 percent in 1991 from 46 percent in 1990. If the increase is real and not some statistical abnormality, that two-point change represents an increase of 3.7 million American adults. The most recent report also combined the answers to a series of questions asked in both surveys to build a "Consumer Privacy Concern Index," a kind of paranoia barometer. Over the year this index rose to 46 percent from 41.

The most troubling revelation in the Harris-Equifax surveys was that executives and ordinary folk alike had begun to change their behavior out of concern for how their personal information might be used. The bodies, in short, had begun piling up.

The 1990 survey found, for example, a startling increase in the percentage of Americans who answered yes when asked, "Have you ever decided *not* to apply for something, like a job, credit, or insurance, because you did not want to provide certain kinds of information about yourself?" In 1990 30 percent (representing roughly 55 million adults) said yes, compared with only 14 percent in 1978.

Here again the responses of the executives of the privacy-intensive industries deserve special note. Twenty-eight percent of direct-marketing executives said they too had decided against applying for something to avoid providing the required information; 67 percent said they had refused to provide personal information requested by a business. Of the credit executives, 23 percent said they had not applied for something; 59 percent had refused requests for information.

At first glance these findings may not seem terribly worrisome. After all, they describe only subtle changes in behavior. What is significant here, however, is not the behavior being modified, but the scale: the fact that tens of millions of us have begun altering our behavior in response to the increasing abilities of companies and government to collect and use our personal information. The results are quantitive evidence that our society is substantially more guarded in 1990 than it was just a decade before.

Companies already have begun to experience a backlash from their snooping. For business 1991 became the year of living cautiously. Lotus withdrew Lotus Marketplace. Equifax, ostensibly as a result of its surveys and a series of "privacy audits" by Alan Westin, ended its practice of using credit data to help direct-marketers build mailing lists. TRW confronted the attorneys general of nineteen states. The credit gladiators got more famous, talking and testifying a blue streak as Congress held repeated hearings on mailing lists, telemarketing, and credit-reporting practices. Congress considered fourteen telemarketing bills in 1991; it enacted one that banned junk faxes and the use of automatic dialing machines by telemarketers and authorized the Federal Communications Commission to keep a list of all consumers who did not want to be called. Moreover, the law allowed anyone on that list to recoup up to $1,500 in court from any marketer who dared call more than once in a twelve-month period.

Privacy had even become a material concern for hard-nosed investors. The 1991 prospectus for Advanced Promotion Technologies, the Florida company that uses a smart-card in its "Vision" frequent shopper program, warned: "There can be no assurance that consumer privacy concerns will not affect consumer acceptance of the Vision System or otherwise have a material adverse effect on the company."

What about the future? The consumer marketers have installed the most sophisticated mass intelligence system in history. Despite its banal current uses, it constitutes the infrastructure of invasion, ready to disrupt the lives of millions of Americans but restrained from doing so only by a reasonably benign political climate, the absence of an overwhelming national enemy, and the good judgment of the system's corporate masters. But technology, as Jacques Ellul, the French technophilosopher, argued in *The Technological Society,* advances along a path of its own choosing, exhausting every conceivable application along the way until restrained by law or obsolescence. By Ellul's reasoning the infrastructure of invasion *will* be used one day to cause vast harm across the land. "History," he wrote, "shows that every technical application from its beginnings presents certain unforeseeable secondary effects which are much more disastrous than the lack of the technique would have been."

The marketers ask us to trust that they will use the information they collect only in morally judicious ways (and to ignore, of course, the fact that much of the information was in the first place collected secretly or by deception). The problem with their assurances is that control over the migration of the information amassed remains in the hands of a few corporate executives and that no external body can reject or approve their decisions. Indeed, control is becoming more concentrated as large data companies, like Dun & Bradstreet, acquire smaller ones. Moreover, the marketers' assurances underestimate the irresistible demand of all data *to be used*, with such use governed by my four laws of data dynamics—that data must merge with complementary data; will be used for purposes other than originally planned; eventually will cause harm to one or more of the group that supplied it; and remains confidential only until someone decides it's not.

These laws become particularly ominous when considered against another trend of our information-obsessed age: the blurring of boundaries between government and private data banks. The migration of personal information to and from government data banks has become routine, in some cases even mandated by law.

The Debt Collection Act of 1982, designed to help the federal government track down citizens who default on nontax debts to the government (such enemies of the state as students who don't pay back their federally guaranteed college loans), allowed agencies to pass along the names and addresses of deadbeats to private credit-reporting bureaus and debt collection companies and even to supply those companies with addresses pulled directly from IRS files. Every month federal agencies supply the largest credit bureaus, including TRW and Equifax, with computer tapes listing the names of delinquent debtors; the bureaus then match the names against their own files. The Office of Management and Budget gleefully projected that the new system would yield $500 million the government might otherwise fail to collect. As of September 1991, however, collections under the act had recouped only about $90 million; another $45 *billion* in delinquent nontax debt remained outstanding.

States use credit data to track down deadbeat parents. The Nebraska Child Support Enforcement Unit, a member of the Federal Parent Locator network, routinely runs the names of parents, usually fathers, against credit records held by TRW and Trans Union. The agency needs a court order to get a look at the full credit file of an AP (that's "absent parent" in parent-trap jargon) but need only punch the keys of an on-line terminal to get each suspect's "header" file containing name, last known address, age, and Social Security number. The header file alone, while skimpy, is a valuable investigative tool. Investigators typically retrieve a man's header file when they believe he may have sired a child out of wedlock and need to find him in order to conduct a paternity screen. The Nebraska Child Support Enforcement Unit has eight credit-reporting machines deployed throughout the state. Byron Van Patten, unit manager, told me that in 1991 his operation retrieved up to eight hundred records a month, most from TRW.

A 1990 General Accounting Office survey of how federal agencies collect, use, and protect personal data found that for 75 record systems, or roughly 8 percent of the 910 surveyed, the agencies in charge did not know the purposes for which outside parties had accessed their records. For 42 of these systems, the outside parties gaining this unacknowledged access were private organizations.

It's unfair, of course, to look into the future and see only dark doings, still less fair to cite the past in doing so. The bad old days are behind us; we have entered the age of electronic enlightenment.

Yes, but: Who would have thought that in 1991, just nine years from the millennium, an ex-Klansman would run for governor and, worse, be taken seriously; that the U.S. Supreme Court would uphold a federal law prohibiting doctors at federally funded clinics from even mentioning abortion as a choice for women confronting an unwanted pregnancy; that the governor of Rhode Island would release the names of 994 bank customers—all citizens who had deposited $100,000 or more in a group of failed credit unions—arguing the "public interest in the information outweighed any privacy concerns"; that gays in the so-called outing movement would begin forcing their peers out of the closet through uninvited disclosure?

Margaret Atwood, in *The Handmaid's Tale*, sketched with chilling understatement how the electronic networks that make shopping and banking so easy could be turned overnight into tools of oppression simply by eliminating the access of select groups of consumers to routine consumption channels. In the book, a shadowy fundamentalist government takes over an America that has grown dependent on a single card to conduct most of its daily business, the "Compucard," a debit card capable of deducting purchases directly from one's bank account. The new rulers simply voided all cards coded with an F, for female, instantly disenfranchising half the population.

"All they needed to do [was] push a few buttons," one woman tells the book's main character, also a woman. "We're cut off."

The narrator protests that she still has $2,000 in the bank.

"Women can't hold property anymore," her friend counters. "It's a new law."

For another exercise, imagine the consumer data bases put to use in other times, other places, by less trustworthy souls. How much simpler would it have been for the Western Defense Command to round up Japanese-Americans if it could have acquired a list of every consumer with a Japanese last name living along the West Coast? The FBI could have gone a step further and subpoenaed a list of every Waldenbooks "preferred reader" who displayed an inordinate interest in books on sake, warfare, and obscure Pacific atolls. Think what mischief Joe McCarthy could have made just by the act of matching his enemies list against the records, say, of TRW, thereby injecting the taint of communism into its data banks for all credit-grantors to see. For that matter, think what Hitler could have done with a list of Jewish households like that compiled by AB Data of Milwaukee.

Extreme thoughts, of course.

For a less extreme exercise, however, consider how the consumer intelligence network could be put to work today. What might health insurers do with the subscription lists of such gay publications as *The Advocate* and the *New York Native*? For that matter, what might the "outing" movement do with such a list in finding still closeted gays? What mischief might the right-to-life lobby work with a list of pregnant teenage girls?

Lists can do harm all by themselves, and occasionally the urge to use them for such becomes simply too overwhelming. Just ask the august journalists of the *Dartmouth Review* who in 1981 published a list of members of Dartmouth's Gay Students Association. In the public interest, of course.

■ ■ ■

George Orwell recognized that although surveillance alone caused harm, what made it even worse was the uncertainty about just how much the watchers knew. "There was of course no way of knowing whether you were being watched at any given moment," he wrote. "How often, or on what system, the Thought Police plugged in on any individual wire was guesswork. It was even conceivable that they watched everybody all the time." The solution, he wrote, was to live life as if "they" were watching at all times.

Clearly no one is watching us at all times, and today's data bases, at least for now, pose no *direct* threat to our daily freedom of movement and speech. Once we know how the mass surveillance network functions— once we notice and understand how and where our secrets migrate—the network becomes much less a threat and more an intriguing and at times amusing installment in the continuing quest of the marketers to understand us.

The privacy debate, however, masks another class of effects that may prove far more damaging to the vibrance of our daily culture. The high-snoop pursuit of the American consumer has produced what I— succumbing now to every writer's need to devise cosmic labels—will call the Culture of the Second Guess.

THE CULTURE OF
THE SECOND GUESS

To be unaware that a technology comes equipped with a program for social change, to maintain that technology is neutral, to make the assumption that technology is always a friend to culture, is, at this late hour, stupidity plain and simple.

—Neil Postman,
Amusing Ourselves to Death, 1985

Technique, as Jacques Ellul observed, "tends to be applied *everywhere* it *can* be applied." And indeed, the techniques of mass surveillance have migrated well beyond the consumer products arena. The effect of this migration, however, has been to blunt creativity and imagination in an ever-expanding range of pursuits, from the creation of our TV shows to the governing of the nation.

The technology is not to blame. The root of the problem lies in man's willingness to subjugate human judgment and vision to the rule of surveys, ratings, and other disembodied measurements. The crimping of the national imagination began when marketers first made the mistake of seeing consumers as natural phenomena whose shopping behavior one day could be reduced to a series of immutable laws and equations. The technology merely automated and accelerated the trend. The trouble is, these tools of the Second Guess, far from anticipating future needs, assume that time has frozen. They measure the opinions and behaviors of consumers grounded firmly in the here and now and capable of expressing their wants only in terms of known and familiar phenomena. Ask a consumer if he likes the latest Pillsbury frozen pizza and he is likely to say yes; ask him what he'd like Pillsbury to make in the future and he'll draw a blank. No consumer could have imagined a microwave oven, let alone told a surveyor he would like such a machine, until after that fateful day in 1945 when a Raytheon engineer noticed that a laboratory radar system had melted the candy bar in his pocket. Until air bags were invented, who among us could have looked Lee Iacocca in the eye and said, "Lee, you know what I'd really like in my next LeBaron? I'd like a big balloon to inflate at the instant my car crashed. That'd be neat."

The oldest and most obvious demonstration of the unhappy consequences arising from the migration of mass surveillance technology occurred in television, where the networks transformed ratings from a simple measure of audience size into a powerful arbiter of creative content and taste. The tools of the Second Guess have since migrated to the movie industry, where a director's creative genius increasingly takes a backseat to the collective opinion of movie viewers intercepted at malls and invited to attend special screenings of rough-cut films. Preview audiences now turn dials to express delight or dissatisfaction with each portion of a movie, producing a collective Richter-like graph that can be superimposed over the film to highlight the dead spots. But testing, warned Steve Martin, who showed his film *Roxanne* to preview audiences to see how well the jokes worked, "can reduce movies to a formula, where you eliminate any judgment and appeal to the lowest common denominator. The danger, as with any medicine, is that an overdose could be poisonous."

In the Culture of the Second Guess, editors too allow numbers to stand in for intuition and judgment. Most of America's most heavily read magazines, including *Vogue, GQ, Self, McCall's,* and *Glamour,* submit every issue they publish to ratings panels recruited by Mark Clements of Mark Clements Research, New York. Clements ships copies of each magazine to as many as 250 subscribers at a time—a different panel *every* month for *each* issue of *each* magazine—asking them to rate cover photographs, headlines, articles, columns, and inside photographs. Clements reports his findings in the form of an issue encrusted with computer-generated stickers giving the scores of each component. Given such slavish attention to the mass will, can it be purely an accident that we know more about the life of President Bush's dog than about the life of the second-highest ranking official of the U.S. government?

Record companies ship tapes containing dozens of unreleased songs to sample panels of music lovers, who then pick which ones ought to grace the musician's next record. The National Geographic Society's book division routinely ships off *ideas* for books to readers and asks whether they would buy such volumes if published. Even attorneys have adapted the tools of the Second Guess: for big-ticket cases they now hire market research firms, such as Strategy Research Corporation of Miami, to help them figure out what arguments will play best in court and what kinds of jurors will be most receptive.

In the Culture of the Second Guess, no one escapes the rating process. Even individuals are rated. The credit bureaus rank us all by the probability we will go bankrupt. Anyone with a high national profile will find himself assigned a numerical "Q" rating, calculated by Marketing Evaluations/TV Q of Long Island, which rates such commodities as actors, authors, TV newscasters, and cartoon characters. In 1984 California State senator Art Torres sponsored an unsuccessful bill to ban the use of Qs in casting decisions, calling the ratings a "tyrannical, discriminatory, and totally unfair employment tool."

Nowhere, however, have the tools of the Second Guess been embraced more wholeheartedly and with greater and more troubling impact than in the American political process. Once upon a time—and we may be talking ancient history here—a candidate ran for office because he had something he wanted to accomplish. Opposing candidates fought it out with brains and wit, crafting articulate arguments that they delivered in the course of true debates meant to persuade voters as well as to demonstrate their own mental agility. Before television came along, Neil Postman observed in *Amusing Ourselves to Death*, candidates were made of sterner stuff. They spoke for hours at a time, and not just in short phrases tailored to the needs of TV broadcasters, but in long, syntactically opulent sentences that would lull any contemporary audience into an irreversible coma.

Television drove the shift to today's image politics and remains the most powerful factor in any major campaign, but in the 1980s candidates again followed the marketers' lead and began experimenting with the techniques of mass surveillance and the targeting they allowed. Now targeting companies compete with image spinners for the campaign dollar, promising to give candidates the power to tell voters exactly what they want to hear. What they promise in the long run, however, is an end to public political discourse. In the politics of the Second Guess, passion and conviction have been eliminated.

The target is the message.

In the vanguard of the new generation of political targeters is John Aristotle Phillips, president and co-founder of Aristotle Industries Inc., Washington, D.C. His offices occupy the top floors of a town house on Pennsylvania Avenue on the cheap rent side of the Washington Mall. A bleak and battered staircase took me to the reception desk on the second floor. From there on up the place looked like the campaign office of some progressive candidate, buzzing with lean, earnest, and attractive young people. It was the McGovern campaign updated, with bell-bottoms traded in for black tights.

Phillips, a man of medium height with full dark hair and preppy glasses, sat at his desk in the topmost room, a kind of cupola with windows on three sides and barely large enough for his oblong desk. He had a clear view of the Capitol dome glowing like pale blue ice against the night sky.

His name had sounded familiar to me from the moment I first heard it, but I could not remember why until he tipped his chair, propped his feet on his desk, and launched into a quick autobiography. He was no stranger to target-related projects: "As an undergraduate," he began, "I designed an atomic bomb."

Ah, *that* John Phillips. Using public documents, he had designed a cheap, feasible thermonuclear device compelling enough to draw the attention of two foreign governments. He later ran for Congress twice, losing both times but learning enough about campaigns and personal computers to develop, with his brother Dean, a software package called Campaign Manager. They founded Aristotle in 1983.

Aristotle's newest product was a collection of compact discs containing the names, addresses, and voting records of 118 million of the nation's 128 million registered voters. The company gets the records, typically on magnetic tape, from 3,400 electoral agencies, then runs the tapes against its existing data base to update records and eliminate duplications. Aristotle ships the list to Donnelly Marketing, which adds census geography, phone numbers, and other information. (R. L. Polk and Metromail provide additional phone numbers.) In the process,

Aristotle has transformed a lowly, widely dispersed body of public information into a concentrated, easy-to-use political weapon, something state election authorities could not have envisioned when they fashioned their electoral disclosure laws. "The point is," Phillips told me, "it's accessible for the first time."

Buyers can search Aristotle CDs by any kind of information, be it age, address, phone number, sex, party affiliation, precinct, whatever, thus allowing candidates and fund-raisers pinpoint precision from a personal computer literally at the touch of a few keys—the same portable capability that caused the privacy revolt against Lotus Marketplace, the CD-housed data base produced by Lotus Development and Equifax.

For a demonstration, Phillips led me downstairs to a rough-edged little room furnished with a table, an ordinary personal computer, cardboard boxes, and miscellaneous debris. Phillips flashed a Robert Kennedy smile. "You're gonna love these CDs," he said.

The CDs give politicians wholly new intelligence-gathering powers. Often, Phillips told me, politicians receive mail from voters with illegible names or return addresses. Using the CD, an official can type in the readable details to retrieve the rest of the writer's file and, perhaps most important, figure out how much his opinion matters—that is, whether or not he is a registered, active voter and a member of the candidate's party. The CDs can also serve as petition busters, giving politicians a quick way to check the voter status of people who sign opposing petitions.

Moreover, the CDs provide elected officials an unprecedented opportunity to conduct quick, "snapshot" polls of neighborhoods, even individual streets or blocks, to monitor reactions to such local events as zoning changes, dam construction, and placement of homeless shelters. They also give politicians the power to respond immediately by mail (or phone) to political attacks or to such awkward events as indictments, lawsuits, and self-granted pay hikes—and to do so cheaply by arranging mailings to take advantage of the same postal delivery discounts afforded direct marketers.

With Aristotle's CDs, elected officials can step up the levels of intimacy in their districts. Birthday cards have always been a staple of constituent relations, with officials mailing a few cards to the oldest people in their districts. "But now," Phillips said, "you can mail 250,000 cards!"

Phillips slipped in a CD emblazoned with a Chesapeake crab, Maryland's best-known product. (The Texas CD features a cactus, Ohio's a silhouette of grain.)

"What street do you live on?" Phillips asked.

I told him; he punched it in. A number appeared in the far right corner. "There are 268 registered voters on your street," he said.

He typed my house number. The file came up immediately, with one little flaw: according to the disc, my house was still occupied by the previous owner.

Where was I?

Phillips typed in my name. The address of my previous Baltimore house appeared, the one I had sold almost three years before. There I was. Still.

My outdated records demonstrated two problems that confront the managers of any automated surveillance technology. First, in our mobile society information ages quickly and must be updated continually. Second, the computer by its nature masks error, conferring the illusion of accuracy on anything that appears on its screen. No political staffer using the Maryland CD would have any reason to suspect that I had moved from that address or that in the meantime I had moved to California and returned to live at yet another Baltimore address.

Phillips inserted another CD, named Fat Cats, a data base of everyone in the country listed in Federal Election Commission files as a contributor to a federal campaign. First he typed in my zip code. This time the number 135 appeared, meaning that 135 of my neighbors had contributed to one or more federal campaigns. I saw that one neighbor contributed $6,800 to various campaigns in the 1989–90 electoral "cycle"; she listed her occupation as "Homemaker."

Phillips and I began joyriding through the data base, searching specific individuals in hopes of discovering their political orientations and their willingness to throw money around. I checked the names of some of my past editors; tight-fisted by nature, none had contributed any money. I checked the names of friends—no luck there, either. We fifties boomers were a stingy bunch.

On a whim I typed the name of one of Maryland's more famous writers, Tom Clancy, author of *The Hunt for Red October* and other raging best-sellers.

The hunt for Tom Clancy took a couple of moments. We couldn't find him by name alone; ultimately we tracked him down by searching the data base by occupational category, in his case "Author." When his name surfaced, we gave a little cheer.

On September 5, 1990, Clancy contributed $1,000 to the "Sullivan for Congress" campaign. A month later, on October 6, he contributed $1,000 to the Committee to Elect "Duke" Cunningham. I tried to call him to give him an opportunity to share our delight, but a recording told me his was an unlisted number. It is an irony of this information age that I could learn intimate details of Clancy's politics, but not his phone number.

Phillips's magazine, *Campaign*, makes shameless use of the data base. In November 1991 the magazine used Fat Cats to reveal political contributions made by dozens of actors, writers, athletes, and other celebrities, including Frank Zappa, who contributed $800 to a congressional campaign in California, and Bob Hope, who paid $4,000 to various Republican forces, including Jesse Helms of North Carolina. The magazine also ran a list of deep-pocket private donors, revealing simultaneously that about sixty of them had exceeded the $25,000 federal limit on aggregate contributions from individuals. A San Diego couple, Stephen and Susan Schutz, had contributed $129,000 to Democratic organizations, $80,000 of it to the Democratic Senatorial Campaign Committee. They had not known of the cap, Mrs. Schutz told the magazine; moreover, none of the organizations they gave money to had seen fit to mention such a limit. "We didn't even know these contributions were a matter of public record," she said. "If we had, we might not have made them."

Phillips and I searched for a few more names on Fat Cats. I felt just a tad wicked. I was Merlin observing my neighbors through a digital crystal ball. This was fun; I wanted to stay for hours. Phillips, however, was already late for a dinner engagement.

"You're welcome to come back and play with this anytime you like," he said.

Targeting is useful only if there is something you'd like delivered to the target, be it diapers or election fliers. To figure out what to say to targeted voters, today's politicians certainly don't do anything so antique as turning to their own deep-set convictions and passions. They turn to the polls.

Polls have done to the electoral process what ratings did to television.

In shifting the emphasis from content to market, polls and targeting have deadened the political process while at the same time creating a feedback loop that has begun to shape the decisions and policies of the White House. As the tools of mass surveillance evolve toward "real-time" surveillance, the deadening effect will accelerate to produce a government run by national mood, not national need: government of the polls, by the polls, for the polls.

Every major campaign hires a pollster, who typically begins his work with a "benchmark" poll designed to learn what voters would most like to hear. Sophisticated pollsters may use so-called split samples to test differing descriptions of the candidate to see which sells best. The wealthiest campaigns try to gather as many responses as they can from important demographic segments in order to judge how the same message can be tailored to appeal to each. As the season progresses, pollsters conduct "tactical" polls to gauge how well voters have accepted the message, what attacks to use against their opponents, and whether or not the campaign is gaining ground.

These messages, in turn, get fed back to voters through direct mail and telephone calls using voter lists like those sold by Aristotle Industries. This kind of targeting, by its ability to aim specific messages directly into the homes of likely voters without context or rebuttal, challenges the principles of open political debate on which the American brand of democracy was founded.

The classic example of how targeting can skirt public debate and change the expected outcome of a vote occurred in 1978 in Missouri, when the United Labor Committee of Missouri, a coalition of major unions, set out to defeat a state antilabor referendum and hired the Matt Reese Organization (later absorbed into a Virginia target-marketing company called RTC Group) to orchestrate the battle. Reese, in turn, hired Hamilton & Staff, a Chevy Chase polling firm, to figure out who supported the measure, who didn't, and how both groups differed. He also contracted with Jonathan Robbin, founder of Claritas Corp., to use Robbin's PRIZM clustering system for targeting.

Hamilton conducted a large initial poll in February of 1978 that found that the Missouri electorate as a whole favored passage of the measure by a 60–40 margin. Things did not look good for organized labor. In late August, however, Matt Reese called Hamilton back. Using PRIZM clusters as a guide, Hamilton & Staff conducted 1,400 poll interviews to figure out how each cluster felt about the right-to-work measure. "There were ten or twelve clusters that we wished we could have moved out of the state of Missouri," Hamilton recalled. "They were never going to vote for us. And there were ten or twelve that we knew we just had to turn out. And there were five, six, seven, maybe eight in the middle that could go either way."

Conventional strategy might have called for a TV blitz to get opponents of the measure to step forward, but TV posed a danger. "If you ran the traditional mass media campaign where 65 or 70 percent of your money was in television, you were going to excite just as many of the people who were against you, because they watched it the same as the people who might be for you."

Instead the campaign turned to targeting. The campaign bombarded voters in the most favorable clusters with 536,000 phone calls and letters in eighteen different formats tailored to the different clusters. "You could have lived just one block away from me, and if I was in the target, I would have gotten six letters and four phone calls and you would have gotten nothing," Hamilton said. "You might not even have known a campaign was on."

The right-to-work measure was defeated 59–41, almost the exact inverse of the ratio Hamilton had found in the poll he conducted before the campaign began.

In the 1989–90 election cycle, Hamilton used similar techniques to construct a data base for Florida's Democratic party, containing the names and addresses of any voter who fit the profile of "ticket splitter"— that is, who might vote Republican in one race, Democrat in another. The result was a handy directory of potentially persuadable voters for use by Democrats throughout the state.

Targeting has become common enough now to be the stuff of how-to articles in political trade magazines. In an article in *Campaigns & Elections* magazine entitled "Precision Politics," David Beiler, president of a Washington political consulting firm called Democracy Inc., noted the increased political use of data bases kept by such giants as Metromail and R. L. Polk. "The tactical advantages resting in these databanks [are] astounding," he wrote. "They can direct your brochure on child care to parents of newborns, your paper on insecticides to home gardeners, your speech on moral decay to religious contributors, with each group further segmented to include only likely swing voters."

One piece of Beiler's advice captured the spirit of the new politics. "Afraid of sounding contradictory while being all things to all people?" Beiler wrote. "Employ a merge/purge to avoid embarrassing combinations of messages."

The tendency of politicians to deliver only what the polls command would be troubling enough, without the addition of another phenomenon of the Culture of the Second Guess: the media obsession with polls.

Polling by and for the media is nothing new. Newspapers began reporting electoral straw polls as early as 1824, and they weren't particularly picky about statistical formalities. The *Harrisburg Pennsylvanian* reported the number of toasts made to candidates in the upcoming presidential election. By the 1950s some two hundred newspapers routinely published the results of Gallup polls supplied to them by Gallup in the form of syndicated columns, which reporters were free to rewrite or quote from at will. As the costs of polling rose, broadcasters and newspapers began forming the polling combines we hear so much from today, such as the CBS/*New York Times* poll. In 1976, a presidential election year, the *Times* and CBS together or individually conducted twenty-eight polls; in 1984, also a presidential year, they more than doubled the number to sixty-eight.

What has changed over time is not merely the frequency of polls, but the speed of their delivery and the prominent role they play in daily news coverage. I was struck by this one morning in 1991, a week *after* election day, when I glanced at a copy of the *San Francisco Chronicle* and found three major poll stories in the first three pages, including the lead story on the front page. Because of this new emphasis, polls have attained an inordinate power to shape government policy. Any future archaeologist reading newspapers published in 1991 would be forced to conclude the White House functioned less like a center of wisdom and judgment, more like a player piano run by a continuously scrolling supply of public-opinion statistics. The polls, for example, ousted John Sununu from his job as chief of staff. Polls even caused the economy to switch from recovery to recession, at least in terms of White House rhetoric. Two sets of headlines appearing on November 18, 1991, on the front pages of *The New York Times* and the *Baltimore Sun* captured the extent to which the tools of the Second Guess had migrated to government.

Both attributed the change in rhetoric, respectively, to a "fall in ratings" and a "drop in ratings."

A common argument in favor of polls is that they inject the lowly voter more deeply into the process of government. "You can say that's good or bad," says pollster Hamilton. "In a democracy, at least, it's supposed to be good." He agrees, however, that polling limits the political imagination. "There is no doubt it's depressive of new ideas." It tends, too, he said, to cause politicians to ignore crucial, long-term issues that don't happen to be in the news at the moment—"the issues which if not solved today will blow you up ten years from now."

There is another problem with polls: their crisp, clean numbers beckon the unwary with a handy illusion of truth.

When newspapers report polls, they often warn that the results are subject to a sampling error of 3 or 4 percent. Such warnings produce an aura of "misleading precision," argues Mervin Field, an opinion researcher. Any pollster knows, he wrote, "that survey data contain the probability of a number of significant nonrandom errors, any of which could produce numerical variance many times larger" than the minuscule percentages included in the disclaimers would dictate. Alex C. Michalos, editor of the *Journal of Business Ethics*, estimated that the true error rate of most polls was probably twice the rate of sampling error—enough error, in short, to invalidate most "horse race" polls taken during closely contested campaigns.

Error can seep into a poll from anywhere. Just the order in which questions are asked can dramatically alter results. Question order, for example, is believed to have caused the *Times* and the *Hartford Courant* to report on the same day that Lowell Weicker was both the leader and the underdog, respectively, in the 1982 race to be U.S. senator from Connecticut. The *Times* had him leading by five points, the *Courant* trailing by sixteen, a twenty-one point difference.

The timing of a poll also can influence results, especially in volatile primary elections. In the New Hampshire primary of 1988, for example, Gallup closed its polling with the conclusion that Robert Dole had won with a 33 to 25 percent margin over George Bush. In fact, Bush won the primary, and by over nine points. Gallup sent an apology to its media clients. The memo, cited in *Campaigns & Elections* magazine, explained that Gallup had failed to take into account the softness of Dole's support and to put "enough emphasis on the fact that in primary elections voter sentiment can change literally overnight."

Still more subtle factors can bedevil pollsters. Two researchers from the University of Michigan Institute for Social Research conducted a study to see what effect open or closed questions had on survey results. An open question invites the respondent to come up with his own answer, a closed question directs him to pick from a menu of choices. The researchers asked people to name "the most important problem facing this country today." They allowed half the respondents to name whatever problem they wished but gave the other half a choice: Choose from a list of four obscure problems (found in a previous survey to be of little concern to anyone), or name a problem not on the list. Sixty percent of this last group chose one of the four listed problems. Only 3 percent of the first group spontaneously mentioned any of them.

Even an interviewer's voice can markedly affect response rates. Three more researchers from Michigan's institute set out to explore a mystery known by every professional pollster—that some interviewers consistently draw higher response rates than others. The institute's own interviewers, for example, had constant rates of refusal that ranged from a low of 6 percent for the best interviewer to 42 percent for the worst. The researchers discovered that people who consistently drew the best response rates had "higher-pitched voices, greater ranges of variation in pitch, greater loudness, faster rates of speaking, and clearer and more distinct pronunciations." The best interviewers were also those perceived through voice alone to be more attractive and of higher social status.

A more fundamental question must be asked of polls: What do they measure—informed opinion or merely top-of-mind reactions that might change with a little more information or a little more time for thought? As Jack Germond, the veteran political writer, once observed: "One of the things that both pollsters and newspaper reporters quickly discover is that most people don't know a great deal about what is going on—and that their opinions might be quite different if they did."

Often people respond to questions simply to please the interviewer or to avoid seeming uninformed, even though they know nothing of the issues at hand. Three researchers, funded by Procter & Gamble, captured this phenomenon when they asked people for opinions about several fictitious legislative bills, including "the monetary control bill." The researchers gave one group of respondents an explicit opportunity to say they didn't have an opinion. Even so, 14.3 percent took a stand on the monetary control bill anyway. A second group wasn't given as easy an out; 54.7 percent expressed an opinion on the fake proposition.

A Roper poll on polls captured some of the most convincing evidence that polls do not measure any great reservoir of knowledge. In response to one question, 56 percent of the people surveyed said "it's not possible" to capture the views of the nation accurately using the small samples pollsters typically use. In response to another question in the same survey, however, 56 percent—the same percentage—said polls are "usually" or "almost always" accurate.

Polls are destined to become more flawed. Increasing competition, rising costs, and the inherent drive of any technology to exhaust its potential will drive pollsters to look for ways of tapping public opinion more and more quickly, a demand for speed that will pressure them to sacrifice the principles of scientific sampling in favor of shortcuts.

Closed questions, for example, will become the format of choice, because faster polling will involve computers, and computers demand that information be entered in readily processed bits and pieces—a yes or no, a numeral, a letter. Pollsters will also feel pressed to save time by reducing the amount of effort they take to reach the originally designated members of their samples, thus compromising the statistical value of the results. In an article in *Science* magazine, Philip Converse and Michael Traugott, both of the Institute for Social Research, reported that short deadlines had compelled media pollsters to complete their surveying in one to three days, thus sharply limiting their ability to make "callbacks"—that is, to keep trying to reach people in the original sample who for one reason or another weren't available early in the poll. "In the face of these pressures," the researchers wrote, "the hastier polls freely substitute other accessible people for designated respondents who cannot be found quickly, or they completely abandon probability designs that designate specific respondents."

To illustrate the dangers, they cited a political survey they conducted during the 1984 presidential campaign. For some reason their interviewers were able to reach more Democrats in the early stages of the poll than Republicans: the first round of calls gave Ronald Reagan only a three-point lead over Walter Mondale. As the institute's pollsters continued making callbacks, they reached more of the Republicans in the original sample, and Reagan's lead increased to six points. The pollsters tried still harder to reach all the originals, in some cases making as many as thirty calls. Reagan's lead increased to thirteen points.

Most visions of future electronic polling include the involvement of television and the interactive TV services that futurists keep telling us will soon be available. Yet the increased involvement of even ordinary TV worries social scientists. An image-dependent medium, television simply was not made for conducting and communicating surveys. To truly understand a poll, researchers warn, you need to be able to read the actual wording of the survey questions and see the tables in which the percentages are presented. Magazines and newspapers can provide this information, thus allowing a reader to judge for himself whether a poll really shows what the accompanying journalistic interpretation claims it shows. He can check the numbers at will. Television, however, abhors numbers and text. Even when a newscast does display questions and responses, it presents them only briefly. Those bits of unsightly typography disappear immediately, forever.

An example of how the demands of good TV and good social science don't mix occurred in September 1989 when NBC broadcast "R.A.C.E."—the Racial Attitudes and Consciousness Exam—a two-part special in which studio audiences in four cities were asked questions about their attitudes and beliefs regarding race in the context of six broad areas: work, neighborhood, crime, politics, school, and general social interaction. Host Bryant Gumbel interviewed the audiences in the first installment; during the second, a six-person panel of national personalities, including quarterback John Elway, filmmaker Spike Lee, and Patrick Buchanan (when he was still a lowly pundit, not yet a presidential contender), discussed the responses. NBC recruited two nationally respected opinion researchers—Tom Smith, of the University of Chicago's National Opinion Research Center, and Lawrence Bobo, of the University of Wisconsin—to serve as the show's scientific conscience—and no doubt to impart to the program an aura of credibility.

On TV, apparently, even surveys need visual action. NBC grouped the questions by the six subject areas but introduced each group with a dramatic vignette intended to capture some element of the topic at hand. Just before the questions on crime, for example, the survey audience watched a vignette in which a black man held up a white store owner. Before the questions on interracial contacts, the audience saw an interracial marriage. The vignettes may have advanced the cause of television, but not that of social science. They undoubtedly influenced the responses of some members of the studio audience, much the way, say, a film showing a doctor smashing the skull of a laboratory dog might tend to alter the results of a subsequent poll on animal rights. Eleanor Singer, a Columbia University social scientist, reviewed the "R.A.C.E." survey for *Public Opinion Quarterly* and found it deeply flawed for this and other reasons. Before writing her review, she conveyed her concerns to Tom Smith, one of the show's consultants, and quoted his reply. "I agree with almost everything you say," he wrote. "What may scare you is how much worse the show would have been without Larry and me winning several battles."

In one such battle, Smith said, he and Bobo managed to fight off a network proposal that the show include a 900 number call-in poll. Such polls produce results that may seem just as precise as those generated by legitimate sampling techniques, but they have little validity, reflecting only the opinions of those people who bother to call. Bobo, too, agreed with Singer's review. In the next issue of the *Quarterly*, he described how at one point he even considered withdrawing from the program—this after NBC rejected a list of questions he and Smith had written for the survey. "We had the temerity," he wrote, "to use complex response formats and to ask about other groups (i.e. Asians and Hispanics)." NBC laid down three commandments: All questions had to be designed for yes or no answers so the answers could be scored easily and displayed readily on TV. All questions had to be limited to black-white relations. All questions had to be short.

Bobo argued most strongly against the first rule mandating the closed yes or no questions "since it would not leave respondents much leeway for offering complex or nuanced opinions and might force people into categories that did not adequately reflect their opinions." He asked: "Will the glitz and marketability demands of television make it impossible [for television] to treat social science findings and methods in a thoughtful way?"

Too much democracy—too much direct input from a populace widely acknowledged to be ill informed about current and past events—may be too much of a good thing. Today's emphasis on polls, and the coming emphasis on quicker and more automated polls, threatens to disrupt the measured pace of government and to sacrifice sober debate to the instant guidance of the masses. As Harold Mendelsohn, a noted public-opinion researcher, observed: "The Founding Fathers anticipated the danger of basing public policies and legislation on rapidly constituted and emotion-grounded public opinions in the absence of thorough debate. Their solution for avoiding self-serving demagogic manipulation of rashly developed opinions on consequential issues was to establish a checks and balances republic based on representations of public opinion—not on direct individual expressions of support or opposition."

In this he echoed Edmund Burke, who said: "Your representative owes you not his industry only, but his judgment, and he betrays [you] instead of serving you if he sacrifices it to your opinion."

The increased dependence on polling was the logical next phase of image politics. Like scanners in the consumer products arena, polls refine the art of selling, not the product itself, the product in this case being government. Like the other mass surveillance technologies, polls also add a compelling if illusory degree of precision to the study of things that defy precise calculation. Together the technologies of the Second Guess have turned magazines to mush (albeit chronically upbeat mush), bleached the vibrance from TV, and saddled us with a roster of political candidates who pursue public service with all the conviction of sidewalk peddlers selling stolen goods.

This could be just the beginning. Mass surveillance may soon allow marketers, TV producers, and politicians to make good at last on their often proclaimed desire to give us exactly what we want. The question is, do we really want to live in a society whose horizons are so limited as to deliver only what we ask for? From our politicians we need wisdom and human judgment, not decisions tailored to the current whim. From our companies we need products that delight and enthrall and trigger global demand not through protectionist threat, but because they are the best, most innovative products in the world. From our directors, writers, and producers we need inspiration and challenge and that human spark that lifts us briefly from our lives. We need a little magic, a little serendipity.

Isn't that, after all, what we pay these people for?

WHAT TO DO

New Laws for a New Age

The real danger is the gradual erosion of individual liberties through the automation, integration, and interconnection of many small, separate record-keeping systems, each of which alone may seem innocuous, even benevolent, and wholly justifiable.

—U.S. Privacy Protection Study Commission, 1977

A century after Louis Brandeis and Samuel Warren wrote their influential *Harvard Law Review* article describing privacy as the right to be left alone, Federal Judge Robert H. Bork was able to sit before his inquisitors on the Senate Judiciary Committee, flushed with that school-yard playfulness toward humanity that so marked the hard-right ideologues of Reagan's Roaring Eighties, and question whether a fundamental right to privacy really did exist—not just question it, but invoke the holiest of holy domestic documents, the Constitution itself, as the basis of his challenge. As Bork and other constitutional fundamentalists delight in pointing out, the Constitution nowhere includes the word *privacy*, let alone sets privacy as an inalienable right. In the absence of such constitutional underpinnings, Bork told the committee, the right to privacy "evaporates."

Fortunately, most of America's lawmakers and jurists gave the Founding Fathers a bit more credit for understanding the needs of the human

231

spirit. Instead of dismissing privacy as a right, they looked for signs of it elsewhere in the Constitution and found it in the protections of the First, Fourth, Fifth, Ninth, and Fourteenth amendments. They have been hampered by the omission of those seven little letters, however. Our so-called right to privacy is a mélange of constitutional interpretations and too specific legislation that fails utterly to take into account the passage of America into "cyberspace," the age of ephemera, where computers, fiber-optic superhighways, interactive cable television, smart-cards, and invisible telecommunications networks promote the constant, liquid transfer of personal information across all boundaries in a fraction of a heartbeat. In cyberspace, it seems, we have at last outrun the ability of our Founding Fathers to anticipate the needs of the future.

There are two roots to this problem. The first is our innate tendency to ignore privacy as an urgent, fundamental issue until something shocking occurs—some White House–sponsored burglary, for example—to make us appreciate how fragile our right to privacy has become. The second is our persistent misjudgment of "technique" and its inherent power to outstrip whatever controls we seek to place on its expansion. "The weight of technique is such that no obstacle can stop it," Jacques Ellul wrote in *The Technological Society*.

America needs new privacy laws. The public, clearly, is ready. A 1988 poll by Cambridge Reports Inc., of Cambridge, Massachusetts, found that the proportion of Americans who favored a law to restrict the exchange of personal information between government and private institutions had increased to 69 percent from 56 percent just two years before. A *Time* magazine poll conducted in 1991 by Yankelovich Clancy Shulman reported that 93 percent of Americans believed that companies "that sell information to others" should be required by law to ask permission from individuals first. Ninety percent said the sale of information on household income should be prohibited; 68 percent said selling information about product purchases should likewise be barred. The 1990 Harris-Equifax survey found that only 31 percent of Americans favored sticking with the current privacy-protection system of "specific laws, congressional oversight, and individual lawsuits." By an "overwhelming" margin of 79 to 19 percent, Americans agreed: "If we rewrote the Declaration of Independence today, we would probably add privacy to the list of 'life, liberty and the pursuit of happiness' as a fundamental right."

But what manner of law can shepherd our passage into cyberspace?

How can Congress hope to confront the privacy problems posed by today's supernova of technological advance and avoid simply adding more disjointed laws to those that already exist?

First, Congress should look backward and understand how we got to where we are today.

From the start, the Supreme Court proved itself an imperfect instrument for setting down so fundamental a principle as privacy. The Court's actions necessarily were limited by the specific circumstances of the cases it reviewed and by the oblique phrasing of the privacy-related amendments, in particular the "search and seizure" protections of the Fourth. Congress had the power to legislate more broadly but settled instead into a reactive pattern of enacting privacy law only in response to unpopular Supreme Court rulings or to specific violations of privacy that raised the public ire.

In its earliest privacy-related rulings, the Supreme Court steadfastly considered privacy from the perspective of an economy based on visible, tangible transactions and behaviors. You held your letters, deeds, and receipts within the confines of your home. Your home was inviolable. Once you stepped outside and made your communications and other behaviors more public or allowed others to store your important documents, your right to privacy began to evaporate. The Court stuck to this view even as the economy evolved rapidly into one that relied on telephones, telegraphs, and radios and on the storage of personal records outside the home.

In 1928, in the landmark *Olmstead* case, the Court ruled that tapping a man's phone did not violate the Fourth Amendment because the amendment protected only tangible objects—not such ephemera as speech—and certainly could not be expected to protect one's speech when it was projected beyond the confines of home. In a dissent from the 5–4 ruling, Justice Louis Brandeis proved himself a prophetic thinker, adding the kind of future-encompassing breadth absent from most privacy legislation. "The progress of science in furnishing the Government with means of espionage is not likely to stop with wiretapping," he wrote. "Ways may some day be developed by which the Government . . . will be enabled to expose to a jury the most intimate occurrences of the home. Advances in the psychic and related science may bring means of exploring unexpressed beliefs, thoughts and emotions. . . . Can it be that the Constitution affords no protection against such invasions of individual security?"

It took forty years for the Court to overturn the *Olmstead* decision and bring wiretapping under the protection of the Fourth Amendment. This ruling, in 1967, established "zones of privacy" within which an individual holds an expectation of privacy "that society is prepared to recognize as 'reasonable.' " The Court ruled the "Fourth Amendment protects people, not places," and expanded the amendment's protections to include an individual's thoughts and communications.

This was progress—but in establishing the "reasonable" standard, the Court once again proved shortsighted as to the sheer power of technology to overrun conventional protections of privacy. The U.S. Office of Technology Assessment, in a 1985 study on electronic record systems and individual privacy, said the standard "had not offered the courts sufficient policy guidance to deal with the range and uses of new surveillance technologies. 'Reasonable expectation of privacy' is an inherently nebulous phrase, and, despite twenty years of judicial application, predicting its meaning in a new context is difficult."

The Court, in effect, had institutionalized the idea that privacy was relative to whatever era was under consideration. As ACLU attorneys Janlori Goldman and Jerry Berman wrote in 1990, the reasonableness standard "can only reflect, not prevent, deterioration in societal respect for privacy."

In 1976 the Supreme Court both applied the reasonableness standard *and* dusted off its obsolete perception of how society conducts its business and ruled, in *United States* v. *Miller,* that a bank customer's financial records were the property of the bank and that the customer therefore had no reasonable expectation the records would be kept private. The Court exercised similar reasoning when it ruled in 1979 that telephone records were not private, and in 1988 that the Fourth Amendment did not protect the sanctity of garbage after it was removed from the home.

Justice William Brennan dissented from the *Miller* ruling, arguing that in fact depositors did expect their banking records to be kept private. Such records, he wrote, could reveal "many aspects" of a depositor's "personal affairs, opinions, habits, and associations. Indeed, the totality of bank records provides a virtual current biography." Echoing Brandeis's concerns of sixty years before, Brennan cast a worried eye on future technology: "Development of photocopying machines, electronic computers, and other sophisticated instruments have accelerated the ability of government to intrude into areas which a person normally chooses to exclude from prying eyes and inquisitive minds. Consequently, judicial interpretations of the constitutional protection of individual privacy must keep pace with the perils created by these new devices."

Congress compounded the Court's failure to set down principles capable of guiding the nation into cyberspace with its narrow reactions to Court rulings and national events. In 1978, for example, Congress responded to the Court's ruling on bank records by passing the Right to Financial Privacy Act, which made bank records private. In 1986 Congress enacted the Electronic Communications Privacy Act, which nullified the Court's ruling on telephone records.

The best example of Congress's too sharp focus occurred, ironically, soon after a Washington weekly, *City Paper*, obtained and analyzed records of the movies rented by Judge Bork and his family. Bork's skepticism about privacy may have worried the Senate panelists, but *City Paper's* brazen invasion of the sanctity of the man's cinematic tastes shocked them. Driven perhaps by awareness of their own randy tastes and the nightmare vision of hordes of *Washington Post* reporters camped outside Blockbuster Video on election eve, senators and their House peers reacted with blinding speed to pass the Video Privacy Protection Act of 1988, an excruciatingly narrow one-issue, one-industry law that barred video retailers from disclosing specific details about the movies their customers rent.

The last time Congress made a broad proactive attempt at protecting privacy occurred when it passed the Privacy Act of 1974. However well intended, the greatest value of the act now is as a case study of what not to do the next time around. In fairness to Congress, however, the act also serves as proof of the difficulty involved in trying to keep up with the rapid pace of information technology—and of the urgent need to do so.

The Privacy Act applied only to federal agencies and set out rules for how they were to store and transfer personal information about individuals. It also gave individuals the right to file civil and criminal suits in cases where an agency willfully, intentionally violated the act. A fundamental tenet was that information collected for one purpose should not be used for another purpose, without first getting the permission of the individual involved, a concept central to contemporary thought on privacy.

In the early 1970s information technology was still in its infancy; as late as 1975, according to a federal audit, 73 percent of the government's personal record files involved manual systems. Advances in computer technology quickly changed the electromagnetic terrain of government, sharply increasing the number of computerized records systems and, more important, generating new ways those records could be searched, collated, matched, and processed. The advance of technology made even the sixties nightmare of a huge central data bank obsolete: on-line access and local and long-distance networks allowed the instant assembly of data from widespread sources in any of the hundreds of thousands of large and small computers, federal and private, sprinkled around the globe. Suddenly any networked desktop computer commanded powers far beyond those of any nightmare Big Data Base.

The advent of personal computers and cheap, swift networks made it virtually impossible to keep track of the migration of personal information and markedly increased the opportunity for inappropriate use of personal records. Microcomputers and networks, moreover, also made it virtually impossible for agencies to insure, as the privacy act requires, that personal data be kept current and accurate. Data retrieved from a main storage memory and stored on floppy or hard disks in far-flung locations can't be updated automatically with each change in the main memory—a problem familiar to anyone who has corrected his credit record with one credit bureau only to move to a new region and discover the same mistake reproduced by another.

The Privacy Act moreover failed to anticipate the advent of new ways of using the emerging technologies—the matching, merging, and profiling techniques now used so heavily by marketers and federal agencies alike. At first glance the act's explicit limits on the use of personal information for purposes other than originally intended would seem to bar such matching. Here, however, the act ran headlong into another characteristic of technological progress observed by Jacque Ellul—that "technique" has a life all its own and drives toward maximum efficiency.

A clause in the Privacy Act exempted agencies from the information-use restriction in cases where such alternate use could be called "routine." Agencies quickly decided that matching and profiling were routine uses, arguing they had always shared information with one another in the past. Their interpretation was reinforced, moreover, by a pronounced federal shift in the early 1980s away from concerns about privacy and toward bureaucratic efficiency. In 1980 the Paperwork Reduction Act gave the Office of Management and Budget, overseers of the Privacy Act, new powers to promote more effective use of information technology in government. In 1981 President Ronald Reagan established the President's Council on Integrity and Efficiency to help reduce fraud and waste; the council saw large-scale computer matching as a terrific way to cut down on excess expense. The following year Congress, leaping into the spirit of things, passed the Debt Collection Act of 1982, which made the migration of data between the government and the private sector—between agencies and the big credit bureaus—not just an impromptu occurrence, but a formal arrangement. The efficiency movement climaxed appropriately enough in 1984 with Reagan's formation of the so-called Grace Commission, which claimed to find "hundreds of billions of dollars" of needless federal expenditures, and passage of the Deficit Reduction Act of 1984, which specifically authorized the sharing of IRS and Social Security records with any federal, state, or local agency administering the country's welfare programs. From 1980 to 1984, according to an audit by the Office of Technology Assessment, the number of computer matches conducted by federal agencies tripled.

The OTA concluded that new electronic technologies "appear to have outpaced the ability of individuals to protect their interests by using the mechanisms available under the Privacy Act."

The result of the interplay between narrow Court rulings and constricted congressional vision is today's loosely linked, gap-filled mosaic of laws, some covering the federal government, some covering private industry, none covering in any broad, cohesive way the information issues Congress *will* face for the remainder of the decade. As of 1991 Congress showed no inclination to change its ways. Members of both houses proposed a flurry of precisely targeted bills aimed in particular at telemarketers, telemarketing fraud, and the credit bureaus—all, needless to say, prominent in the news and thus on voters' minds.

Another paradox of privacy in the age of silent electronic intrusion, however, is that the technologies and applications that should concern us most tend to be those that have not yet come to our attention. To paraphrase Janis Joplin, you don't know you have privacy until it's gone.

The Privacy Act was obsolete the day it was signed into law. Needed now is a reassessment and consolidation of privacy law, an Omnibus Privacy Act incorporating and superseding the patchwork quilt of legislation and Supreme Court rulings that exist today. The act would not come easily. Privacy is pivotal to such sensitive politician-muting issues as abortion, the right to die, and freedom of the press. The fight for such a bill would be hard, long, and—given the past penchant of antiabortion groups to bomb offending institutions and dispatch children into the paths of oncoming cars—perhaps even bloody. Nonetheless, privacy is long overdue for a thorough examination. The way to start is by setting down a few crucial, forward-looking principles.

Here are my candidates:

First, any new legislation must acknowledge that America and the world have entered cyberspace, where information is power and new electronic technologies for gathering and amassing such information have concentrated great reserves of power in the hands of a few corporations and agencies. Congress must also recognize that the new technologies have indeed created wholly new strains of information infinitely more revealing than the sum of their innocuous components, and that such recombinant data is just as ill understood as the creations of genetic engineering—and must be treated with as much concern and caution.

Second, Congress must stop fighting privacy fires with such narrow laws as the Bork bill and instead recognize the commonalities in the many intrusive technologies and practices it will soon be forced to review. Linkage and coalescence will characterize technology in the age of ephemera. The barrier between government and private-sector information will become increasingly porous. Telemarketers, credit-reporting bureaus, and the IRS already use many of the same technologies and, increasingly, share the same kinds of information. Current technological trends show clear and mounting momentum toward a day when TV ratings, grocery scanning, direct marketing, political polling, tax filing, perhaps even voting and the taking of the decennial census could be accomplished through shared electronic pathways, perhaps even in real time.

There is enough evidence to show where technology is headed to allow us to begin asking future questions now and to frame laws with Constitution-like flexibility to prepare for them. Will a warrant be necessary to peer into the silicon memory of a supermarket smart-card? We saw how the New York City Police Department used Nielsen's TV-rating technology as part of a homicide investigation; could such use in the investigation of a still-breathing suspect constitute an illegal search? What happens in the future when Nielsen's passive meter can recognize the members of a household—when a husband is accused of killing his wife during "L.A. Law" and the prosecutor subpoenas the night's record? Will the administrators of our food stamp programs be allowed access to scanner records of our shopping trips to verify our eligibility? Will the male defendant in a date rape case be allowed to present his victim's frequent shopper records—her repeated purchase of condoms—as evidence in his defense?

Congress must recognize too that the intelligence-gathering techniques of business and government cause a kind of harm that defies precise dollar enumeration. When we lose control of our personal records, when we begin to suspect that someone somewhere is keeping a file we know nothing about, we experience a subtle diminution of self, the kind of harm our laws and courts have trouble addressing. Congress acknowledged this characteristic of privacy in the 1991 Telephone Consumer Protection Act—known more commonly as the junk-fax or auto-dialing bill—when it set a penalty of $500 for each call prohibited by the law, such as calls involving a prerecorded voice or made by an auto-dialing machine. A consumer need not prove that he was harmed by the call, just that the call was made. (If he can prove the telemarketing company "willfully" broke the law, he can sue for up to $1,500 for each violation.) To restore trust, any new law must give individuals real, effective control over how the information they give to the government is used. We need concrete, actionable assurance that the information we give to the IRS goes only to the IRS, not to Joe's Repo Company, and likewise that whatever we reveal to Metromail won't make its way to the Immigration and Naturalization Service—regardless of what the efficiency experts demand. The law must acknowledge that trust and peace of mind are national assets that far exceed the short-run savings of efficiency. At the same time, of course, Congress must take extreme care to assure that any future privacy laws and their attendant penalties don't erode other fundamental rights, in particular freedom of speech and freedom of the press.

Above all, it's time to acknowledge what the courts, Congress, and the public have more or less agreed on all along—that privacy is indeed an inalienable right. It's time, in fact, for a constitutional amendment to insert the word—almost anywhere would be a relief—if only to avoid the inevitable congressional and high-court dithering caused when the next generation of juridical ideologues rises to ask, "Privacy? What's that?" There's even an efficiency angle to satisfy the bean counters at the Office of Management and Budget: think of how much court time and energy could be saved if no one ever again had to debate the existence of a right to privacy.

SOURCES, NOTES,
MINUTIAE

The fundamental problem with reporting a book like this is that marketers are notoriously squeamish about revealing material details about anything they do, for fear of arming the competition with some valuable tidbit of information. Consider Procter & Gamble, America's foremost consumer products marketer. In 1991 the company persuaded the Cincinnati police to investigate a news leak made to a reporter for the *Wall Street Journal*. The police proceeded to commandeer the telephone records of countless innocent American citizens to find out who among its many employees had called the *Wall Street Journal* numbers. Newspapers throughout the country condemned Procter & Gamble for its intrusive, rights-trampling investigation. The company eventually apologized and, dusting off that classic dodge of culpability so heavily relied on through the Reagan era, called the investigation an error of "judgment." One always wonders what people mean when they use this word. Did Procter & Gamble mean it should never have conducted the investigation at all? Or rather that it should have taken stronger measures from the start, such as kidnapping the family members of suspect managers or forbidding everyone at company headquarters to go to the bathroom until the loose-lipped miscreant confessed? Regardless, the investigation accomplished what certainly was its goal—to cut off communication with reporters by scaring the daylights out of every employee in its empire.

I encountered the chilling effect of Procter & Gamble's investigation twice in the course of my reporting, first when I called the company's public relations office to try to arrange interviews on the company's use of scanner-generated market intelligence, later when Paco Underhill of Envirosell (introduced in "The Hidden Observers" chapter) invited me to observe a project involving Noxell Corporation, a major cosmetics marketer and, although I did not know this at the time, a subsidiary of Procter & Gamble. Noxell approved in principle of my observing Underhill at work but wanted to know more about me, so I faxed my résumé and a letter describing my book to Underhill, who relayed it to Noxell. Noxell saw that I had once been a *Journal* staff writer and, as Underhill replayed the response, said "No fucking way."

I came across this kind of aversion to publicity often in the reporting for this book.

Resistance, however, was by no means universal. Many companies take the position that they do what they do and thus might as well discuss it. In researching this book, I relied as much as possible on well over two hundred substantial interviews—most of them taped—with marketers and other live sources, a number that does not include the many dozens of short hit-and-run encounters with direct-mailers in tracking my mail backward to its sources.

Where interviews were out of the question or inappropriate, I relied on reporting techniques honed by I. F. Stone and Jessica Mitford and turned to four broad classes of primary documents:

- The many reports and surveys produced by marketers and market research associations. I discovered that marketers keep statistics and write reports on virtually every marketing phenomenon known to man. Among the most prolific report generators are the American Marketing Association in Chicago, the Marketing Science Institute in Boston, and the Advertising Research Foundation in New York. One of the enduring mysteries of marketing is that the Advertising Research Foundation, an organization of men and women tuned to the subtleties of marketing, could choose a name with the canine acronym ARF.
- Brochures, rate cards, fliers, and catalogs produced by the marketers to market their own services and wares. I relied heavily on the mailings of LBMI Direct Marketing, because of their charming enthusiasm for targeting the poor and the gullible. The mother of all direct-mail catalogs is the immense and always entertaining *Direct Mail Lists, Rates & Data* catalog, available in most libraries.
- Court documents and transcripts of congressional testimony. I include here federal reports published by the Census Bureau, the General Accounting Office, and the Office of Technology Assessment.
- Professional magazines and journals where marketers speak among themselves in the privacy afforded by limited circulation, in particular *Direct Marketing* magazine, *Credit* magazine, *The Friday Report* (a newsletter), *Journal of Consumer Research, Journal of Consumer Marketing, Journal of Advertising Research, Journal of Marketing, American Demographics, Campaign, Campaigns & Elections*, and *Government Information Quarterly*. I found *The Friday Report* to be of particular value. A weekly newsletter, it tracks every new advance in data-base marketing. I first encountered the newsletter when an anonymous soul sent me a copy containing a critical review of a "Nova" documentary that tracked a portion of my journey through the marketing data bases. The price of a subscription was steep—$165 a year—but I quickly subscribed.

Also worthy of note is *The Privacy Journal* published by Robert Ellis Smith, whose tireless chronicles of the erosion of privacy should keep the microphones out of our beds for a good while longer. (It costs $109 a year.)

Among the libraries that proved invaluable to my research: the Census Library in Suitland, Maryland; the Advertising Research Foundation library in Manhattan; and that greatest gift to mankind, the U.S. Library of Congress, where even the copy machines work.

The following notes detail many of the sources I used to write each chapter. The notes are not exhaustive. I have identified sources wherever a fact or observation promises to be controversial or where I have extracted some valuable nugget of information from the work of another author who deserves credit for having been first to uncover it. Where appropriate, and occasionally where utterly inappropriate, I have thrown in bits of information that I could not wedge into the main text but that I found to be tantalizing nonetheless.

1. THE TROJAN TEDDY

The Trojan teddy letter was part of the "First Birthday" co-op mailing by *American Baby* magazine. Ours arrived on January 31, 1989, six days before my daughter's birthday. It went to three million mothers of one-year-olds. As I note in a later chapter, *American Baby* suspended the mailing later that year.

Estimates of advertising spending came from the June 21, 1991, issue of *The Friday Report*, which reported forecasts made by Veronis, Suhler & Associates. Data on the increasing speed of commercials and the high volume of new product introductions appeared in "Marketing Is Everything," by Regis McKenna, in the *Harvard Business Review*, January–February 1991. My information on the increasing numbers of distinct ads came from "Advertising and Mass Marketing," by Peter F. Eder, in *The Futurist*, May–June 1990.

My list of unorthodox advertising media comes from various sources, including the *New York Times*, *San Francisco Chronicle*, *Wall Street Journal*, and *Privacy Journal*. I sat through *Rain Man's* Buick commercial one night in 1991. I found the telemarketing figures in the text of the federal "Telephone Consumer Protection Act of 1991."

I learned about Sprint's use of telephone records in a January 1989 interview with a Sprint official who asked not to be identified. The dollar-laden letter came from Step Consumer Research, New York, and was postmarked January 12, 1989. I learned of Coke's monumental survey at an American Marketing Association conference in Miami Beach in January 1991. An ARF report presented at an ARF meeting in New York produced the statistics on the numbers of group and individual interviews marketers conducted in 1989.

Lotus's troubles with its "Marketplace" CDs were widely reported; I pulled the $8 million loss estimate from the January 25, 1991, edition of *The Friday Report*.

I learned of the changing treatment of tax records in "Access to Tax Records for Statistical Purposes," an article in the journal *Review of Public Data Use*, 1984.

Additional Sources

Anderson, Paul F. "Marketing, Scientific Progress, and Scientific Method." *Journal of Marketing*. Fall 1983.
Bogart, Leo. "Advertising: Art, Science or Business?" *Journal of Advertising Research*. December 1988–January 1989.
———. "Progress in Advertising Research?" Ibid. June–July 1986.
"Cat and Mouse." *Privacy Journal*. June 1991.

"Change in Consumer Markets Hurting Advertising Industry." *New York Times.* October 3, 1989.

Eder, Peter F. "Advertising and Mass Marketing." *The Futurist.* May–June 1990.

Friday Report. May 5, 1991; June 21, 1991; December 13, 1991.

Johnson, Henry A. "Computer Technology Is Key to Segmentation and Service." *Direct Marketing.* June 1985.

"Making the Grade with the Customer." *Wall Street Journal.* November 12, 1990.

McKenna, Regis. "Marketing Is Everything." *Harvard Business Review.* January/February 1991.

Passavant, Pierre. "Beware!—Big Database Is Watching You." *Direct Marketing.* August 1985.

Posch, Robert. "Do We Have Constitutionally Protected Access to Our Customers?" *Direct Marketing.* June 1988.

"The Snap Has Turned to Slog." *New York Times.* November 18, 1990.

Zinkhan, George M., et al. "MBAs' Changing Attitudes Toward Marketing Dilemmas: 1981–1987." *Journal of Business Ethics.* 8:963–974, 1989.

2. SEX, PRUNES, AND VIDEOTAPE

For historic perspective I relied in particular on Erik Barnouw's *The Sponsor: Notes on a Modern Potentate;* Susan Strasser's *Satisfaction Guaranteed: The Making of the American Mass Market;* Roland Marchand's *Advertising the American Dream;* Ernest Dichter's *The Strategy of Desire;* and of course Vance Packard's *The Hidden Persuaders.* I consulted Robert Bartels's *The History of Marketing Thought*—a painfully dry and businesslike work—to get a sense of how marketers pursued the consumer at different points over the century. Todd Gitlin's *Inside Prime Time* provides a good grounding in how commercial forces govern television. Eric Clark's *The Want Makers* captures the range of techniques used by marketers to get the rest of us to buy more stuff.

In places I have committed the no doubt unpardonable sin of lifting quotations directly from some of the above works and failing to credit the writers who discovered them in the first place. I make amends here: Clark produced the remarks of Dr. Johnson and Claude Hopkins; Marchand the scare advertisements, John Benson's appraisal of the consumer intellect, the *Printer's Ink* admonitions against fouling the airwaves, and much of the surrounding detail.

I borrowed many of Susan Strasser's discoveries about the early efforts at market intelligence gathering made by Coke, Bon Ami, and Sears. Clark provided the facts about Lord & Thomas, Nielsen, and Gallup.

Dichter's remarks come from several sources: a story I wrote for the *Wall Street Journal* in 1983 about a latter-day prune campaign; an article in the now defunct *Reporter,* called "Adman's Nightmare: Is the Prune a Witch?" October 13, 1953; and Dichter's own observations, which I found in *The Strategy of Desire* and other articles listed below.

Additional Sources

"Admen Try to Make Juice-Loving World Swoon for a Prune." *Wall Street Journal.* February 15, 1983.

Appel, Valentine. "Brain Activity and Recall of TV Advertising." *Journal of Advertising Research*. August 1979.

Belk, Russell. "Possessions and the Extended Self." *Journal of Consumer Research*. September 1988.

Dichter, Ernest. "Case Histories in the Study of Motivation." Unpublished paper. 1951. Advertising Research Foundation Library.

———. "These Are the Real Reasons Why People Buy Goods." *Advertising & Selling*. July 1948.

Levitt, Theodore. "M-R Snake Dance." *Harvard Business Review*. November– December 1960.

Olson, Jerry, and William Ray. "Exploring the Usefulness of Brain Waves as Measures of Advertising Response." Marketing Science Institute. Report No. 89-116. October 1989.

———. "Using Brain-Wave Measures to Assess Advertising Effects." Marketing Science Institute. Report No. 83-108. September 1983.

"Psyche & Sales: 'Consumer Motivations' Are Probed for Industry by Clan of Researchers." *Wall Street Journal*. September 13, 1957.

Wilcox, Gary B. "Cigarette Brand Advertising and Consumption in the United States: 1949–1985." *Journal of Advertising Research*. August–September 1991.

3. THE CEMENT ELEPHANT

I built this chapter primarily from interviews with census officials, veterans of the early demographics industry, executives of Claritas, and, above all, Jonathan Robbin, who granted me three Saturdays of conversation in his cozy home high atop the Potomac River—the house, as he put it, that Claritas built. I trace the sourcing in two sections focused on the census and on Robbin.

The Census Bureau

Although I quoted only a few census officials in my narrative, I interviewed many, and their observations became the fabric of the census portion of the chapter. Those I did not name include Carolyn Hay and Alvin L. Etzler, both supervisory survey statisticians, who explained how the bureau puts together its mailing list; Susan Miskura, chief of the Year 2000 Research and Development Staff, who told of the bureau's plans to study the marketers' data collection techniques as one component of preparations for the millennial census; Frederick G. Bohme, chief of the census history staff, who steered me to many excellent sources of census history, in particular the bureau's own procedural histories available in the census library at Suitland; Richard Griffin, chief of the census design branch, who described the statistical tricks the bureau uses to prevent accidental disclosure of identities; Brian Greenberg, assistant division chief for research and methodology; John Beresford, the Census Bureau statistician who is most credited with opening the bureau to outside users; Marshall L. Turner, Jr., chief of the data user services division, also instrumental in making the "cement elephant" dance; Velma Lacy, of the program and policy development office, who gave me a copy of her study on census surveys commissioned by private organizations; and Larry Carbaugh, chief of the state and regional program staff, who told me about Vincent Barabba's impact on the bureau.

Greg Russell, assistant division chief of current surveys, told me that Ralston-Purina in February 1987 petitioned the bureau to add a question about pet ownership to the bureau's Current Population Survey. The bureau declined the request. "It just seemed out of place," Russell told me.

In recounting the Census Bureau's distant history, I relied primarily on the following:

• *The American Census: A Social History*, by Margo J. Anderson. It was here that I first read of the biblical taboo against census taking. Anderson also made a glancing reference to General Sherman's use of census data and told me exactly where to look for Sherman's thank-you note: the Walter Willcox Papers, Box 36, Joseph C. G. Kennedy file, Library of Congress.

• *Census: 190 Years of Counting America*, by Dan Halacy. He too described the biblical taboo and set down those marvelous names collected by the daring census takers of yore.

For details of Sherman's march, I consulted *This Hallowed Ground*, by Bruce Catton, and *The March to the Sea and Beyond*, by Joseph T. Glatthaar.

For the history of information processing: *Big Blue: IBM's Use and Abuse of Power*, by Richard Thomas DeLamartz; *Creating the Computer: Government, Industry and High Technology*, by Kenneth Flamm; and *Herman Hollerith: Forgotten Giant of Information Processing*, by Geoffrey D. Austrian. Austrian noted that Hollerith threw a lavish celebration after the successful use of his machine during the 1890 census, noteworthy here because he held the party on Glen Echo Heights, a bluff over the Potomac very near where Jonathan Robbin lives today. I gathered additional details about the bureau's use of computers from the census procedural history for 1970.

I first read of the bureau's involvement in the World War II internment of Japanese-Americans in David Burnham's *The Rise of the Computer State*. Burnham also described the episode in his testimony before a congressional joint hearing on May 14, 1987, called "1990 Census Planning—Questionnaire Subjects."

I found Tom C. Clark's remarks in an oral history interview published in *Japanese-American Relocation Reviewed*, volume 1, *Decision and Exodus*, Bancroft Library, University of California, at Berkeley. (The Supreme Court Library in Washington graciously allowed me to examine its copy.) I also consulted Robert Jenkins's *Procedural History of the 1940 Census of Population and Housing*, published by the University of Wisconsin Press in 1985, and the *30th Annual Report of the Secretary of Commerce*, 1942.

A particularly valuable document materialized almost at my side—and utterly by accident—while I was thumbing through unrelated materials in the bureau's Suitland library. A census librarian walked into the reading room and told another librarian of something she had just found. I didn't hear the document described; I heard only the tinge of sorrow in the librarian's voice. Being a snoop by occupation, I caught up with her and asked what she had discovered. She handed me a brown binder containing a report typed on onionskin, dated April 19, 1942, called "Forms and Procedures of the Civilian Evacuation Program: Preliminary Report" and containing detailed census tabulations of the numbers of Japanese on the West Coast. (The term *evacuation* would have made George Orwell smile.) The report, signed by the Census Bureau's Calvert Dedrick, also included a collection of forms and cards to be filled out by the Japanese, and brought the whole episode to life. Here, for example, was a medical card with a category to be filled out called "General Appearance." Here too were identification tags to be attached to the internees' baggage and a form titled "Agreement Regarding Disposition of Motor Vehicle."

The report also contained a curious ad hoc addition, a letter from a chicken farmer to the California Baby Chick Association, concerning the farmer's plan to cope with the shortage of Japanese chicken sexors caused by the internment. Dedrick, the bureau's liaison with the Western Defense Command, had inserted the letter into the binder for comic relief. On a small piece of paper appended to the farmer's letter, Dedrick wrote, "Lest you think that this work is entirely tragedy . . ." The farmer's letter had been part of a petition by the California chicken industry to exempt Japanese chicken sexors, who constituted 90 percent of the coast's trained sexors, from the evacuation. "Sexing," the farmer stated, "is an art which cannot be learned in a short period of time, and one which demands a long period of intensive study and application."

For more recent history I turned to the bureau's own procedural histories; various editions of the bureau newsletter, "The Census and You"; and the minutes of meetings of the Census Advisory Committee of the American Marketing Association (October 11–12, 1984; November 14–15, 1985; October 8–9, 1987; April 14–15 and October 13–14, 1988; April 13–14 and October 19–20, 1989; April 18, 1990).

I learned of the sole arrest for a breach of bureau confidentiality laws in a May 18, 1990, letter from a bureau official to an unidentified individual who had requested information about confidentiality. With a little more research, I found that on November 18, 1981, a field operations supervisor from Nashville, Tennessee, was indicted for, among other things, allowing bureau address registers to be removed from the Nashville district office and copied by a former employee, who then allowed other nonbureau employees to make more copies. She pleaded guilty on January 13, 1982, to three counts of the original fifteen-count indictment, including the wrongful disclosure charges, and was sentenced to three years in jail for each count. The judge suspended all but 120 days. Her file is number 81-30245, in the Nashville Division, U.S. District Court, Middle District of Tennessee.

Lawrence Cox made his remarks about confidentiality and the use of summary census data in "Confidentiality Issues at the Census Bureau," written with four coauthors and presented at the bureau's First Annual Research Conference, March 20–23, 1985.

Andrew Hacker's quote at the opening of the chapter was published in "The business of Demographics," *Population Bulletin*, June 1984, published by the Population Reference Bureau, Washington, D.C.

Jonathan Robbin and Claritas

Interviews with Jonathan Robbin can be taxing affairs. Each morning I arrived with a carefully crafted set of questions; each afternoon I left with few of them answered but with tapes and notebooks crammed nonetheless. Questions aimed at gathering simple historic detail somehow became triggers for fulsome lectures on statistics and mathematics. To gather the mundane details of Robbin's life and work, I relied on a variety of reports and publications, including Robbin's own ten-page curriculum vitae (the February 1990 edition); the history, explanations, and descriptions in the "User's Guide" volume of Claritas's REZIDE (the *National Encyclopedia of REsidential ZIp Code DEmography*, 1974); the newsletter of Claritas's current parent, VNU; Claritas's November 1981 client list; and a copy of Robbin's 1969 "Index of Susceptibility to Civil Disorder."

I interviewed several other Claritas executives, including Mark Capaldini, Terry Pittman, and David Miller. I visited Doug Anderson in 1989, while doing research on a story for *Harper's* magazine about the marketers' intelligence system.

June Barnes of Satellite Music Network gave me a rundown on how the company uses Claritas's PRIZM system; Jeffrey T. Pescatello, of WMMW, told me how his station joined Satellite Music Network and saw its ratings soar.

Additional Sources

"Army Recruits Claritas to Find Who Uncle Sam Wants." *Washington Post*, September 1, 1980.

"Clusters." *The New Yorker*. February 1, 1982.

"Congress Orders U.S. Marshals To Take First Decennial Census in August 1790." *Census and You*. Census Bureau. August 1990.

Courtland, Sherry. "Census Confidentiality: Then and Now." *Government Information Quarterly*. Vol. 1, no. 4, pp. 407–418.

"Developing Mailing Lists for the 1990 Census." Joint Hearing, Subcommittee on Census and Population, and Subcommittee on Postal Operations and Services. Committee on Post Office and Civil Service. House of Representatives. 99th Congress. Second Session. March 13, 1986.

Gates, Gerald W. "Census Bureau Microdata: Providing Useful Research Data While Protecting the Anonymity of Respondents." Paper presented at American Statistical Association annual meeting. August 1988.

"New Census Era Opened 100 Years Ago." *Census and You*. June 1990.

"Placing Products: Marketing Firm Slices U.S. into 240,000 Parts to Spur Clients' Sales." *Wall Street Journal*. November 3, 1986.

Schwartz, Joe. "The Census Means Business." *American Demographics*. July 1989.

Weiss, Michael J. *The Clustering of America*. Harper & Row. 1988.

Wilson, Oliver H., and William J. Smith. "Access to Tax Records for Statistical Purposes." *Review of Public Data Use*. 12: 195–205. 1984.

4. NAKED CAME THE CONSUMER

I first conducted research for this chapter in 1989 for an article for *Harper's* magazine. I expanded the reporting in 1990 and 1991 to include information from a vast array of additional sources; this chapter now bears little likeness to the original magazine story.

I scanned *The Friday Report* for announcements of the newest lists, among them the Chemlawn, Sunoco, and Minnesota State Lottery lists. I found references to other new lists in *Direct Marketing* magazine and in the huge catalog of mailing lists, *Direct Mail List Rates & Data*, available in most public libraries. My information about U.S. Sprint came from a 1989 interview with a reluctant Sprint marketing executive who asked that he not be identified by name.

To trace my junk mail, I did not bother taking the coy route of writing away for things and using different variations of my name. I simply called the companies and asked for the people who signed the mail. The hardest part was finding a telephone number to dial, as the marketers' letters rarely contain a telephone number (unless they invite you to call a

900 number or to order by mail) and typically list only post office boxes as return addresses. In such cases I first called the post office where the box was rented and asked for the identity of the renter—postal law states that the post office must disclose the name if the renter is a commercial organization—and simply called Directory Information for the phone number.

Occasionally I got to speak to the person named on the letter, as in the case of Elizabeth Fediay of the National Security Pac, who clearly was delighted to have the opportunity to chat with a pen pal. More often I wound up transferred from one phone extension to the next until I reached the poor soul at the bottom of the corporate food chain, the list manager. List managers tended to be pleasant and cooperative, aware, I think, that the process by which they acquired my name verged on larceny. They asked me to read back the special code on the envelope that indicated the specific list from which they had drawn my name and address. (Never let a marketer tell you he doesn't know how he got your name; marketers keep careful track in order to gauge which lists win the most responses.)

Whenever I met serious resistance, I dusted off my atomic rebuttal: "It's *my* name." Usually it worked.

Details of *The New Yorker* list were provided by a broker with the Kleid Company of New York, which handles high-brow lists, including the subscription list of *Harper's* magazine. I learned of additional gay mailing lists from LC List Marketing in New York. LBMI sent me a steady supply of its newest list offerings. I also watched my own mail.

I did not quote or name many of the people I interviewed, although together they provided that critical mass of knowledge every writer must accumulate before putting words on the page. The list includes, in order of contact, Joe Dawson, Equifax; Daniel Klibanoff, Listworld; Jerold L. Heisler, Metromail; Ellen Farley, Donnelly Marketing; Ron Friedman, Group 1 Software; Jock Bickert, National Demographics & Life-styles; Eugene Mahaffey, BancOne Corp.; F. James O'Neill, CACI; Stan Fridstein, the Right Start Catalog; Michael Curry, Quality Paperback Books; Beth and Steffie (first names only) at CPC Associates; Sheila Rohner, Pennsylvania Dutch Resorts; Elgie Holstein, Bankcard Holders of America; Dennis W. Benner, TRW; Alan Westin, Columbia University; Mary Culnan, Georgetown University; and John Baker, Equifax.

I relied heavily on brochures, list catalogs, and other marketing materials prepared by the marketers in order to sell their services to other marketers. I acquired many of these simply by requesting them; I picked up others at the big 1991 Advertising Research Foundation meeting in New York; still others were mailed to me by the sources I interviewed and by other journalists. The state of Texas graciously sent me several hundred pages of court documents related to the multistate suit against TRW, settled in December 1991.

For an excellent primer on direct marketing, I recommend Ed Burnett's 744-page how-to guide, *The Complete Direct Mail List Handbook*, published in 1988 by Prentice-Hall Inc.

Additional Sources

Bloom, Paul N., et al. "Identifying the Legal and Ethical Risks and Costs of Using New Information Technologies to Support Marketing Programs." Unpublished paper. University of North Carolina. 1991.

"Credit Data Suit Settled by TRW." *New York Times.* December 11, 1991.

Fost, Dan. "Privacy Concerns Threaten Database Marketing." *American Demographics.* May 1990.

"Hot Lists: Data Mills Delve Deep to Find Information About U.S. Consumers." *Wall Street Journal.* March 14, 1991.

"The Junk Mail Explosion." *Time* magazine. November 26, 1990.

Larson, Erik. "What Sort of Car-Rt-Sort Am I?" *Harper's* magazine. July 1989.

"1988 Survey of List Practices." *Direct Marketing.* August 1988.

Schwartz, Joe. "Databases Deliver the Goods." *American Demographics.* September 1989.

"Someone's Got a File on You." *Changing Times.* July 1988.

Townsend, Bickley. "Psychographic Glitter." *Across the Board.* March 1986.

Wheaton, James. "The Meaning of Merge/Purge." *Direct Marketing.* January 1990.

"Why Melinda S. Gets Ads for Panty Hose; Melinda F., Porsches." *Wall Street Journal.* May 6, 1988.

5. MOTHERS AND OTHER TARGETS

My sketch of the baby formula industry is based on information from various published and interview sources. For details about the Gerber and Carnation programs, I interviewed Jim Lovejoy, Gerber's director of corporate communications; Steve Poole, director of public relations for Gerber's Gerber Products Division; Laurie McDonald, Carnation's director of public affairs.

Mead Johnson's spokesperson, Holly De More, declined comment on the advice of legal counsel. I also interviewed, but did not quote or name, Antoinette Eaton of the American Academy of Pediatrics; David Waldman of 21st Century Marketing, which manages the Growing Child prenatal list; and officials of the University of Maryland Medical Center in Baltimore, the Children's National Medical Center in Washington, D.C., and the Maryland Department of Health and Mental Hygiene. I also read testimony of Laurie MacDonald and of Mary Lou Steptoe, deputy director of the Federal Trade Commission's bureau of competition, prepared for a hearing on formula marketing held March 14, 1991, by the Senate Judiciary Subcommittee on Antitrust, Monopolies, and Business Rights and the Senate Agriculture, Nutrition, and Forestry Committee.

Nielsen Marketing Research and Information Resources Inc. both said sales of formula through stores totaled $1.6 billion.

The UCLA study on formula marketing, "Hospital Influence on Early Infant-Feeding Practices," appeared in the December 1985 issue of *Pediatrics.* For additional reading on the subtle tactics used by formula companies, see "Providing Free Samples of Baby Items to Newly Delivered Parents: An Unintentional Endorsement?" in *Clinical Pediatrics,* March 1987.

I gathered information on the National Change of Address program primarily from interviews with Dick Strasser, senior assistant postmaster general, and Bob Krause, director of address information systems. In addition, I drew information from the following postal service documents: the January 3, 1991, list of NCOA licensees; the 1990 "Comprehensive Statement on Postal Operations," which sets out the number of addresses processed through NCOA; the Annual Report of the Postmaster General, 1990; and the U.S. Postal Service Request for Proposal No. 104230-91-A-0033, which lists the first-year licensing fee and sets out the requirements that any company must meet to become a licensee.

"Brighton Man" is Peter Gleason, M.D., Brighton, New York, whose enthusiasm for the semiotics of junk mail is rivaled only by my own.

6. WHOSE NAME IS THIS ANYWAY?

The opening quote comes from a letter included as an exhibit in testimony presented by Mary Culnan, associate professor of business administration, Georgetown University, to the House Subcommittee on Postal Operations and Services in October 1991.

An official of the U.S. Selective Service, who asked not to be identified by name, told me details about the agency's use of the Farrell's Ice Cream list. Frank Keith, a spokesman for the Internal Revenue Service, described his agency's attempt to use the Dunhill list to track down tax evaders. The Dunhill List Company of Washington, not to be confused with Dunhill & Co. and Dunhill International, confirmed that it indeed had provided the two million names.

7. SEEING IS BELIEVING

The late Hugh Malcolm Beville, Jr., remains the undisputed master of ratings history: I and the television industry as a whole owe him a great debt for chronicling the evolution of this little understood yet supremely influential phenomenon. His *Audience Ratings: Radio, Television and Cable* is not the most enthralling read, but it speaks with sedate authority. In places he allowed himself a little freedom, revealing, for example, the profound differences in the way Arthur C. Nielsen, Sr., and C. E. Hooper lived—and died. Nielsen was conservative; he always took the train because of the heightened statistical odds of dying in an air crash. Hooper was flamboyant and loved to fly. Nielsen died after a long illness, Hooper in a spume of blood and bone when he fell into a whirling airplane propeller on December 15, 1954. I relied on Belville's book for most of the chronology of the early years of ratings.

Erik Barnouw's *The Sponsor: Notes on a Modern Potentate* provides an excellent account of how television and the promotional needs of the consumer products industry became inextricably linked. Todd Gitlin's *Inside Prime Time* likewise offers a glimpse at how ratings attained so much influence. *Television and Human Behavior,* by George Comstock et al., steered me to some marvelous, arcane studies of how people watch television and what television in turn does to people. For a sense of how TV's best creative minds viewed ratings, I turned to *The Producer's Medium: Conversations with Creators of American TV,* by Horace Newcomb and Robert S. Alley, and found the Norman Lear quote that heads this chapter.

The Committee on Nationwide Television Audience Measurement (Contam) provided the core of this chapter. The text of Contam's "People Meter Review" is hard going, but for anyone interested in how ratings really get produced, it's a must read. The volumes I found particularly useful were, in order of their appearance in the box, "Exit Interviews," "Household Contacts," "Engineering Review," "Sampling and Field Implementation," and the "Final Report."

Nielsen, no slouch at consuming paper, publishes its data in a vast array of reports, from weekly ratings booklets—the "pocketpieces"—to annual compendia of television facts. I extracted information from the following Nielsen publications: "The Pocketpiece" for April 22–28, 1991; "The System for Success," a brochure published in November 1988; a "Nielsen Media Research Backgrounder" on the company; "Television Audience 1990," a yearbook of ratings facts; and "Television Viewing Among Blacks: The 1989–90 Television Season," a report on the black audience. Several one-page Nielsen handouts provided details of network TV's shrinking share of audience and a record of the highest-rated shows in TV history.

I conducted a wide range of interviews but once again cited only a few of those who kindly gave me their time and thoughts. Those I interviewed but did not name are, in order of contact, Terry Pittman, Claritas Corp.; Terry D'Angona, Strategy Research Corp.; Alex P. Pentland, Media Laboratory, Massachusetts Institute of Technology; William Benz, Busch Media Group, Anheuser-Busch Inc.; Richard J. Montesano, ABC Television Network Group, Capital Cities/ABC; Steve Douglas, The Douglas Group; Lee Weinblatt, the PreTesting Company; Rick Dellacquila, Campbell Soup Co.; Abbott Wool, Vitt Media International; Robert P. Seiber, Turner Broadcasting System Inc.; Arnold Becker, Columbia Broadcast Group, CBS Inc., Los Angeles; and Melvin A. Goldberg, Electronic Media Rating Council Inc., a.k.a. the ratings police.

Arbitron granted me interviews with Gerald Cohen and Claire L. Kummer, who gave me a demonstration of the Motivac machine at Arbitron's Maryland technology center. Dr. Cohen told me that fireplaces, with their tendency to spread romantic but unruly shards of light throughout a room, tended to hamper Motivac's ability to count. In a test apartment curtains blown by an air conditioner also bedeviled the system. Big dogs, of course, remained a problem. The big dog effect has become the subject of an industry joke that may or may not be based on fact. A network executive, on seeing an early attempt at passive measurement, is supposed to have quipped: "You show me a dog who can pop a beer and handle a remote, and I'll count him."

Nielsen gave me ready access to many of its executives, both in New York and at its Dunedin Center in Florida. Each had an interesting story to tell, but once again, and perhaps to their relief, I could not name them all. The executives I did not cite are, in New York, Barry Cook, Nielsen's new research ombudsman; in Dunedin, Florida, Ed Aust, Bill Thomas, and Scott Brown.

I was surprised when I first learned that Nielsen's ratings originated from Dunedin, such a sleepy, out-of-the-way suburb of Tampa. On seeing the place, however, I was struck by the appropriateness of the location: the center rises directly from the green lawns and rectangular blocks of a bland residential neighborhood of the kind one might find anywhere in suburban America.

I conducted most of my research for this chapter with the support of *The Atlantic Monthly*, which published a shorter version in March 1992. The magazine undoubtedly opened doors that otherwise might have been closed.

Additional Sources

Allen, Charles L. "Photographing the TV Audience." *Journal of Advertising Research.* 1965.

Beville, Hugh Malcolm, Jr. "People Meter Will Impact All Segments of TV Industry." *Television/Radio Age.* October 27, 1986.

Buckman, Adam. "People Meter Era Arrives in Confusion." *Electronic Media*. September 7, 1987.

"CBS Cancels Its Contract with Nielsen for Ratings." *New York Times*. July 8, 1987.

"Fast Forwarding into TV's Past." *New York Times*. February 15, 1991.

"French Try World's First Passive People Meter." *Electronic Media*. April 22, 1991.

"Hawkeye and Company in a 'M*A*S*H' Salute." *New York Times*. November 25, 1991.

"Interested in Commercial Avoidance? Why Not Exhume and Study Percy's Data?" *Media Matters*. October 1990.

Lu, Daozheng, and David A. Kiewit. "Passive People Meters; a First Step." *Journal of Advertising Research*. June–July 1987.

Marin, Rick. "Loved the Pilot, Hate the Show." *Channels*. September 10, 1990.

Measuring the Audience. Gannett Center Journal. Summer 1988.

"No Laugh Track, No Deal." *New York Times*. June 9, 1991.

Ratings at a Crossroads. Transcript proceedings. Advertising Research Foundation Electronic Media Workshop. December 6–7, 1990.

Reeves, Jimmie L., and Richard Campbell. "Misplacing 'Frank's Place': Do You Know What it Means to Miss New Orleans?" *Television Quarterly*. No. 1, 1989.

Schiavone, Nicholas P. "Truth or Consequences." Talk presented to Media Research Club of Chicago. April 1991.

Trachtenberg, Jeffrey. "Diary of a Failure." *Forbes*. September 19, 1988.

"TV's Venturesome Programmers Find It's Lonely Out Front." *New York Times*. November 19, 1990.

8. THE THIN RED LINE

David J. Collins, who now runs the Data Capture Institute, Duxbury, Massachusetts, walked me through the early history of scanning and bar codes. His book, *Using Bar Code: Why It's Taking Over*, proved an invaluable reference when I sat down to write this chapter. Thomas V. Brady of the Uniform Code Council, Dayton, Ohio, gave me a precise chronology of the greatest moments in scanning and a short course in the structure of codes. He also sent me a thick packet of detailed council booklets designed for manufacturers about to use bar codes for the first time. I learned of Congress's early interest in scanning from "In a Fishbowl," an article in *Forbes*, December 1, 1975.

Giant Food's Robert W. Schoening briefed me on the history of Giant's experience with scanners. Two other Giant officials, Joanne Anderson, manager of data-processing field support, and Dave Herriman, vice-president of grocery operations, provided additional detail about Giant's use of scanners.

Mary Ellen Burris, the veteran director of consumer affairs for Wegmans Food Markets Inc., Rochester, New York, told me about the Wegmans Shoppers Club. Ron Jaffe, senior director of marketing for Waldenbooks, told me about his company's preferred reader program.

I learned of Frito-Lay's use of BehaviorScan to test its Sun Chips snack through an interview with Dwight R. Riskey, the company's vice-president of new business and market research. Frito-Lay first tested the product in November 1989 and began a national roll-out in February 1991. Among the nuggets of snack food intelligence exposed by that interview was the fact that Cleveland and the surrounding Ohio valley have the highest craving for "salty snacks," as the chips and puffs category is called. Southern California had the lowest demand.

Arbitron's ScanAmerica information on diet Pepsi and diet Coke appeared in a report given me during an interview with Ken Wollenberg, executive vice-president, sales and marketing. Tom Mocarsky, Arbitron's spokesman, gave me a demonstration of the ScanAmerica scanner wand. Pierre R. Megroz, vice-president, sales and marketing, of Arbitron's television network and station service, explained how ScanAmerica evolved and, with the help of a couple of computer jockeys at Arbitron's Laurel, Maryland, office, showed me the kinds of ratings information the system can provide.

I extracted the statistics on coupons and coupon redemption from a June 1989 IRI report, "Coupon Misredemption Analysis," and from the April 12, 1991, issue of *The Friday Report*, which described the results of a coupon study by the Advertising Checking Bureau, New York. For an idea of how much buying power is pent up in all those coupons, imagine that by some fluke (or by the nefarious designs of some econoterrorist) consumers redeemed every single coupon ever issued in 1990. Extrapolating from the redemption cost of $4.8 billion, the total cost to the marketers would have been $120 billion, or $1,290 per U.S. household.

Catalina's Dan Granger explained the rules of competitive engagement that allow competitors to share the same Checkout Coupon cycle: If Coke buys rights to the cola subcategory, it can target shoppers who buy Pepsi but not those who buy Slice, a noncola drink also made by PepsiCo. During the same cycle, Slice can buy rights to the noncola subcategory and gleefully ambush buyers of 7Up, a Coca-Cola product. However, Slice cannot target buyers of Coke itself.

David E. Brandkamp, VideOcart's northeast regional manager, met me at Giant's Frederick store and joined me in a quick tour of a few aisles to explain the workings of the cart. I spent another hour or so alone with the cart, mumbling to myself and jotting notes and occasionally shaking my head in wonder, no doubt prompting worried glances and hurried exits from surrounding shoppers. I interviewed Robert McCann, Jr., the company's executive vice-president, in his Chicago office.

The numbers of products stocked by grocery stores come from a survey by *Progressive Grocer*, published in the magazine's April 1991 issue. A Safeway official, Louise Booth, disclosed the number of products its stores sell in a paper presented to the American Marketing Association, January 1990. The estimate of the number of product introductions came from remarks made in January 1991 by Patrick W. Collins, of the Ralph's supermarket chain.

Mary J. Culnan, Georgetown University, sent me an advertisement for mailing lists generated by the Citicorp POS data base, which she picked up at the Direct Marketing Association annual meeting in January 1992. The list broker was Qualified Lists Corporation of Armonk, New York, which announced that Citicorp could also deliver lists of 334,345 cosmetic buyers, 1,112,351 coupon clippers, 578,354 health-conscious consumers, and 692,757 pet owners.

My information on Advanced Promotion Technologies, a Procter & Gamble affiliate, came primarily from APT's June 26, 1991, prospectus regarding a planned stock offering.

Sources interviewed but not named in the text are Robert Warrens, J. Walter Thompson Co.; Thomas F. Mandel, SRI International; Scott A. Neslin, Dartmouth College; and Andrew Tarshis, NPD/Nielsen Inc.

Additional Sources

Abraham, Magid, and Leonard Lodish. "Advertising Works: A Study of Advertising Effectiveness and the Resulting Strategic and Tactical Implications." Information Resources Inc. 1989.

"The ARF Scanner-Based Services Fact Sheet." Advertising Research Foundation, April 1989.

Andersson, Edmund P. "A Historical Perspective of Bar Code Technology." *ScanJournal.* Fourth quarter, 1984.

Coyle, Joseph S. "Scanning Lights up a Dark World for Grocers." *Fortune.* March 27, 1978.

Curry, David J. "Single-Source Systems: Retail Management Present and Future." *Journal of Retailing.* Spring 1989.

"Don't Blame Television, Irate Readers Say." *Wall Street Journal.* March 1, 1989.

Levine, Joshua. "The Ultimate Sell." *Forbes.* May 13, 1991.

Metzger, Gale D. "Single Source: Yes and No." *Marketing Research.* December 1990.

Petersen, Laurie. "Study Confirms Impulse Buying on Rise." *Adweek.* October 12, 1987.

"Read Me First: Getting Started with the Universal Product Code." Uniform Code Council. July 1991.

"Ready, Set, Scan that Melon!" *New York Times.* June 14, 1990.

Sylvester, Alice K. "Single Source . . . Single Force." Paper presented at Advertising Research Foundation Behavioral Research and Single Source Data Workshop, June 26–27, 1990.

"Television Ads Ring up No Sale in Study." *Wall Street Journal.* February 15, 1989.

Tellis, Gerard J. "Advertising Exposure, Loyalty, and Brand Purchase: A Two-Stage Model of Choice." *Journal of Marketing Research.* May 1988.

_____ "Does TV Advertising Really Work?" Point-of-Purchase Advertising Institute. Undated.

_____ "Point of View: Interpreting Advertising and Price Elasticities." *Journal of Advertising Research.* August–September 1989.

"UPC Symbol Specification Manual." Uniform Code Council. January 1986. (Reprinted August 1990.)

Woods, Bob. "Throwing the Electronic Switch." *Food & Beverage Marketing.* March 1991.

9. THE HIDDEN OBSERVERS

For this section I relied heavily on encounters with observational researchers, in particular Saatchi's Penelope Queen and Paco Underhill of Envirosell, who gave me generous amounts of his time in both New York and Tannersville, Pennsylvania. Allison Cohen of Ally & Gargano showed me a video of some of her chocolate research and cheerfully recounted many of her other exploits. I made two visits to Lee Weinblatt's Englewood, New Jersey, headquarters.

The revelations about music and dining came from research by Ronald E. Milliman, of Western Kentucky University, who published his findings in the *Journal of Consumer Research*, September 1986.

Langbourne Rust told me about his past research and some of the tricks of the observation trade. In addition I drew information from a variety of written materials: the text of a speech Rust delivered to the Market Research Council on November 17, 1989; a speech he gave before the Advertising Research Foundation, April 6, 1988; two of his articles from the *Journal of Advertising Research:* "Children's Advertising: How It Works, How to Do It, How to Know If It Works," August–September 1986, and "Using Attention and Intention to Predict At-Home Program Choice," April–May 1987. I gathered additional information from the ARF progress report "An Observational Study of Children: Report on an ARF Pilot Project," by Allan L. Baldinger, ARF's director of marketing research, presented at a foundation workshop April 6, 1988.

I constructed the garbage section primarily from published reports but also drew information from two past interviews with William Rathje.

The studies on lawns, hallucinogenic drugs, and tombstones are all the property of the Arizona State Museum Library, University of Arizona. The fourth study, on cigarette butts, was cited in "Nonreactive Measures in Psychotherapy Outcome Research," in *Clinical Psychology Review,* volume 3, 1983. My references to Joseph Bonano and Mary Kay, two names not often juxtaposed so closely, come from *National Geographic* magazine, April 1983, and *Business Week,* April 1, 1991, respectively.

I consulted the following articles by Rathje: "Archaeologists Bust Myths About Solid Waste and Society," *Garbage* magazine, September–October 1990; "The Garbage Decade," *American Behavioral Scientist,* September–October 1984; "Rubbish!," *The Atlantic Monthly,* December 1989; "The Telltale Garbage of Tucson," *Early Man,* Winter 1979; and "Why We Throw Food Away," *The Atlantic Monthly,* April 1986.

Melanie Wallendorf and Michael Reilly described their research on Mexican-American garbage in "Ethnic Migration, Assimilation, and Consumption," *Journal of Consumer Research,* December 1983. Reilly described his novel consumer espionage tactics in "Household Refuse Analysis and Market Research," *American Behavioral Scientist,* September–October 1984.

Safeway's Louise Booth (cited also in the notes to the previous chapter) used the nickname "coffin" to describe horizontal freezer cases.

Nielsen's Bill Thomas, also cited previously, told me about the coding of TV broadcasts.

Additional Sources

Clark, Eric. *The Want Makers.* Viking. 1988.

"Delving into the Consumer Unconscious." *New York Times.* July 22, 1990.

"Destron/IDI of Boulder plays ID tag for profits." *Denver Business Journal.* April 16, 1990.

The Hot Line (newsletter). PreTesting Company. Englewood, New Jersey. Vol. 1, nos. 4, 6–10.

"The 'Spy' of Madison Ave." *Los Angeles Times.* May 5, 1990.

Taylor, W. M. Wadman. "Microchip Implant Report." Dogs Home Battersea. London. July 31, 1990.

Weinblatt, Lee. "Flat Switch Insertable into a Magazine and Usable as Part of a Survey Technique for Readership Publications." U.S. Patent, 4,726,771. February 23, 1988.

10. INVADED!

Heloise sent me a box filled with dozens of examples of junk mail targeting vulnerable Americans. One advertisement struck me as particularly compelling, although less clearly targeted than those I cite in the text. A yellow note, saying "Don, This really works!—J," had been stuck to a full-page ad for the "amazing Sex Scent that makes 3 out of 4 women give in!" (I learned that a " 'normal' man is only successful 1 time in 4.") For reasons I could not grasp, the scent was named "Exit 1," evoking all the romance of a turnpike off ramp. It was sold by New York's "Jean Aubert," who advised: "Spray a little Exit 1 behind your ear, or on your shirt collar, then smile and walk up to the first pretty girl you see." Aubert even provided scientific evidence: "In a dentist's waiting room, some sex scent was sprayed on a chair. During the course of the day, 11 patients out of 13 either sat on that chair or the one next to it."

Within moments, I confess, my check was in the mail.

I acquired my copies of the 1990 Harris-Equifax survey "The Equifax Report on Consumers in the Information Age," from Equifax Corp., which in 1991 kicked off a concerted campaign to become far more responsive to consumer needs and complaints and to transform its image from intruder to good corporate citizen. The company also provided me with the 1991 sister study.

I drew upon other surveys as well, including a review of privacy polls published in the spring 1990 issue of *Public Opinion Quarterly*. The article, by James Katz, a sociologist at Bell Communication Research, and Annette Tassone, a doctoral candidate at the Stevens Institute of Technology, included a caveat that suggests that national concern about privacy may actually be greater than even the Harris-Equifax surveys indicate. "Unlike many other topics of research," the authors warned, "surveys of privacy concerns are by their nature likely not to include members of the population who would be most concerned about invasions of privacy. This is because potential respondents presumably would not be willing to reveal information about themselves to pollsters, judging them to be privacy invaders. Consequently, public opinion polls on the subject are probably underestimating the level of public concern."

I also consulted a rather skimpy poll conducted by Yankelovich Clancy Shulman for *Time* magazine and CNN. I cite it with reluctance. Yankelovich, a respected pollster, contacted only five hundred people and did so in a single day, raising serious questions about the poll's statistical validity. The poll's most interesting finding was that people objected more to the sale of their income records than of their arrest records.

Louis Brandeis made his remarks about the intent of the Founding Fathers in his dissent from the majority opinion in *Olmstead v. United States* (177 U.S. 438. 1928). Edward Bloustein's article appeared in the *New York University Law Journal*, December 1964. In his article Bloustein also made this observation: "The feeling of being naked before the world can be produced by having to respond to a questionnaire or psychological test as well as by having your bedroom open to prying eyes and ears. And the fear that a private life may be turned into a public spectacle is greatly enhanced when the lurid facts have been reduced to key punches or blips on a magnetic tape accessible, perhaps, to any clerk who can throw the appropriate switch."

I found Alan Westin's 1967 definition of the right to privacy in "Electronic Record Systems and Individual Privacy," a report by the Congressional Office of Technology Assessment, one of the few federal agencies that can still be counted on to conduct thorough, dispassionate, and nonpartisan federal investigations. The report was published in June 1986. Vincent Barabba put forth his definition in a speech to the Symposium on Personal Integrity and Data Protection Research, held by the Swedish Council for Social Science Research, Stockholm, on March 16, 1976.

I gathered information about the Debt Collection Act from the OTA report cited above and from interviews with Dean P. Balamaci, manager of the credit programs branch of the Treasury Department's Division of Credit Administration (founded, of course, in 1984), and with Kathleen M. Downs, manager of the division's credit projects branch. I also reviewed two Treasury documents, the July 1991 edition of the "Guide to Credit Bureau Reporting" (intended for use by federal agencies in complying with the Debt Collection Act), and the January 22, 1991, "Federal Supply Schedule: Debt Collection Services," which details the requirements credit bureaus and debt collectors must meet before they can become approved federal contractors. Even this schedule contained a market research survey. At one point the survey asked contractors to state whether they agreed or disagreed with this statement: "The cover page is eye-appealing and provides an adequate description of the major types of items included in the schedule."

The General Accounting Office survey, published in August 1990, is titled "Computers and Privacy: How the Government Obtains, Verifies, Uses and Protects Personal Data" and can be ordered from the Government Printing Office. The order code is GAO/IMTEC-90-70BR.

Privacy Journal reported on the Rhode Island governor's disclosure of depositors' names in its February 1991 issue. The report noted that even the Providence Journal, the state's spunky leading newspaper, refused at first to publish the list.

The New York Times, October 7, 1990, reported the Dartmouth Review's sensitive handling of the gay student list. Given other disclosures in the Times article, the Review's behavior should come as no surprise. The Times reported that in 1980—the year the Review was founded—it "sponsored a free lobster-and-champagne feast to coincide with a campus fast for the world's hungry."

The Orwell quote came, of course, from 1984.

11. THE CULTURE OF THE SECOND GUESS

The process of second-guessing directors is by no means new. Alfred Hitchcock wanted to end The Birds with a shot of birds covering the Golden Gate Bridge, an ominous ending true in spirit to the original Daphne du Maurier short story. Universal wanted a more upbeat ending and got it. In 1932 Paramount shot two endings for A Farewell to Arms. In one, as in the Hemingway novel, the heroine died; in the other she survived. Paramount chose the latter, prompting Hemingway to fire off a telegram advising Paramount executives "to use your imagination as to where you can put the prints of Farewell to Arms." Censors wanted Rhett Butler to really let Scarlett have it at the end of Gone With the Wind, by telling her, "Frankly, my dear, I don't give a darn."

Today, however, movie production and distribution costs are far higher, and the process of second-guessing the creative instinct has become automated. One result, as Mark Crispin Miller wrote in an April 1990 Atlantic Monthly piece, is that "going to the movies has become about as memorable as going to the airport."

Steve Martin made his remark about advance testing in "Facing the Test," the Dallas Morning News, March 14, 1988.

My information on how record companies use advance testing comes from "Do Marketers Control What We See?," *Psychology Today*, June 1989. I learned of National Geographic's methods of testing books while preparing several chapters for one such book, compellingly titled *America's Great Hideaways*. The book division also sends out copies of the manuscript to every source interviewed, practically guaranteeing that nothing controversial will ever appear. In one chapter on the Minnesota north woods I remarked that a heater in my cabin came on with a *"whoosh*, like the arrival of the devil himself." This annoyed the owner of the cabin, who told the fact checker that if I didn't like the cabin, I should have asked for another one. The devil got bounced from the chapter.

Dick Thomas, of Strategy Research Corporation, told me of his company's court-related market research but steadfastly refused to discuss any specific examples.

I drew my information on the Q ratings from *TV Guide* ("Those Hush-Hush Q Ratings . . . ," December 10, 1988), *USA Today* ("We Know Ye," August 14, 1991), and Hugh Beville's *Audience Ratings*, cited previously.

For information about how contemporary politicians use polls and practice targeting, I relied heavily on articles in *Campaigns & Elections* magazine, in particular the following: "Against All Odds," May–June 1988; "Benchmark Basics & Beyond," May 1991; "Precision Politics," February–March 1990; and "Strategic Polling: The Fine Art of Honing in on Voter Preferences," September 1991. William Hamilton, of Hamilton & Staff, filled in the blanks.

The story of Matt Reese's victory in Missouri has been widely told. David Burnham described it in *The Rise of the Computer State*. For my account, I relied on interviews with Jonathan Robbin (cited previously), pollster Hamilton, and Charles B. Welsh, a marketing consultant in Arlington, Virginia, but formerly president of a political targeting company that relied on Claritas's PRIZM system. I also drew details from Robbin's own account of the Missouri campaign, "Geodemographics: The New Magic," which appeared in the spring 1980 issue of *Campaigns & Elections*.

I drew my brief reference to the 1824 political polls from an excellent history, "The First Straw: A Study of the Origins of Election Polls," by Tom W. Smith, in *Public Opinion Quarterly*, volume 54, 1990. (He recounts how another newspaper totaled the bets made for and against certain candidates.)

For a rich perspective on the use and abuse of polls over time, I recommend these additional sources: "Polling and the News Media," by Albert E. Gollin, in *Public Opinion Quarterly* (volume 51, 1987); "Why the 1936 *Literary Digest* Poll Failed," by Peverill Squire, also in the *Quarterly* (volume 52, 1988); "Fifty Years of Survey Sampling in the United States," Martin R. Frankel and Lester R. Frankel, the *Quarterly* (volume 51, 1987); and, especially, "Lyndon Johnson and the Public Polls," by Bruce E. Altschuler, the *Quarterly* (volume 50, 1986). My statistics on the *Times* and CBS polls came from the Gollin article.

The poll-laden edition of the *San Francisco Chronicle* was published November 13, 1991. The front-page story was a report on a *Chronicle*-sponsored poll on a mayoral runoff election. A wire service story on page two reported on a poll aimed at figuring out who was likely to win the New Hampshire primary, still three months away. The page three story appeared under the byline "The Gallup Organization" and reported the results of a Gallup poll asking how many Americans agreed with various campaign statements made by David Duke in his just failed run to be governor of Louisiana.

Mervin Field disclosed his statistical qualms in *Polling on the Issues*, a collection of articles edited by Albert H. Cantril, published by Seven Locks Press, Cabin John, Maryland, in 1980. Alex Michalos estimated the degree of total error in his article "Ethical Considerations Regarding Public Opinion Polling During Election Campaigns," *Journal of Business Ethics*, volume 10, 1991.

Lowell Weicker's experience was reported in "Benchmark Basics & Beyond," cited above. Gallup's 1988 New Hampshire embarrassment was recounted in "Bad Year for the Polls," *Campaigns & Elections*, March–April 1989.

Howard Shuman and Jacqueline Scott of the Michigan Institute for Social Research described their research on closed questions in "Problems in the Use of Survey Questions to Measure Public Opinion," *Science*, May 22, 1987. Jack Germond made his observation in the above-cited *Polling on the Issues*. The survey on phantom legislation appeared in "Opinions on Fictitious Issues: The Pressure to Answer Survey Questions," George F. Bishop et al., in *Public Opinion Quarterly*, volume 50, 1986. Burns W. Roper reported the results of his poll on polls in "Evaluating Polls with Poll Data," in the same volume.

The study by Philip Converse and Michael Traugott appeared in the November 28, 1986, issue of *Science*.

Eleanor Singer's review of R.A.C.E. and Lawrence Bobo's response appeared in the *Public Opinion Quarterly*, volume 54, 1990, and volume 55, 1991. Harold Mendelsohn, University of Denver, raised his concerns about the effect of polling on government in "The Future Study of Public Opinion," *Public Opinion Quarterly*, volume 51, 1987.

Additional Sources

Bartels, Larry M., and C. Anthony Broh. "The Polls—A Review: The 1988 Presidential Primaries." *Public Opinion Quarterly*. Vol. 53, 1989.

Clark, Eric. *The Want Makers*. Viking. 1988.

Groves, Robert M. "Research on Survey Data Quality." *Public Opinion Quarterly*. Vol. 51, 1987.

Kohut, Andrew. "Rating the Polls: The Views of Media Elites and the General Public." *Public Opinion Quarterly*. Vol. 50, 1986.

McCurry, Michael. "The New Electronic Politics." *Campaigns & Elections*. March–April 1989.

Porado, Philip. "Finding Faster Feedback." *Campaigns & Elections*. December 1989.

Smith, Tom W. "The Art of Asking Questions, 1936–1985." *Public Opinion Quarterly*. Vol. 51, 1987.

"Studios Shifting to Mad Ave's Savvy Sell." *Variety*. April 1, 1991.

"21st Century Politics." *Campaigns & Elections*. March–April 1989.

12. WHAT TO DO

I relied here on the legal research of others more skilled than I at tracing the development of law. To gain an appreciation of the complexity likely to be involved in producing any new legislation on privacy, I interviewed privacy advocates Alan Westin and Eli Noam of Columbia University, Janlori Goldman of the ACLU's privacy project, Marc Rotenberg of the Computer Professionals for Social Responsibility, and Mary Culnan of George-town University. Not all would agree with the observations I make in this chapter.

A number of reports and legal reviews provided an excellent overview of how bureaucrats and technology have undermined existing privacy protections. Two reports by the Office of Technology Assessment provide richly detailed examinations of the interplay of surveillance technology and privacy law: "Electronic Record Systems and Individual Privacy," June 1986, cited earlier; and "Electronic Surveillance and Civil Liberties," October 1985.

The August 1990 General Accounting Office survey, "Computers and Privacy: How the Government Obtains, Verifies, Uses and Protects Personal Data," proved useful as well. It presents rather disturbing evidence of the extent to which personal records have become commodities that pass easily among federal agencies and between federal and private data banks. Even more disturbing, as the report's author told me in an interview, is that the GAO had intended to track the flow of personal records more thoroughly but had to settle for the survey because the migration of personal records had become so widespread as to make any other means of tracking them impossible.

An excellent assessment of the current state of privacy law, from the perspective of a privacy advocate, is "A Federal Right of Information Privacy: The Need for Reform," written by Jerry Berman and Janlori Goldman and published by the Benton Foundation Project on Communications & Information Policy Options. I also reviewed ACLU testimony presented in August 1990 before the Senate Judiciary Subcommittee on Technology and the Law and presented in August 1988 before a joint panel considering the merits of what would soon become the "Bork" video bill.

INDEX

Selective binding, 88
Selective Service, U.S., 99
Senate Judiciary Committee, 231
Sesame Street, 63
Sex Over Forty, 80
Shared-name deals, 67
Sherman, William Tecumseh, 33–34
Shoplifting, 176–77
Shopper ID programs, 134–36; Behav-
    iorScan, 139–44, 146, 162–63; initial
    response rates for, 146–48
Shoppers' Association for Value and
    Economy (SAVE), 72, 74
Shopping baskets and carts, 178–79; elec-
    tronic, 152–54
SIDS Alliance, 86
"Simpsons, The," 115, 116
Singer, Eleanor, 229
"60 Minutes," 116, 145
Skylawn Memorial Park, 80
Smith, Randall S., 154, 155
Smith, Tom, 228, 229
Snoopy, 63
Social Security, 11, 83–84, 237
Souter, David H., 10
Southern California Gas Co., 40
Spar, Edward, 45, 57
Speech, freedom of, 21, 98, 239
Spiegel Co., 13, 68
Split samples, 222
Sponsorship, 22, 145–46
Stack, Robert, 116
Starbucks, 173
State Will Co., 86
Statistical Research Inc., 112–13, 146
Statistics, 34, 114, 118
Statistics Canada, 54
Stewart, Carol, 61
Stockouts, 157
Strain, James E., 81
Strasser, Susan, 55–56
Strategy of Desire, The, 23–24
Strategy Research Corp., 13, 217
Strub, Sean, 67–68

Strub/Dawson Inc., 67
Strub Media Group Inc., 67
Struse, Rudolph W., III, 156
Style: "planned obsolescence" and, 20
Sunoco, 63
Sununu, John, 224
Super Bowl, 127
Superlists, 60
Supermarkets, 102; electronic shopping
    carts for, 152–54; parent-child interac-
    tions in, 173–74, 181–82; scanner
    technology in, 129–63 (*see also* Scan-
    ner technology)
Supreme Court, U.S., 53, 212, 233–35,
    237
Surveillance, 167–98; eavesdropping
    and, 174–75; of employees, 133–34; of
    garbage, 188, 189–91, 234; hidden
    cameras in, 9, 25, 170, 172, 174–75,
    195–97; in homes, 9, 171–72; im-
    plants in, 191–94; privacy and, 174;
    reasons for, 169–71; in retail stores,
    167–69, 172–80, 181–82; in search
    for symbolic links between consumers
    and products, 182–88; wristwatch sys-
    tem in, 197–98
Surveys, 8–9, 19, 23, 60, 64, 91, 108;
    attached to warranty cards, 8, 72; dis-
    sembling in, 170, 189–90; human
    judgment subjugated to, 215–18,
    221–22, 229–30; of supermarket shop-
    pers, 134–35. *See also* Political
    polls
Sweethearting, 133–34
Sylvania Electric, 131
Sylvester, Alice, 147
Symbolism: in consumption, 182–88
Synchographics, 12, 79–97; childbearing
    and, 79–93; and milestones in life of
    child, 3–5, 11, 86, 87, 92–93, 208;
    moving and, 93–96

Tabulating Machine Co., 35
Tactical polls, 222